Understanding the European Union

A Concise Introduction

Second Edition

John McCormick

palgrave

First edition 1999
Reprinted five times
Second edition 2002

Published by
PALGRAVE
Houndmills, Basingstoke, Hampshire RG21 2XS and
175 Fifth Avenue, New York, N.Y. 10010
Companies and representatives throughout the world

ISBN 0–333–94868–8 hardback
ISBN 0–333–94867–X paperback

This book is printed on paper suitable for recycling and made from
fully managed and sustained forest sources.

A catalogue record for this book is available
from the British Library.

Library of Congress Cataloging-in-Publication Data
McCormick, John, 1954–
   Understanding the European Union: a concise introduction / John
   McCormick.—2nd ed.
      p. cm
   Includes bibliographical references and index.
   ISBN 0–333–94868–8—ISBN 0–333–94867–X (pbk.)
   1. European Union. I. Title. II. Series.
JN30 .M38 2002
341.242'2—dc21   2001057740

Copy-edited and typeset by Povey–Edmondson
Tavistock and Rochdale, England

10   9   8   7   6   5   4   3   2   1
11 10 09 08 07 06 05 04 03 02

Printed and bound in Great Britain by
Creative Print & Design (Wales), Ebbw Vale

Contents

List of Boxes, Tables, Figures and Maps   vii

List of Abbreviations   ix

Introduction   xi

Acknowledgements   xv

1 What is the European Union?   **1**

    The international system   2
    Levels of cooperation   6
    The logic of integration   12
    Regional integration around the world   18
    Conclusions   27

2 The Idea of Europe   **29**

    The changing nature of Europe   30
    Where is Europe?   38
    Europe today   41
    Conclusions   54

3 The Evolution of the EU   **56**

    Domestic and international background   57
    First steps towards integration (1945–58)   63
    Deepening and widening (1958–86)   68
    Economic and social integration (1979–92)   72
    From Community to Union (1992–)   76
    Conclusions   82

4 The Institutions of the EU   **84**

    A constitution for Europe   85
    The European Commission   88
    The Council of Ministers   95
    The European Council   99
    The European Parliament   103
    The European Court of Justice   109
    Conclusions   113

5 **The EU and the Member States**   **115**

   The changing powers of the member states   116
   Reducing regional differences   122
   Improving environmental quality   128
   An emerging European civil society   132
   The changing character of the EU   135
   Conclusions   139

6 **The EU and its Citizens**   **141**

   The democratic deficit   142
   The people's Europe   149
   Social policy   156
   Improving accountability   162
   Conclusions   165

7 **Economic Integration**   **167**

   The single market   168
   Effects of the single market   173
   The common agricultural policy   180
   Inside the euro zone   186
   Conclusions   191

8 **The EU and the World**   **193**

   Building a European foreign policy   194
   Towards a European defence policy   200
   Europe as an economic superpower   204
   Relations with the United States   209
   Relations with eastern Europe   212
   Development cooperation   214
   Conclusions   218

Appendix: A Chronology of European Integration, 1944–2002   220

Sources of Further Information   223

Bibliography   226

Index   233

List of Boxes, Tables, Figures and Maps

Boxes

1.1 International organizations   5
1.2 What is sovereignty?   10
1.3 Regional integration: costs and benefits   16
2.1 Paneuropa   37
2.2 The quality of life in Europe   52
3.1 The Marshall Plan, 1948–51   61
3.2 The 1986 Single European Act   75
3.3 The 1992 Treaty on European Union   78
4.1 European Union law   89
4.2 Specialized EU institutions   97
4.3 Parties in the European Parliament   107
5.1 The rise of regional identity   123
5.2 Environmental policy   130
5.3 Intergovernmental conferences   137
6.1 The knowledge deficit   145
6.2 Cultural policy   153
6.3 The Social Charter   158
6.4 Consumer protection policy   161
7.1 Europe and the aerospace industry   176
7.2 The Common Fisheries Policy   183
7.3 The European Central Bank   188
8.1 The EU on the world stage   196
8.2 Prospects for a European army   203
8.3 The implications of eastward expansion   213

Tables

1.1 Regional integration associations   19
2.1 Demographic, economic and political indicators   42
4.1 The European Commissioners, January 2002   91
4.2 Presidents of the European Commission   92
4.3 Directorates-general of the European Commission   93
4.4 Qualified majority voting in the Council of Ministers   100

4.5 Seats in the European Parliament, 2002   104
5.1 The division of policy responsibilities   121
8.1 The EU in the global economy   205
8.2 The ACP states   215

Figures

1.1 Confederalism and federalism compared   7
2.1 Population indicators   53
4.1 The European policy process   86
6.1 Public opinion on EU membership   143
8.1 The EU share of world trade   206
8.2 EU trade with the world   208

Maps

1   The EU   xvi
2   Growth of the EU   71
3   Potential new members of the EU   80

List of Abbreviations

ACP	African, Caribbean, Pacific
CAP	Common Agricultural Policy
CFSP	Common Foreign and Security Policy
CoR	Committee of the Regions
COREPER	Committee of Permanent Representatives
DG	directorate-general
EAGGF	European Agricultural Guidance and Guarantee Fund
EC	European Community
ECSC	European Coal and Steel Community
ecu	European Currency Unit
EDC	European Defence Community
EEA	European Economic Area
EEC	European Economic Community
EFTA	European Free Trade Association
EMS	European Monetary System
EMU	economic and monetary union
EP	European Parliament
EPC	European Political Cooperation
ERDF	European Regional Development Fund
ERM	Exchange Rate Mechanism
ESF	European Social Fund
EU	European Union
G8	Group of Eight industrialized countries
GAC	General Affairs Council
GDP	gross domestic product
GNP	gross national product
IGC	intergovernmental conference
IGO	intergovernmental organization
IO	international organization
MEP	Member of the European Parliament
NAFTA	North American Free Trade Agreement
NATO	North Atlantic Treaty Organization
OECD	Organization for Economic Cooperation and Development
OEEC	Organization for European Economic Cooperation
PR	proportional representation
SAP	Social Action Programme
SEA	Single European Act
TEN	trans-European network
VAT	value-added tax
WEU	Western European Union

Introduction

The creation of the European Union will go down in history as one of the most remarkable achievements of the twentieth century. In the space of just forty years – less than two generations – Europeans fought two appalling wars among themselves, finally appreciated the dangers of nationalism and the futility of violence, and sat down to design a system that would make it inconceivable that they would ever take up arms against each other again.

The results have been substantial. A set of treaties, laws and institutions has been created that has altered the political, economic and social landscape of western Europe. They have changed the way Europeans relate to each other, made Europe into a new economic superpower, and helped bring to the region the longest uninterrupted spell of general peace in its recorded history. The European Union is the world's biggest trading bloc, is one of the two largest markets in the world, has adopted a common currency, and has planted the seeds of a common foreign and defence policy.

Of course not everyone agrees that European integration has been a good idea, nor is everyone ready to give it credit for bringing peace to the region. Europeans have mixed opinions about the wisdom of shifting powers from the member states to a new level of government, and while opinion polls show that about half approve of the European Union, the other half either disapproves or is not yet sure what to think. Critics point accusing fingers at 'interfering Eurocrats', and worry about the costs of giving authority to institutions that are often secretive and unaccountable. They also question the extent to which integration can be credited with the economic growth and prosperity that has come to western Europe since 1945.

But like it or not, the European Union is here to stay. The changes it has brought have spun a web of links among the states of western Europe that would be difficult to unravel. Free trade and the free movement of people have dissolved the barriers that for so long reminded Europeans of their differences, and while national and regional identities are still alive and well, they no longer threaten to bring conflict or war.

Under the circumstances, Europeans are having to learn about the nature and structure of the European Union. Fifteen years ago it was only a marginal factor in most of their lives, but with the completion of the single market, the adoption of the euro, and moves towards a common foreign policy it has become difficult to ignore. Where once they could be ignored, it has now become important to understand the powers of the European institutions, the content of the treaties, and the meaning of concepts such as structural funds, cohesion and the democratic deficit.

This is an introductory book about the European Union, written for anyone who wants to understand how it works and what it means for the 375 million people who live under its jurisdiction. Unfortunately confusion seems to be the order of the day – Europe has been busy integrating itself for nearly fifty years, but three in four of its inhabitants confess to a poor understanding of the EU, its policies and its institutions, and about one in eight admit that they know nothing at all about how it works (see Box 6.1 on page 145).

This is a worrying state of affairs. As long as the confusion persists, Europeans will keep their distance from the EU, integration will continue to be driven by the elites who have made most of the major decisions since the outset, and the values and priorities of the European people may not be reflected in those decisions. A common criticism of the EU is that it is undemocratic, and that bureaucrats have too much power and too little accountability – but little will change unless Europeans learn how it works, and increase the pressure for accountability.

From my vantage point as a British citizen living in the United States, I have watched with fascination as my fellow Europeans have strengthened their bonds, and with concern as so many have admitted their doubts about the consequences. My annual trips back to Europe have allowed me to compare public and media responses to the EU on both sides of the Atlantic, and to gain the kind of perspective that distance often allows. At the same time my students at Indiana University have presented me with the challenge of convincing them why they should care about something that is happening 4000 miles away.

Part of that challenge involved finding a book that explained the EU clearly and approachably, but while publishing on the EU has been a major growth industry in recent years, there are remarkably few books that really introduce the EU, and even fewer that successfully convey the significance of the EU. Too many authors become bogged down in treaty articles and Eurojargon, and – the worst sin of all – they often make one of the most fascinating developments in European history sound dull and bureaucratic.

These problems prompted me to write *The European Union: Politics and Policies*, which was published in 1996 by Westview Press and aimed mainly at college and university classes on the EU in the United States and Canada. In 1997, Steven Kennedy at Palgrave asked me to write a shorter book that was more introductory and broad-ranging, and aimed at a wider readership. The first edition of *Understanding the European Union* was published in 1999, its main goal being to demystify the European Union, to help readers come to grips with this strange new economic and political entity, and to do this all as clearly and as concisely as possible.

Apparently it struck a note, and it was very gratifying to hear from Steven in 2000 that a second edition was needed, bringing in the changes made by the Treaty of Nice, and covering the adoption of the euro and the upcoming enlargement to central and eastern Europe. Like its precursor, this second edition includes all the important details about how the EU works and what it does, and provides context by introducing, explaining and assessing the history of the EU, the goals and motives behind European integration, the impact of integration on the member states, the changes the EU has made to the lives of Europeans and the long-term implications of the European experiment. It also provides critical analysis of the EU, offering thoughts on where it has done well and not so well, and on where improvements need to be made.

This second edition has been thoroughly revised and updated, and large parts of it have been fine-tuned in response to comments from reviewers and from instructors who have used it in their classes, and in light of developments since the first edition. Several new sections have been added, several boxes have been replaced, and the arguments and analysis have been developed.

Above all, *Understanding the European Union* is an introduction, and it does not set out to cover every aspect of European integration in depth. It is a survey of key developments, institutions, and policies. It takes a broad view, offering some depth where necessary, but ultimately providing a route map to the rapidly growing number of more specialist studies of the many different facets of the EU.

Chapter 1 looks at the nature of regional integration, exploring the motives behind international cooperation, showing how the EU is different from conventional international organizations, and placing it in context by briefly describing several other exercises in regional integration around the world.

Chapter 2 provides historical background by discussing the evolution of the idea of Europe, and showing how the terms 'Europe' and 'European' have changed and evolved. The chapter also includes a political, economic and social survey of Europe today, which serves as a foundation for the discussions about integration in later chapters.

Chapter 3 offers a short history of European integration since 1945. It describes and explains the different steps in the process, from the creation of the European Coal and Steel Community, through the treaties of Rome, Maastricht and Nice, to the completion of the single market and adoption of the euro.

Chapter 4 looks at the five major European institutions – the Commission, the Council of Ministers, the European Council, the European

Parliament and the Court of Justice – and explains how they are structured, how they function, how they relate to one another and how they fit into the process of making European law and policy.

Chapter 5 assesses the relationship between the EU and its member states, and the changing character of the EU. It looks at the constitutional issues raised by integration, and illustrates the effects of integration by looking at developments in regional and environmental policy, explaining what they have meant for the member states.

Chapter 6 does much the same for the relationship between the EU and its citizens. It looks at the problem of the democratic deficit and examines the impact that EU policies on citizenship, culture, workers' rights, unemployment and worker mobility have had on the lives of Europeans, ending with a discussion of the need for democratic reform.

Chapter 7 focuses on the economic impact of European integration, with particular emphasis on the changes that have resulted from the single market programme. It looks at the ups and downs of the Common Agricultural Policy, and finishes with an assessment of the implications of the introduction of the euro.

Chapter 8 puts the European Union in a global context. The chapter begins with a survey of the attempts that have been made to develop a European foreign and defence policy, then assesses the role of the EU as the world's newest economic superpower and looks at the EU's relations with different regions of the world.

Acknowledgements

The students in my classes have been the most important influence on this book because it was written mainly with the needs of students in mind. So I want to thank them for providing the points of reference that helped me decide what to include, what to leave out and what questions to address. I would also like to thank Steven Kennedy for his usual excellent judgement and for his advice and prodding on this second edition. My thanks also to Neill Nugent and Willie Paterson for their work as series editors, to John Peterson for his comments, and to all the production staff at Palgrave. Finally my thanks and love to Leanne for her support, and to our son Ian for providing me with plenty of happy diversions from the PC. He was born in April 2001, just as I was beginning work on this second edition, so it is dedicated to him in the hope that he grows up to be as much a European as an American.

JOHN McCORMICK

Map 1 *The EU*

EU member states

Chapter 1

What is the European Union?

The international system
Levels of cooperation
The logic of integration
Regional integration around the world
Conclusions

To understand Europe you have to be a genius or French.
Madeleine Albright, US Secretary of State, 1998

When we study world politics and economics, and try to understand our place in the global system, most of us think in terms of states, and of ourselves as citizens of one or other of those states. Maps of the world show continents and regions divided by state frontiers, demarcating areas that come under the administration of different governments and separate systems of law. When we travel from one state to another, we usually have to show passports or other documents, and are reminded that we are in transit until we return to the state to which we 'belong'.

We think in terms of states because they have been the primary actors in the global system for more than 200 years, and because the study of international relations has for decades meant the study of alliances, changing patterns of cooperation and conflict, and fluctuations in the balance of power between and among states. However, the state is not the only kind of administrative unit, nor is it even necessarily the best. In fact there are many who argue that the state system is declining, its credibility undermined by its association with the nationalist ideas that led to the outbreak of two world wars, and its inability to deal with many of the demands of modern international society.

Those who sought peace after the Second World War placed a new premium on cooperation in place of competition, but plans to build a new global order dominated by western Europe and North America were disrupted by the Cold War. For critics of the state system, the Cold War once again showed how states seemed unable to guarantee the safety of their citizens except through a balance of terror with other states. The resulting tensions led to renewed support for the idea of peace through international cooperation, which led in turn to a dramatic growth in the number of international organizations after the Second World War, spearheaded by the United Nations and covering a wide field of different functions and policy areas.

The desire for peace also led to experiments in regional integration, a process by which countries remove the barriers to free trade and the free movement of people across national borders, with the goal of reducing the tensions that can lead to international conflict. The European Union is just one of those experiments, but the one that has evolved the furthest and brought the greatest changes for its citizens. Regional integration has also been attempted in North America, Latin America, the Caribbean, south and southeast Asia, and parts of Africa, but so far on a more modest scale. Some argue that the European Union could provide a model that might eventually lead to the breakdown of the state system, and to its replacement by a new community of bigger political and economic units and networks.

The European Union has become a major new actor on the world stage, has changed the lives of more than 375 million Europeans, and has indirectly impacted the lives of everyone who trades with western Europe. Yet it is still a puzzle and a mystery to most people, and we are still some way from agreeing just what it is. It is more than a typical international organization, because it has much greater powers over its members, but it is not yet a state or a superstate. So what is it? In an attempt to provide some answers, this chapter looks at the nature of international cooperation, and assesses competing ideas about how the EU has evolved, and what it has become. It also looks at other experiments in regional integration so as to put the EU into a broader perspective.

The international system

Look at a map of the world and you will see it divided into states. These units of administration have dominated the way we think about political relations among humans for generations – some say since the Renaissance, some since the Peace of Westphalia which ended the Thirty Years War in 1648, and others say since the beginning of the nineteenth century and the emergence of the modern state system. A state is a legal and physical entity which has at least four key qualities:

- It operates within a fixed *territory* demarcated by borders, and controls the movement of people, money and goods across the borders.
- It has *sovereignty* over that territory and over the people and resources within its borders, and has the right to impose laws and taxes within its borders.

- It is legally and politically *independent*, and creates and operates the system of government under which its residents live.
- It has *legitimacy*, meaning that it is normally recognized both by its people and by other states as having jurisdiction and authority within its territory.

None of these qualities is absolute, because there are practical limits to all four – there may be border disputes that interfere with the definition of territory, there may be moral, economic or political difficulties that compromise the notion of sovereignty (for example, standards and obligations set by international law), no state is truly independent because it is subject to economic and security pressures from outside, and levels of legitimacy vary according to the extent to which the citizens of a state respect the powers and authority of that state. States may also be divided within themselves into different nations.

While the state is a legal/political entity, a nation is a group of people tied together by history, language and culture. Occasionally, a nation will coincide with a state, but most states are home to multiple different national groups, a problem that makes the distinction among countries less clear. Thus Spain, for example, is a state, but its population is divided into multiple different nationalities, including Andalusians, Aragonese, Basques, Cantabrians, Castilians, Catalans, Galicians, Navarese, and Valencians. The result of multinationalism is that loyalties and identities are often divided, making it difficult always to be sure about which label to apply to different groups of people.

The power of states has declined in recent years, for several reasons:

- The world has become a more complex place, with many interstate political and economic ties, driven by the need to trade, build security alliances, and borrow money.
- People have become more mobile, with complex new patterns of emigration developing, the movement of professionals employed by multinationals, and the rise of mass tourism that has broken down the psychological borders between states.
- The focus of allegiance has changed as national minorities within states have become more assertive and demanded greater self-determination, even independence in some cases.
- States have been unable always to meet demands for security, justice, prosperity, and the promotion of human rights.
- The inability of states to provide all the demands of their citizens for goods and services has combined with the rise of multinational corporations in search of new markets and profits to change the nature of production and to increase the pressure for the reduction of barriers to free trade.

- Revolutions in technology, science and communications – and the need to deal with shared problems such as transboundary pollution and the management of the oceans – have demanded new systems of regulation.

With the declining ability of states to respond to the needs of citizens, there has been growing international cooperation on matters of mutual interest. This cooperation has taken many forms, from the narrowly focused to the broadly idealistic, and has resulted in the development of many different methods and systems for promoting cooperation. The most common has been the creation of international organizations (IOs) (see Box 1.1), within which different countries, interest groups, corporations and governments cooperate. Such cooperation usually involves the coming together of equals, who each have the same voting power and meet to make decisions jointly.

Where governments participate in international cooperation, decision making is described as intergovernmental. States use IOs as forums within which they can meet, share views, negotiate, and work to reach agreements. To have much real impact, these agreements usually need to take the form of international treaties. The membership of IOs is voluntary, and they lack the power to raise taxes, usually depending for revenue on contributions from their members. They do not have independent powers, their decisions being the result of the joint will of their members. They do not have the power to enforce their decisions, and normally cannot impose fines on recalcitrant members, or impose sanctions other than those agreed by the membership as a whole. In most cases, the only pressure they can impose on members is moral pressure, or the threat of expulsion from the organization.

At first glance, the European Union looks much like a standard IO. It is a voluntary association of states in which many decisions are taken as a result of negotiations among the leaders of the states. Its taxing abilities are limited and its revenues small. It has few compelling powers of enforcement, and its institutions have little independence, their task being to carry out the wishes of the member states. None of its senior officials are directly elected to their positions, most being either appointed or holding *ex officio* positions (for example, members of the Council of Ministers are such by virtue of being ministers in their home governments).

However, on closer examination, it is obvious that the EU is much more than a standard IO. Its institutions have the power to make laws and policies that are binding on the member states, and in areas where the EU has authority EU law overrides national law. Its members are not equal, because many of its decisions are reached using a voting system that is weighted according to the population size of its member states. In some areas, such as trade, the EU has been given the authority to negotiate on

Box 1.1 International organizations

Most definitions of 'international organization' (IO) describe a body that promotes voluntary cooperation and coordination between or among its members, but has neither autonomous powers nor the authority to impose its rulings on its members. The emergence of IOs has been a relatively recent phenomenon, underwritten by desires to encourage cooperation as a way of avoiding international conflict. In 1900 the world had just 220 IOs; by 1969 the number had grown to about 2000, by 1981 it had reached 15 000 and it now stands at more than 40 000 (Union of International Associations Homepage, 2001).

Different kinds of IO have developed for different reasons and with different structures, methods and goals. Most fit broadly into two main categories:

- *Intergovernmental organizations* (IGOs) have national governments as members, and work to promote voluntary cooperation among those governments on matters of shared interest. IGOs have little or no autonomy in decision making, because their members make all the key decisions, and they usually have little or no ability to enforce those decisions. Examples include the United Nations, the Commonwealth, the World Trade Organization, the Organization for Economic Cooperation and Development (OECD) and the North Atlantic Treaty Organization (NATO).
- *International non-governmental organizations* (INGOs) are either bodies that work internationally outside government, or that consist of groups of national non-governmental organizations. They include multinational corporations such as Royal Dutch/Shell, Sony or General Motors, but most are non-profit-making interest groups that cooperate in order to pursue the collective goals of their members, or to bring pressure on governments for changes in policy. Examples include the International Red Cross (relief activities), Amnesty International (human rights) and Friends of the Earth (environmental issues).

behalf of the 15 member states, and other countries work with the EU institutions rather than with the governments of the member states. In several areas, such as agriculture, the environment, and competition, policies are driven more by decision making at the level of the EU than of the member states.

Where cooperation leads to the transfer of this kind of authority, we move away from intergovernmentalism and into the realms of supranationalism. This is a form of cooperation within which a new level of authority is created that is autonomous, above the state and has powers of coercion that are independent of the state. Rather than being a meeting place for governments, and making decisions on the basis of the competing interests of those governments, a supranational organization rises above the individual interests of its members and makes decisions on the basis of the interests of the whole.

Debates have long raged about whether the EU is intergovernmental or supranational, or a combination of the two. At the heart of these debates has been the question of how much power and sovereignty can or should be relinquished by national governments to bodies such as the European Commission and the European Parliament. Britons and Danes (and even the French at times) have balked at the supranationalist tendencies of the EU, while Belgians and Luxembourgers have been more willing to transfer sovereignty.

Some observers question the assumption that intergovernmentalism and supranationalism are the two extremes of a continuum (Keohane and Hoffman, 1990), that they are a zero-sum game (one balances or cancels out the other), that supranationalism involves the loss of sovereignty, or that the EU and its member states act autonomously of each other. It has been argued, for example, that governments cooperate out of need, and that this is not a matter of surrendering sovereignty, but of pooling as much of it as is necessary for the joint performance of a particular task (Mitrany, 1970). The EU has been described as 'an experiment in pooling sovereignty, not in transferring it from states to supranational institutions' (Keohane and Hoffmann, 1990, p. 277).

It has also been argued that it is wrong to assume that 'each gain in capability at the European level necessarily implies a loss of capability at the national level', and that the relationship between the EU and its member states is more symbiotic than competitive (Lindberg and Schein-gold, 1970, pp. 94–5). Ernst Haas argues that supranationalism does not mean the exercise of authority over national governments by EU institutions, but rather that it is a process or a style of decision making in which 'the participants refrain from unconditionally vetoing proposals and instead seek to attain agreement by means of compromises upgrading common interests' (Haas, 1964, p. 66).

Levels of cooperation

There are many different degrees of cooperation, depending upon the degree to which authority is shifted from the states, but the two options most often discussed in relation to the EU are confederalism and federalism.

Confederalism is a loose system of administration in which two or more organizational units keep their separate identities but give specified powers

Figure 1.1 *Confederalism and federalism compared*

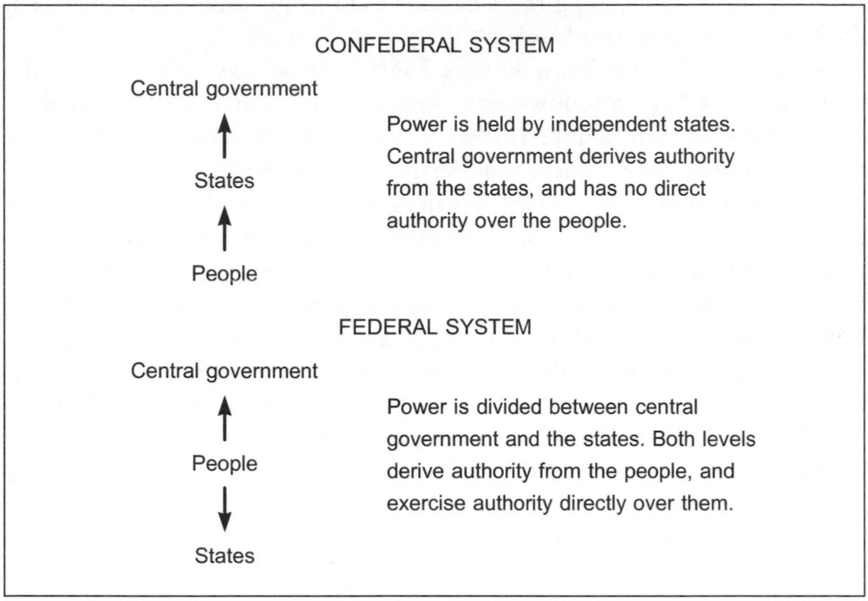

CONFEDERAL SYSTEM

Central government

↑

States

↑

People

Power is held by independent states. Central government derives authority from the states, and has no direct authority over the people.

FEDERAL SYSTEM

Central government

↑

People

↓

States

Power is divided between central government and the states. Both levels derive authority from the people, and exercise authority directly over them.

to a central authority for reasons of convenience, mutual security or efficiency. The members are sovereign and the central authority is relatively weak, existing solely at the discretion of the members and doing only what they allow it to do. If states were to form a confederation, then the citizens of those states would continue to relate directly to their own governments, and only indirectly to the higher authority (Figure 1.1). The latter would draw up laws and regulations for the states, but would exist solely at their discretion and pleasure.

Among the best known examples of confederalism are the United States in 1781–89, Germany in 1815–71, and – to some extent – Switzerland today. In the case of the United States, its original 13 states cooperated under a loose agreement known as the Articles of Confederation, which created little more than a 'league of friendship'. Central government could declare war, coin money and conclude treaties, but could not levy taxes or regulate commerce, and founded its system of 'national' defence on a network of state militias. The Articles could not be amended without the approval of all 13 states, and treaties needed the consent of at least nine states. There was no national executive or judiciary, and the powers of the confederation lay in the hands of an elected Congress in which each state had one vote. Congress rarely met though, and had no permanent home, so its powers were exercised by committees with variable membership. The assumption was that the states might cooperate enough eventually to form a common system of government, but they did not. It was only in 1787 that work began on developing the federal system of government upon which the United States is based today.

In the case of Germany, a 39-state confederation was created under the domination of Austria following the Congress of Vienna in 1815. Based on the old Holy Roman Empire, it was more an empire than a new state. Very few restrictions were placed on the powers of the member kingdoms, duchies, and cities, whose representatives met sporadically (just 16 times in the 56-year history of the confederation) in a Diet in Frankfurt. Amendments to the constitution needed near-unanimity, and most other measures required a two-thirds majority. Regular business was conducted by an inner committee in which the 11 largest states had one vote each and the smallest had six between them. There were no common trade or communications policies, and the development of a common army was frustrated by the refusal of smaller states to cooperate (Carr, 1987, pp. 4–5).

For its part, Switzerland was almost entirely confederal until 1798, and although it now calls itself a federation, it has given up fewer powers to the national government than has been the case with other federations, such as Germany, the United States and Russia. The 1874 constitution allocates specific powers to the federal government, the rest being reserved to the 20 cantons and 6 half-cantons. The Swiss encourage direct democracy by holding national referendums, have a Federal Assembly elected by proportional representation and are governed by a seven-member Federal Council elected by the Assembly. One of the members of the Council is appointed by the Federal Assembly to a one-year term as head of state and head of government.

The European Union has never been formally or informally described as a confederation by the member states, and yet it has several of the features of a confederal system:

- The citizens of the member states do not relate directly to any of the EU institutions (except Parliament, which they elect), instead relating to them through their national governments. Despite their powers of making and implementing policy, the key institutions of the EU – the European Commission, the Council of Ministers, the European Council, and the European Court of Justice – derive their authority not from the citizens of the member states, but from the leaders and governments of the member states. They are run either directly by national government leaders (the Council of Ministers and the European Council) or are appointed by those leaders (the Commission and the Court of Justice).
- The member states still have their own separate identities, have their own systems of law, can sign bilateral treaties with other states, can act unilaterally in most areas in foreign policy, and can argue that the EU

institutions exist at their discretion. There is no European government in the sense that the EU has obvious leaders – such as a president, a foreign minister or a cabinet – with sole power to make policy for the EU member states. The most important elected political leaders in the EU are still the heads of government of the member states.

- There is no generalized European tax system. The EU raises funds in part through levies and customs duties, which are a form of tax, but the vast majority of taxes – income, corporate, property, sales, capital gains, and so on – are raised by national or local units of government, which also make most tax policy.
- There is no European military or defence system. The armies, navies and air forces of the member states still answer to the governments of the member states, although contingents have come together as the seeds of a European security force (see Chapter 8), and in that sense are the functional equivalent of the militias that existed in the American confederal system.
- The EU may have its own flag and anthem, but most of the citizens of the member states still have a much greater sense of allegiance to their own national flags, anthems and other symbols, and there has been little progress towards building a sense of a European identity (see Chapter 6).

By contrast to a confederation, a federal system is one in which at least two levels of government – national and local – coexist with separate or shared powers, each having clearly defined and independent functions but neither having supreme authority over the other. Unlike a confederal system, where the higher authority does not exercise power directly over individuals, a federal government exercises power over both its constituent units and its citizens, and there is a direct relationship between citizens and each level of government.

Federalism usually involves an elected national government with sole power over foreign and security policy, and separately elected local governments with powers over such issues as education and policing. There is a single currency and a common defence force, a written constitution that spells out the relative powers of the different levels of government, a court that can arbitrate disputes between them, and at least two major sets of law, government, bureaucracy and taxation. The cumulative interests of the local units tend to define the interests of national government, which only deals with those matters that are best dealt with at the national rather than the local level.

There are several federations in the world, including Australia, Canada, Germany, India, Mexico and Nigeria, but the best known and most thoroughly studied is the United States. It has been a federal republic since 1789, when the original 13 states agreed to move from a confederal

Box 1.2 What is sovereignty?

One of the most controversial of the issues surrounding the discussion of European integration relates to sovereignty – what is it, who has it, and what impact will integration have on the powers enjoyed by the member states? Has European integration involved a loss of sovereignty by the member states of the EU?

Sovereignty is commonly defined as the right to hold and exercise authority. So a state is sovereign over its territory, for example, meaning it has the power to determine what happens within that territory, and to make laws that govern the lives of the people who live there. More specifically, sovereignty is usually said to lie in the hands of the person or institution that exercises control over the territory. In democratic systems, this usually means the national legislature. Theoretically, there are no legal constraints on a sovereign, only moral and practical ones – the sovereign is not answerable to any higher authority, but can only exert its powers to the extent that those under its authority will tolerate, and to the extent that it can practically implement its decisions.

In a democracy, the sovereign may not answer to any higher authority, but does answer to the people, because it is the will of the people that decides where sovereign power lies. So sovereignty really lies with the people, even though sovereign power is exercised by the institution that the people elect to represent their interests. This means that the common complaint made by Eurosceptics that integration means a loss of sovereignty is not entirely accurate. Sovereignty has not been lost in the European Union, but rather has been redistributed. Where sovereign power was once monopolized by national governments in the member states, it is now shared by those governments and by the institutions of the European Union.

The real issue in the European Union is not so much a loss of sovereignty as the inability of European citizens to influence directly the decisions taken by all the EU institutions; that is, to exercise their sovereignty. This is the problem of the democratic deficit, which is discussed in detail in Chapter 6.

relationship to a federal union, voluntarily giving up power over such areas as common security but retaining their own sets of laws and a large measure of control over local government. For example, the states can raise their own taxes, and they have independent powers over such policy areas as education, land use, the police and roads. They are not allowed to make treaties with other states or foreign nations, have their own currencies, levy taxes on imports and exports, or maintain their own armies. For its part, the federal government cannot unilaterally redraw the borders of a state, impose different levels of tax by state, give states different levels of representation in the US Senate (where every state has two representatives), or amend the constitution without the support of two-thirds of the states. Meanwhile – an important point – the US constitution reserves to the states all the powers not expressly delegated to the national government or prohibited to them by the national government.

The EU member states can still do almost everything that the states in the US model *cannot* do: they can make treaties, operate their own tax systems, maintain an independent military and so on. The EU institutions, meanwhile, have few of the powers of the federal government in the US model: they cannot levy taxes, operate a common military, do not yet enjoy the undivided loyalty of most Europeans, and do not have sole power to negotiate all agreements on behalf of the member states with the rest of the world. The EU is not yet the kind of federation that ardent Europeanists would like, but it does have some of the features of a federal system:

- It has a complex system of treaties and laws that are uniformly applicable throughout the European Union, to which all the member states and their citizens are subject, and that are interpreted and protected by the European Court of Justice.
- In those policy areas where the member states have agreed to transfer authority to the EU – including intra-European trade, the environment, agriculture, and social policy – EU law supersedes national law. In other policy areas, national law is still dominant.
- It has a directly elected representative legislature in the form of the European Parliament, which has growing powers over the process by which European laws are made. As those powers grow, so the powers of national legislatures are declining.
- Although still small by comparison to most national budgets (just €98 billion ($86 billion) in 2002), the EU budget gives the EU institutions an element of financial independence.
- The European Commission has the authority to oversee negotiations with third parties on behalf of all the member states, in those areas where its has been given authority by the member states.
- The EU has its own currency – the euro – which has replaced the national currencies of most of the member states. Thus authority over fiscal policy has been transferred from the governments of the countries that have adopted the euro to the European Central Bank in Frankfurt.

One way of looking at the practice of European federalism is to picture the EU as a network in which individual member states are increasingly defined not by themselves but in relation to their EU partners, and in which they prefer to interact with one another rather than third parties because those interactions create incentives for self-interested cooperation (Keohane and Hoffmann, 1991, pp. 13–14). It has been argued that the EU is 'cooptive', meaning that its participants have more to gain by working within the system than by going it alone (Heisler and Kvavik, 1973). Once they are involved, governments of the member states must take some of the responsibility for actions taken by the EU as a whole, and find it increasingly difficult to blame the European institutions.

Federalism is not an absolute or a static concept, and it has taken on different forms in different situations and at different times according to the relative strength and nature of local political, economic, social, historical and cultural pressures. For example, the US model of federalism was in place long before that country began its westward expansion, explicitly includes a system in which the powers of the major national government institutions are separated, checked and balanced, and was adopted more to avoid the dangers of chaos and tyranny than to account for social divisions. Furthermore, it has changed over time as a result of an ongoing debate over the relative powers of national and local government. In India, by contrast, federalism was seen as a solution to the difficulty of governing a state that was already in place, and that had deep ethnic and cultural divisions; the national government has a fused executive and legislature on the British model, and while India is a federal republic like the United States, political reality has ensured that powers have often been much more centralized in the hands of the national government.

The most enthusiastic European integrationists would like to see a federal United States of Europe in which today's national governments would become local governments, with the same kinds of powers as the *Länder* governments have today in Germany or state governments in the United States. Before this could happen, there would need to be – at the very least – a directly elected European government, a common tax system, a single currency, a common military, and EU institutions would have to be able to act on behalf of all the member states in foreign relations. But just how far the process of integration would have to go before there was a federal Europe is a debatable point. There is no reason why European federalism would have to look exactly like the US, Indian or even German models – it could be much looser.

The logic of integration

What are the motives behind regional integration, and how do they help explain the European Union? People or states usually cooperate or create alliances for one of four reasons: they may be brought together by force, they may share common values and goals and reach agreement on how to govern themselves as a whole, they may come together out of the need for security in the face of a common external threat, or they may decide that they can promote peace and improve their quality of life more quickly and effectively by working together rather than separately.

Interstate cooperation in western Europe was long influenced and driven by one or other of the first three motives, but since 1945 there has been a shift to the fourth. Economic integration was seen as a means of achieving peace, so barriers to trade have been pulled down, national monetary policies harmonized, and arrangements made for the free movement of people, goods, money and services, all in the hope of bringing new levels of prosperity. The most ardent supporters of economic integration have never seen it as an end in itself, however, and as the EU member states have built closer economic ties, so some of their leaders have flirted with the idea of political integration. Which came first is debatable; there were undoubtedly political motives behind the first steps in the long process of economic integration, but the development of a European single market and the adoption of the euro have had political consequences.

Political integration can be defined as the process by which political leaders and citizens in separate countries are encouraged to create a new set of common governing institutions, to give those institutions jurisdictional powers, and to shift some of their loyalties and expectations to that new level of government. Instead of making separate decisions over foreign and domestic policy, they either make joint decisions or delegate decision making powers to the new institutions. The countries cease to function separately and independently, and instead work as one, with the result that political competition expands beyond the national arena to incorporate multinational values and priorities (see Lindberg, 1963, pp. 6–7, and Haas, 1968, p. 16).

The study of international relations after the Second World War was dominated by realist theory, which argues that states are the most important actors on the world stage (because there is no higher power), and that states strive to protect their interests relative to each other. Realists talk about the importance of survival in a hostile global environment, and argue that states use both conflict and cooperation to ensure their security through a balance of power with other states. For them, the EU would be a gathering of sovereign states, which retain authority over their own affairs, give power to new cooperative bodies only when it suits them, and reserve the right to take back that power at any time. In short, realist theory argues that the EU exists only because the member states have decided that it is in their best interests.

Realism is a pessimistic way of looking at the world, and was a response to the tensions that arose out of the nuclear age. It did not explain the rising tide of cooperation that followed the Second World War, and also left many questions about the motives behind international relations unanswered. Thus it began to fall out of fashion, and most of the theoretical debates about European integration have since focused on two different sets of explanations: functionalism and neofunctionalism.

Functionalism

While realists talk about competition, conflict, and self-interest, functionalists focus more on cooperation. While realists talk about relations among governments, functionalists argue that the best people to build cooperation are technical experts, not government representatives. They talk about the internal dynamic of cooperation, arguing that if states work together in certain limited areas and create new bodies to oversee that cooperation, they will work together in other areas through an 'invisible hand' of integration. In short, functionalists argue that European integration has its own logic that the EU member states find hard to resist. Although membership involves contracts that could be broken, in reality they have an almost irresistible authority, and integration has now become so much a part of the fabric of western European society that if a state left the EU, the costs would far outweigh the benefits.

Functionalism is based on the idea of incrementally bridging the gaps between states by building functionally specific organizations. So instead of trying to coordinate big issues such as economic or defence policy, for example, functionalists believed they could 'sneak up on peace' (Lindberg and Scheingold, 1971, p. 6) by promoting integration in relatively non-controversial areas such as the postal service, or a particular sector of industry, or by harmonizing technical issues such as weights and measures.

The thinker most often associated with functionalism was the Romanian-born British social scientist David Mitrany (1888–1975), who defined the functional approach as an attempt to link 'authority to a specific activity, to break away from the traditional link between authority and a definite territory'. He argued that transnational bodies would not only be more efficient providers of welfare than national governments, but that they would help transfer popular loyalty away from the state, and so help reduce the chances of international conflict (Rosamond, 2000, p. 33). Ironically, Mitrany felt that peace could not be achieved by regional unification, because this would simply expand the problems of the state system, and replace interstate tensions with interregional tensions. Neither did he support the idea of world government, which he felt would threaten human freedom.

Writing in 1943, Mitrany argued for the creation of separate international bodies with authority over functionally specific fields, such as security, transport and communication. They should be executive bodies with autonomous tasks and powers, he argued, and do some of the same jobs as national governments, only at a different level. This focus on particular functions would encourage international cooperation more quickly and effectively than grand gestures. The dimensions and structures of these international organizations would not have to be predetermined, but would instead be self-determined (Mitrany, 1966, pp. 27–31, 72).

Once these functional organizations were created, Mitrany argued, they would have to work with each other. For example, rail, road and air agencies would need to collaborate on technical matters, such as the coordination of timetables, and agreement on how to deal with different volumes of passenger and freight traffic. As different groups of functional agencies worked together, there would be coordinated international planning. This would result not so much in the creation of a new system as in the rationalization of existing systems through a process of natural selection and evolution. States could join or leave, drop out of some functions and stay in others, or try their own political and social experiments. This could eventually lead to 'a rounded political system... the functional arrangements might indeed be regarded as organic elements of federalism by instalments' (ibid., pp. 73–84) .

Although it has been described as 'an approach rather than a tightly knit theory' (Taylor and Groom, 1975, p.1), functionalism has dominated the theoretical debates since the 1950s about how the EU has evolved. The two men often described as the founders of the European Union, French businessman Jean Monnet and French foreign minister Robert Schuman, were functionalists in the sense that they opted for the integration of a specific area (the coal and steel industry) with the hope that this would encourage integration in other areas. As Schuman put it, 'Europe will not be made all at once or according to a single plan. It will be built through concrete achievements which first create a *de facto* solidarity' (Schuman Declaration, reproduced in Weigall and Stirk, 1992, pp. 58–9).

Neofunctionalism

Studies of the early years of European integration led to the expansion of Mitrany's theories as neofunctionalism. This argues that prerequisites are needed before integration can happen, including a switch in public attitudes away from nationalism and towards cooperation, a desire by elites to promote integration for pragmatic rather than altruistic reasons, and the delegation of real power to a new supranational authority (see Rosamond, 2000, Chapter 3). Once these changes take place there will be an expansion of integration caused by spillover: joint action in one area will create new needs, tensions and problems that will increase the pressure to take joint action in another. For example, the integration of agriculture will only really work if related sectors – say transport and agricultural support services – are integrated as well.

Box 1.3   Regional integration: costs and benefits

Public opinion about the European Union is often based on a patchy grasp of how the EU has affected the lives of its citizens, and is often coloured by the populist rhetoric of pro- and anti-European media, political parties and political leaders. In the debate over the merits of integration, it has so far been easier to point accusing fingers at the costs than to outline the benefits. The costs most often quoted include the following:

1. Loss of sovereignty and national independence.
2. Loss of national identity as laws, regulations and standards are harmonized.
3. Reduced powers for national governments.
4. The creation of a new level of impersonal 'big government' in Brussels.
5. Increased competition and job losses brought by the removal of market protection.
6. Increased drug trafficking and crime arising from the removal of border controls.
7. Problems related to controversial issues such as the Common Agricultural Policy.
8. Integration promotes globalization and its related problems.

For pro-Europeans, the benefits of integration include the following:

1. Cooperation will make war and conflict less likely.
2. The single market offers European businesses a larger pool of consumers.
3. Mergers and takeovers are creating world-leading corporations.
4. Greater freedom of cross-border movement within the EU.
5. A pooling of the economic and social resources of multiple member states.
6. New global power and influence for member states working together.
7. Poorer member states 'rising' to standards maintained by more progressive states.
8. Funds and investments creating new opportunities in the poorer parts of the EU.
9. The promotion of democracy and capitalism in weaker member states.

The forerunner of today's European Union was the European Coal and Steel Community (ECSC) (see Chapter 3). This was created partly for short-term goals such as the encouragement of Franco–German cooperation, but Monnet and Schuman also saw it as the first step in a process that would eventually lead to political integration (Urwin, 1995, pp. 44–6). Few people supported the ECSC idea at the start, but once it had been working for a few years, trade unions and political parties became more enthusiastic because they began to see its benefits, and pressure grew for integration in other sectors. Urwin notes that the sectoral approach of the ECSC was handicapped because it 'was still trying to integrate only one part of complex industrial economies, and could not possibly pursue its aims in isolation from other economic segments' (ibid., p. 76). This was partly why it was not until six years after the creation of the ECSC that agreement was reached among its members to achieve broader economic integration within the European Economic Community.

Spillover takes several different forms. For example, with functional spillover, if states integrate one sector of their economies, the difficulty of isolating it from other sectors would lead to the integration of all sectors (George, 1996, p. 24). With technical spillover, differences in standards would lead different states to rise (or sink) to the level of the state with the strictest (or most lax) regulations. Finally, political spillover implies that once different functional sectors become integrated, interest groups such as corporate lobbies and trade unions will increasingly switch their attention from trying to influence national governments to trying to influence the new regional executive, which will encourage their attention in order to win new powers for itself.

Neofunctionalist ideas dominated studies of European integration in the 1950s and 1960s, but briefly fell out of favour in the 1970s, in part because the process of integrating Europe seemed to have ground to a halt in the mid-1970s, and in part because the theory of spillover needed further elaboration. The most common criticism of neofunctionalism was that it was too linear, and needed to be expanded or modified to take account of different pressures for integration, such as changes in public and political attitudes, the impact of nationalism on integration, the influence of external events such as changes in economic and military threats from outside, and social and political changes taking place separately from the process of integration (Haas 1968, pp. xiv–xv).

Joseph Nye (1971, pp. 208–14) gave neofunctionalism a boost when he wrote about taking it out of the European context and looking at non-Western experiences as well. He concluded that experiments in regional integration involve an integrative potential that depends on several different conditions:

- The economic equality or compatibility of the states involved. Questions have long been raised about the wisdom of allowing poorer southern and eastern European states to join the EU. At the same time, differences in the size or wealth of the member states may be less important than the presence of a driving force that helps bring them together, such as the tension between France and Germany.
- The extent to which the elite groups that control economic policy in the member states think alike and hold the same values.
- The extent of interest group activity. Such groups play a key role in promoting integration if they see it as being in their interests.

• The capacity of the member states to adapt and respond to public demands, which in turn depends on the level of domestic stability and the capacity – or desire – of decision makers to respond.

On all these counts the EU has a relatively high integrative potential, in contrast to another key experiment in regional cooperation: the North American Free Trade Agreement (NAFTA) (see below). The United States may be a strong driving force, but it is much wealthier than Mexico, elite groups in Mexico are more in favour of state intervention in the market-place than those in the United States and Canada, trade unions in the United States have been highly critical of NAFTA, and public opinion in Mexico is more tightly controlled and manipulated than in the United States and Canada. NAFTA may help close some of the gaps, leading to an improvement in integrative potential and removing some of the obstacles to a North American single market, but many obstacles remain.

Regional integration around the world

Since 1950, Europeans have built a complex web of economic, political and social ties among themselves. Their successes have drawn new attention to several other exercises in regional integration in other parts of the world. The motives have been similar or the same – peace through cooperation, security from neighbouring and distant enemies, the creation of greater economic opportunities, shared values, convenience, efficiency, and the self-interest of elites – but the levels of integrative potential vary.

North America

The removal of barriers to trade has taken on a new significance for the United States, Canada, and Mexico, which are currently in the process of building a free trade area that – with a combined GNP of $10.2 trillion and a population of 405 million – is wealthier and more populous than the EU. NAFTA was born on 1 January 1989 when a bilateral agreement between the United States and Canada came into force, aimed at reducing their mutual barriers to trade. Because it did not include the removal of all those barriers, the agreement actually promoted *freer* trade rather than free trade. Controversially, Mexico was admitted with the signing of the NAFTA treaty in 1992 that came into force on 1 January 1994.

Compared to the EU, the goals of NAFTA are modest: to phase out all tariffs on textiles, clothing, cars, trucks, vehicle parts and telecommunications equipment over ten years; to phase out all barriers to agricultural

Table 1.1 *Regional integration associations*

Europe	European Union (1951, 15 members)
North America	North American Free Trade Agreement (1994, 3 members)
Latin America	Latin American Free Trade Association (1960–80, 7 members) Central American Common Market (1960, 5 members) Andean Group (1969, 5 members) Latin American Integration Association (1980, 11 members) Southern Cone Common Market (Mercosur) (1991, 4 members)
Caribbean	Caribbean Community and Common Market (1973, 14 members)
Pacific Rim	Asia Pacific Economic Cooperation (1989, 21 members)
Asia	Association of Southeast Asian Nations (1967, 10 members) South Asian Association for Regional Cooperation (1985, 7 members) Commonwealth of Independent States (1991, 12 members)
Middle East	Arab League (1945, 22 members) Council of Arab Economic Unity (1957, 13 members) Arab Cooperation Council (1989, 4 members) Arab Maghreb Union (1989, 5 members)
Africa	Central African Customs and Economic Union (1964, 6 members) East African Community (1967–78, revived 1999, 3 members) Economic Community of West African States (1975, 16 members) Economic Community of Central African States (1983, 10 members) Southern African Development Community (1992, 14 members) African Union (2001, 53 members)

trade over 15 years; to allow banks, securities firms and insurance companies access to all three markets; to open up the North American advertising market; to allow lorry drivers to cross borders freely; and to loosen rules on the movement of corporate executives and some professionals. At the same time, national energy and transport industries are still heavily protected under NAFTA, there is nothing approaching the free movement of people, and all three member states can apply their own environmental regulations. No institutions have been created beyond two commissions to arbitrate disagreements over environmental standards and working conditions; special judges can also be empanelled to resolve disagreements on issues such as fishing rights and trade laws.

For some, NAFTA's real significance lay less in the content of the agreement than in the symbolism of its passage, representing (as it did at the time) a shift in US foreign policy and in the structure of a US economy gearing up for unparalleled competition from abroad. Certainly it is a much looser arrangement than the European Union, or even the European Economic Community in its early years. It is strictly intergovernmental, and although it has reduced trade restrictions, it has involved little surrender of authority or sovereignty.

Whether NAFTA will ever become anything like the EU remains to be seen. Neofunctional logic suggests it might, but many obstacles will need to be removed: Mexico's limited democracy and its centralist/corporatist ideas of government that run counter to traditions in the United States and Canada; large disparities in wealth, education and per capita production; concern among Canadians about the cultural dominance of the United States; concerns about external security in the wake of the September 2001 terrorist attacks on New York and Washington DC; significant gaps in mutual knowledge and understanding among the citizens of the three countries; and myths, misconceptions and sheer ignorance about free trade.

While the signing of the 1989 US–Canadian treaty attracted little public attention or political debate, the inclusion of Mexico raised questions in the United States about job losses, illegal immigration, drug trafficking and environmental standards, but it raised even more fundamental questions for Mexico. First, NAFTA has meant greater competition for Mexican companies and an increased trade deficit for Mexico because imports from the United States have grown more quickly than exports from Mexico. At the same time it offers considerable economic possibilities: Mexican companies now have greater access to the enormous markets to the north, more foreign investment is flowing into Mexico, and more jobs are being created in Mexico as US and Canadian companies take advantage of cheaper Mexican labour.

Second, NAFTA poses a challenge to Mexico's traditional economic policy, which has been heavily interventionist, in contrast to the more free market approach taken by the United States and Canada. In 1960 Mexico was a founder member of the seven-nation Latin American Free Trade Association (LAFTA, see below), but was unable to achieve the very modest LAFTA goals of reducing tariff and trade barriers on selected items. Membership of NAFTA immediately removed tariffs from two-thirds of Mexican exports to the United States and from nearly one-half of imports from the United States. By 2009 all US–Mexican trade should be tariff-free.

Third, the investment and trade offered by NAFTA may improve the quality of life for the average Mexican worker, but there are doubts about whether this will happen quickly enough to reduce illegal immigration to the United States in the short term. Finally, NAFTA is likely to mean substantial political and social changes for Mexico because of the links between economic liberalization and democratization. A free trade partnership with wealthy liberal democracies brings with it greater pressure for democratic reform. Spain, Portugal and Greece all joined the European Union within a few years of shaking off authoritarian regimes; membership of the EU brought all three countries economic benefits, which in turn underpinned their efforts at democratization.

Latin America

While the United States and Canada are relative newcomers to the idea of regional integration, several much older exercises have been under way south of the Rio Grande since the 1960s, with mixed results. A combination of overly ambitious goals, persistent protectionism, authoritarian politics and bad timing has undermined most of the agreements reached so far, forcing the participating states regularly to change their objectives and methods. The result has been a complex and constantly changing web of bilateral and multilateral free trade agreements.

The first step was taken with the signing in 1960 of the Treaty of Montevideo, creating the Latin American Free Trade Association (LAFTA). Seven countries – Argentina, Brazil, Chile, Mexico, Paraguay, Peru and Uruguay – agreed to create a free trade zone by 1972, but the process was quickly derailed by the difficulties inherent in negotiating the abolition of trade barriers, the ambitious timetable and the authoritarian nature of most of the governments involved. In 1969, Chile and Peru – frustrated by the lack of progress – joined Bolivia, Colombia and Ecuador in the creation of the Andean Group, a more dynamic attempt at economic integration involving reduced taxes, a common external tariff and investment in poorer industrializing areas.

In the same year LAFTA postponed the deadline for the free trade zone to 1980, but when even this proved too ambitious it focused instead on establishing a preferred tariff area based on bilateral rather than multi-lateral agreements. Domestic economic problems in most South American countries made it difficult to reach the necessary agreements, so a new Treaty of Montevideo was signed in 1980, replacing LAFTA with the Latin American Integration Association (ALADI). With 11 members – the 7 LAFTA members were joined by Bolivia, Colombia, Ecuador and Venezuela – this emphasized the importance of regional preferences aimed at increasing exports, reducing imports and developing more favourable balances of trade as a prelude to regional integration. Although the replacement of authoritarian regimes by democratically elected governments augured well, the Latin American debt crisis of the 1980s discouraged those governments from opening up their markets.

The focus began to change in 1985–86 when Argentina and Brazil started to concentrate on the reduction of barriers to bilateral trade. Just as Franco–German cooperation provided the early engine for regional integration in Europe, the Argentina–Brazil nexus had a spillover economic effect on neighbouring states. In 1991 the effect expanded with the signing of the Treaty of Asunción between Argentina, Brazil, Paraguay and Uruguay, creating the Southern Cone Common Market, or Mercosur. This involves progressive tariff reduction, the adoption of sectoral agreements, a common external tariff, the agreement of free trade areas with neighbouring countries or subregional groups, and the ultimate creation of a common market. Bolivia and Chile are associate members.

A new dimension has been added to free trade in North and Latin America in recent years with US-led attempts to work towards a free trade zone covering the entire western hemisphere. The idea was raised in 1990 by President George Bush, who spoke of the possibility of a free trade area of the Americas (FTAA), stretching from Alaska to Cape Horn. It was taken up enthusiastically by President Bill Clinton, who played host to the leaders of 34 states at a 'summit of the Americas' in Miami in December 1994, the first meeting among leaders of American states for 27 years. They agreed a target date of 2005, with 'concrete progress' to have been made by 2000, and trade ministers have since held meetings to decide the agenda for negotiations. A second summit of the Americas was held in Santiago, Chile, in April 1998 formally to launch the negotiations. A third was held in Quebec City, Canada, in April 2001. However, while trade within regional subgroupings such as NAFTA, Mercosur and the Central American Common Market has grown substantially in recent years, the FTAA has many obstacles to overcome.

Meanwhile, broader economic integration has been taking place around the Pacific rim under the aegis of Asia Pacific Economic Cooperation (APEC). This is not so much an institution as a forum for the discussion of economic issues affecting 21 Asian, Pacific and American states, including

Canada, China, Japan, Russia, and the United States. Although it has been promoted most actively since 1989 by the United States and Australia, Japan and China are widely seen as the leading contenders for leadership of APEC in the twenty-first century. The medium-term goal is the creation of a free trade zone among these countries by 2020. Progress so far has been slow, and China appears to see Japan less as a partner than as a rival for leadership in the region. At the same time, the Japanese role is welcomed by many of its neighbours as offering a counterbalance to the economic weight of the United States.

APEC members include some of the world's fastest-growing economies, and APEC already accounts for about 60 per cent of global GDP; the economic potential of APEC is enormous, and if the experiment is successful it will almost certainly promote economic liberalization throughout the region.

Asia

Until 1997–98, dynamic economic growth underlined the potential for regional economic integration among the newly industrializing countries of southeast Asia. The most important initiatives have come out of the Association of Southeast Asian Nations (ASEAN), established in August 1967 to replace an earlier organization founded in 1961. Headquartered in Jakarta, Indonesia, ASEAN now has ten members: the founding states were Indonesia, Malaysia, the Philippines, Singapore and Thailand, which were joined in 1984 by Brunei, in 1995 by Vietnam and in 1997 by Burma, Cambodia and Laos. From an initial interest in security issues (protecting the region from big-power rivalry and providing a forum for the resolution of intraregional problems), ASEAN has moved steadily towards economic cooperation and trade, its members agreeing in 1992 to create an ASEAN Free Trade Area within 15 years.

ASEAN has a much looser institutional system than the EU. The major decision making body is the Meeting of the ASEAN Heads of Government, or the ASEAN Summit (equivalent to the European Council). The first such summit took place in 1976, but no plans were made to meet regularly until the fourth summit in 1992, when it was decided that the heads of government would meet formally every three years and informally at least once in between. While summits lay down the general direction of ASEAN activities, foreign ministers meet annually (inviting along other ministers as and when necessary) to develop overall policies, and economics ministers meet annually to work on the development of the free trade area. In recent years, sectoral ministers have also met more regularly to discuss energy, agricultural, tourism and transport issues. When necessary, joint ministerial meetings take place to promote cross-sectoral coordination. A standing committee headed by a secretary-general takes care of business between ministerial meetings, providing a very modest bureaucracy for ASEAN (ASEAN Homepage, 2001).

Further west, the most obvious candidate to head a regional economic grouping is India, with a population of about one billion. India has been reluctant to become involved in regional economic arrangements, however, thanks mainly to strained relations with most of its neighbours, especially Pakistan, with which it has had three wars since 1947. India's giant presence has also caused an unequal distribution of power in south Asia, and successive Indian governments have tended to prefer to deal bilaterally with other countries in the region. For their part, India's smaller neighbours fear that India would inevitably dominate a regional association, and use it to institutionalize its hegemony (Hardgrave and Kochanek, 2000, pp. 431).

Despite these concerns, greater regional cooperation began slowly to emerge in the early 1980s, leading to the creation in 1985 of the South Asian Association for Regional Cooperation (SAARC) with seven members: Bangladesh, Bhutan, India, the Maldives, Nepal, Pakistan, and Sri Lanka. Together they are home to more than 1.3 billion people, or one-fifth of the world's population. Meeting in 1983, the foreign ministers of the seven countries agreed to promote 'collective self-reliance' in nine areas, including agriculture, transport and telecommunications, and since 1985 the leaders have met at annual summits rotating among the different countries, with the host country assuming the chairmanship for that year.

The commerce ministers met for the first time in 1996, a move that was seen as recognition of the need to address what Indian Prime Minister Narasimha Rao called 'neoprotectionism' among SAARC members, notably India and Pakistan. The seven countries had earlier agreed to set up a South Asian Preferential Trading Arrangement (SAPTA) with a view to encouraging the removal of tariff and non-tariff barriers and working towards the creation of a free-trade area (SAFTA) by 2005. At the moment SAARC has no institutional arrangements, its goals are very modest in comparison with those of the European Union, or even NAFTA, and much work still needs to be done if India and Pakistan's long-standing mutual distrust is to be overcome.

The Middle East

The Middle East has had less success with experiments in regional integration than any other part of the world, which is ironic given the Islamic belief in a worldwide community of Muslims transcending race, language and national identity. Greater cooperation among the states of the Middle East makes sense at many levels: several countries are too small to sustain themselves once the oil runs out, the profits of the oil producers could be used to invest in non-producers and help promote manufacturing in the region, cooperation would allow better control of the already considerable flow of workers to the oil-rich states, and intraregional trade could help the Middle Eastern states reduce their dependence on oil exports to the West and develop regional transportation networks.

There have been a number of attempts at regional cooperation. The first began in 1945 with the creation of the Arab League to promote political, economic, social and military cooperation. The League is headquartered in Cairo, and currently has 21 members. A second step was taken in 1957 with the creation of the Council of Arab Economic Unity, whose goal is to promote economic integration. Headquartered in Amman, Jordan, it has 11 members. Another more limited experiment in integration – the United Arab Republic, bringing together Egypt and Syria – took just three years to collapse (1958–61). In 1965 the Arab Common Market was set up to promote economic cooperation and integration, but so far it has attracted only four members (Egypt, Iraq, Jordan and Yemen). Finally, the Arab Monetary Fund was established in 1977 to promote economic and monetary integration. Headquartered in the United Arab Emirates, it has 19 members.

Why has the success of these organizations been so limited? Part of the problem stems from internal dissension, notably differences of opinion on how to deal with Israel: Egypt was expelled from the Arab League for ten years when it signed the 1979 peace treaty with Israel. Further divisions were caused by disagreement over how to respond to Iraq's invasion of Kuwait in 1990. Cooperation has been further undermined by differences between states over the interpretation of Islam, the fact that less than 10 per cent of trade in the Middle East and North Africa is intraregional, the dominance of oil in national economies, protectionist national economic policies and severe cross-border restrictions on the movement of people. It will take a significant shift in attitudes and policies for the Middle East to create the right conditions for greater economic cooperation.

Africa

Africa to date has lacked much integrative potential, because of a combination of poverty, political instability, civil war, border disputes, and the often different political and economic agendas of African states. This has not discouraged several groups of countries from building regional cooperative organizations. One early experiment was the East African Community, under which Kenya, Tanzania and Uganda built elements of a single market and a customs union, adopted a single currency, and developed a common transport system. The Community broke up in acrimony in 1977, in part because of the unbalanced benefits accruing to Kenya, but was relaunched in 1999.

A more substantial experiment – but one that has its own problems – is the 16-member Economic Community of West African States (ECOWAS). Headquartered in Abuja, Nigeria, it was founded in 1975 and now has a total population of more than 220 million people. ECOWAS set out to achieve first a customs union and then a full common market along the lines of the European Union. By harmonizing their policies on agriculture, industry, transport and communications and paving the way for the free movement of people and labour, its members felt they could change the balance of power between themselves and the richer Western countries. To promote cooperation, a development fund was created through which the wealthier ECOWAS members could channel investment funds to the poorer members.

Organizationally, ECOWAS revolves around meetings of the heads of government, which took place annually until 1997, when it was decided to hold them twice a year. A council of ministers, consisting of two representatives from each of the member states, meets twice a year to oversee the running of ECOWAS, which is left to a small secretariat and five commissions dealing with issues such as trade, customs, industry and transport. A tribunal meets to interpret provisions laid down in the founding treaty of ECOWAS and to settle disputes between member states.

With its growing oil revenues in the late 1970s, Nigeria was initially an active member of ECOWAS and exerted a substantial regional influence through grants, loans and technical assistance to other member states. During the 1980s, however, when Nigeria began to tighten its belt and put domestic economic priorities above those of regional cooperation, the cracks in the ECOWAS structure began to show. Some of its members (notably Côte d'Ivoire, Ghana and Senegal) have achieved relative political and economic stability, but others (such as Burkina Faso, Liberia and Sierra Leone) have persistent instability. However, the main problem has been the unequal size of the member states. With 53 per cent of the population of ECOWAS, Nigeria is by far the largest, wealthiest and most powerful member, which has not only caused nervousness among the smaller members (such as Benin, Cape Verde, Gambia and Togo) and poorer members (Guinea, Guinea-Bissau, Mali, Mauritania and Niger), but has also led to resentment among Nigerians, who feel that their country has borne too much of the financial burden of ECOWAS.

Nigeria is a large and valuable market for the smaller states, but they have been unwilling to reciprocate by opening their markets to Nigeria and have long suspected Nigeria of working towards regional domination. Also, ECOWAS members often have conflicting economic and trade policies, have made little progress in stabilizing exchange rates among themselves and regularly fail to pay their membership fees. One of its few tangible achievements to date was its contribution to monitoring a cease-fire in war-torn Liberia in 1990–93, which prompted its members to agree a new treaty in 1993 in which they adopted the additional objective of working together on regional peacekeeping.

European integration has been driven largely by the efforts of its larger member states – notably France and Germany – and the future of NAFTA is closely tied to events and policies in the United States. In few places, however, are the fortunes of an experiment in regional integration so patently dependent upon one of the members as is the case with ECOWAS. If Nigeria were to develop long-term democracy and economic stability, and if its oil wealth were harnessed for the benefit of the national economy and the greater good of all its citizens, it could become a powerful and influential force for democratic change and economic development throughout West Africa. Until that happens, the aspirations of ECOWAS will be more significant than its achievements.

In July 2001, Africa launched the most ambitious attempt yet to build regional cooperation when the 37-year-old Organization of African Unity (OAU) was replaced by the African Union. Inspired by the European Union, the African Union was planning – as this book went to press – to set up an African central bank, a parliament, an executive commission, and a court. All 53 members of the OAU were potentially also members of the African Union, but since conflicts were under way in 21 of those countries, the integrative potential of the Union was questionable.

Conclusions

The European Union is the most highly evolved example of regional integration in the world, but as this chapter reflects, it is far from being the only example. Clusters of states on every continent have found that cooperation on a variety of issues is in their interests, so much so that several have decided to take that cooperation to another level, moving into the realms of economic integration. In other words, rather than simply working together on matters of mutual interest, they have surrendered powers to decision making systems that function beyond the level of the state. Some of these systems are informal, consisting, for example, of regular meetings among ministers or national leaders and agreement to reach decisions jointly rather than individually. Others are more formal and have moved beyond the intergovernmental level to the creation of supranational organizations and bodies of common law.

As a result, regional integration is a concept with which we are all becoming more familiar. This is especially true in Europe, because the laws and decisions that govern the lives of Europeans are being made less at the local or national level, and increasingly as a result of negotiations and compromises among the EU member states. Developments in Brussels, Strasbourg and Luxembourg are becoming as important to understand as those in the national capitals. Not long ago an 'informed citizen' was someone who knew how the national system of government worked, how the national economy functioned and how the national society was structured. To be 'informed' now demands a much broader horizon, and familiarity with a new set of institutions, processes, and political, economic and social forces. It also demands an understanding of the character of the EU, and the extent to which it is a confederal or a federal association.

Yet Europeans are still some way from understanding how and why regional integration happens, or even deciding whether or not it is a good idea. Western Europe has come a long way since 1945, and has survived political and economic crises to become an economic superpower that has enjoyed the longest period of peace in its history, domestic conflicts excepted. But to what extent can this be credited to the European Union? What would Europe look like today without the EU? Would it be richer or poorer, more or less peaceful? Is there anything that the rest of the world can learn from the European experience, and is there anything that Europeans can learn from the steps being taken towards regional integration in the Americas, Asia or Africa?

Opinions on the value of regional integration – and its long-term prospects – will remain divided as long as they are confused and obscured by questions and doubts about the conditions that encourage integration, the logic of the steps taken towards integration, and the end product. Comparing the European case with other examples of regional integration around the world can give us more insight into its advantages and disadvantages, but we are still some way from agreement on what drives the process, and from understanding what we have created. Most confusingly, the goals of regional integration are only very vaguely defined. How will Europe know when it has gone far enough? What exactly is the end goal? The next two chapters will attempt to answer these questions by looking at the evolution, structure and effects of the European Union.

Chapter 2

The Idea of Europe

The changing nature of Europe
Where is Europe?
Europe today
Conclusions

Europe is a continent of energetic mongrels.
H. A. L. Fisher, British historian

We live in a European world. It is a multicultural world, to be sure, but most if it has been colonized at some point by one European power or another, and the majority of people live in societies that are either based on the European cultural tradition or influenced on a daily basis by the norms and values of that tradition. The 'world culture' described by the American political scientist Lucien Pye (1966) is ultimately European in origin, even if it is most actively promoted and exported by the United States (which is itself primarily a product of European culture).

It is all the more ironic, then, that the idea of Europe is so hard to pin down. We know where Europe sits on a map, but we have difficulty in defining its physical and cultural boundaries and in being certain about what makes it distinctive. Europeans have much that unites them, but much more that divides them. They lack a common history, they speak many different languages, they have different social values, their views of their place in the world often differ, they have gone to war with each other with tragic regularity, they have often redefined their allegiances and their identities, and they have frequently redrawn their common frontiers in response to changes in political affiliations.

However, since 1945 the differences have slowly been replaced by common interests, goals and values, prompted in part by a redefinition of Europe's place in the world. Helen Wallace (1992, p. 16) argues that in trying to improve the way they manage their own affairs, taking on more responsibility for each other and dealing with the uncertainties posed by changes in the Soviet Union and then in Russia, Europeans have become more introverted and their internal preoccupations have heavily shaped their attitudes towards the rest of the world. Outsiders have also had to rethink their understanding of Europe, which is now less a collection of freestanding sovereign states and more an economic superstate. North Americans and the Japanese see the EU as a new source of competition for economic power and political influence, while most eastern Europeans see it as a new force for positive economic and political change, and as a club that many of them would very much like to join.

Despite this redefinition of Europe, the idea of European unity that has taken root and expanded since 1945 is nothing new. In fact it is an old idea that has simply been revived and, more importantly, adopted voluntarily by a large number of Europeans for the first time. Monarchs, popes, generals and dictators have dreamed about variations on the theme of unity since the Early Middle Ages, and intellectuals have been writing and talking about unity as a means of defending Europe against itself and outsiders since at least the fourteenth century. The key difference between the times in which they wrote and the contemporary age is that there is now much wider political and public support for the idea of integration than there ever has been before.

This chapter will attempt to draw a portrait of Europe. It begins with a discussion of the meaning of the terms 'Europe' and 'European', providing a brief history both of the idea of Europe and of the arguments in favour of integration and unity, and setting the scene for developments after 1945 (covered in Chapter 3). The second half of the chapter is a political, economic and social profile of Europe today, which compares and contrasts the character of the member states of the EU and their neighbours.

The changing nature of Europe

Defining 'Europe' and 'European' has always been difficult, thanks to disagreements about the outer limits of the region and the inner character of its inhabitants. Today those inhabitants are experiencing political and economic change that is encouraging them to think of themselves less as Spaniards or Belgians or Finns and more as 'Europeans', but this is a trend that begs several questions. What is Europe, where does it begin and end, and what exactly does being a European mean? Is there a coherent and distinctive European identity and a set of core European values with which the inhabitants of the region can identify? When and how did the idea of European unity emerge, and how has it evolved?

Europe has never been united, and its history has been one of fragmentation, conflict and changing political boundaries. Large parts of Europe have been brought together at different times for different reasons – beginning with the Romans and moving through the Franks to the Habsburgs, Napoleon and Hitler – but while many have dreamed of unification, it has only been since the Second World War that Europeans have finally begun to embrace the notion that nationalism might be set aside in the interests of regional cooperation. For the first time in its history, almost the entire subcontinent is engaged in a process of integration that is encouraging its inhabitants to think and behave as Europeans rather than as members of smaller cultural or national groups that just happen to inhabit the same land mass.

The word Europe is thought to come from Greek mythology: Europa was a Phoenician princess who was seduced by Zeus disguised as a white bull, and was taken from her homeland in what is now Lebanon to Crete, where she later married the King of Crete. Just when the term European was first applied to a specific territory or its inhabitants is unclear, but it appears first to have taken on substance when Greeks began to settle on the Ionian Islands and came across the Persians. The expansion of the Persian empire led to war in the fifth century BC, when Greek authors such as Aristotle began to make a distinction between the languages, customs and values of Greeks, the inhabitants of Asia (as represented by the Persians) and the 'barbarians' of Europe, an area vaguely defined as being to the north. Maps drawn up by classical scholars subsequently showed the world divided into Asia, Europe and Africa, with the boundary between Europe and Asia marked by the River Don and the Sea of Azov (Delanty, 1995, pp. 18–19; den Boer, 1995).

The Roman Empire – whose power was at its peak from approximately 200 BC to 400 AD – brought a substantial part of Europe under a common system of government for the first time. However, it was centred on the Mediterranean and took in North Africa and parts of the Middle East as well, and so was not exclusively European. Because the Romans were presiding over an empire, there was no prevailing sense that everyone living under Roman rule was part of a region with a common identity. Furthermore, the inhabitants of Europe were (and still are in some places) known as Franks or Romans by the inhabitants of the Middle East and North Africa. The situation was further confused after the end of Roman hegemony in the last part of the fourth century AD, when Rome was invaded by the northern 'barbarians' and Europe broke up into feuding kingdoms. The invasions separated Europe culturally from its classical past, and the dark ages that followed witnessed substantial movements of people as different tribes – notably the Huns, the Vikings and the Magyars – invaded other parts of Europe.

The birth of Europe is often dated to the Early Middle Ages (500–1050), with the emergence of a common civilization based on Christianity, with Rome as the spiritual capital and Latin as the language of education. The beginnings of a sense of a European identity came with the emergence of a rift between the western and eastern branches of Christianity, the expansion of Frankish power from the area of what is now Belgium and the Netherlands, and the development of a stronger territorial identity in the face of external threats, notably from the Middle East. The retreat of Europeans in the face of Asian expansionism reached its peak in the seventh and eighth centuries with the advance of Arab forces across North Africa. Crossing the Straits of Gibraltar in 711, they conquered most of Spain and southern France, being turned back only in 732 with their defeat by Charles Martel at Poitiers.

The term European was used by contemporary chroniclers to describe the forces under the command of Martel (Hay, 1957, p. 25), but it did not become more widely used until the year 800, when Charlemagne was crowned Holy Roman Emperor by the Pope and was described in poems as the king and father of Europe. The Frankish Empire over which he presided covered most of what are now France, Switzerland, Austria, southern Germany and the Benelux countries. (As proponents of European unity in the 1950s liked to point out, this correlated closely with the territory of the six founding member states of the European Economic Community.) Although the Frankish Empire helped promote the spread of Christianity, it was quickly divided up among Charlemagne's sons after his death in 814, and while the Holy Roman Empire persisted until the middle of the fourteenth century, it was – as Voltaire later quipped – 'neither Holy, nor Roman, nor an Empire'.

Europe at the time was technologically backward in comparison with China, and was to remain peripheral to the development of civilization until well into the Middle Ages. Central authority declined and intra-European trade ended in the wake of further invasions from Scandinavia and central Europe, and feudalism became the norm as large landowners exercised growing authority over their subjects. By the beginning of the High Middle Ages in the mid-eleventh century, however, commerce had revived, agricultural production was growing, population was beginning to increase, towns were becoming centres of intellectual and commercial life, a new class of merchants was emerging, monarchs and the aristocracy were imposing greater control over their territories, and the threat of invasion from outside Europe had largely disappeared. In fact, through the crusades and the development of external trade, Europe – long the target of foreign invaders – now became the aggressor. As Christian armies came together from all over the region to take part in the crusades, Europe developed a tighter identity.

Safe from invasion, European politics and culture began to take root in the High Middle Ages, and by the fifteenth century it had become increasingly common for scholars to use the term 'Europe', which to outsiders became synonymous with 'Christendom'. Indeed the latter term was used more often than the former to describe the region. This was ironic given the turbulence that followed in the wake of famines, the Black Death and the Hundred Years' War (1337–1453), the emerging power of monarchs, and the challenges to the authority of the papacy that led to the Reformation and the growth of the modern state system. Europe became divided among a variety of Protestant churches and the Roman Catholic church, and for much of the sixteenth and early seventeenth century was destabilized by religious warfare. Nonetheless Europeans began voyages of discovery to Africa, the Americas and Asia, there was an expansion of education based on the classical works of Greek and Latin authors, and a scientific revolution was sparked by the findings of Copernicus, Sir Isaac Newton and others. All these developments combined to give Europeans a new confidence and a new sense of their place in the world.

Delanty (1995, p. 42) argues that cultural diversity within Europe ensured that the idea of European unity was restricted to matters relating to foreign conquest. The earliest proponents of unity were motivated in part by their belief that a united Christian Europe was essential for the revival of the Holy Roman Empire and by concern about Europe's insecurity in the face of gains by the Turks in Asia Minor; most of the proposals for unity were based on the argument that the supremacy of the papacy should be revived (Heater, 1992, p. 6). A notable example was the suggestion made in 1306 by the French lawyer and diplomat Pierre Dubois (b. 1255). Noting that war was endemic in Europe despite the teachings of Christianity, Dubois suggested that the princes and cities of Europe should form a confederal 'Christian Republic', overseen by a permanent assembly of princes working to ensure peace through the application of Christian principles. In the event of a dispute, a panel of nine judges could be brought together to arbitrate, with the Pope acting as a final court of appeal (Heater, 1992, p. 10; Urwin, 1995, p. 2).

The Renaissance (roughly 1350–1550) saw the loyalty of individuals shifting from the Church to ideas based on individualism and republicanism, and the state system began to emerge, beginning in England and France. Under the circumstances, the idea of regional unity was far from the minds of all but a small minority of idealists. Among these were King George of Bohemia and his diplomatist Antoine Marini, who proposed a European confederation to respond to the threat posed by the Turks in the mid-fifteenth century. Their plan – which was remarkably similar to the structure eventually set up for the European Union – involved an assembly meeting regularly and moving its seat every five years, a college of permanent members using a system of majoritarian decision making, a council of kings and princes, and a court to adjudicate disputes (de Rougemont, 1966, p. 71).

The church had become so divided by the end of the sixteenth century that the idea of a united Christian Europe was abandoned, and those who still favoured the idea of European unity saw it as based less on a common religion than on addressing the religious causes of conflict and the growing threat of Habsburg power. These were the motives behind the Grand Design outlined by the Duc de Sully (1560–1641) in France in the early seventeenth century. He proposed a redrawing of administrative lines throughout Europe so as to achieve equilibrium of power, and the creation of a European Senate with 66 members serving three-year terms (Heater, 1992, pp. 30–5).

One of those influenced by de Sully's ideas was William Penn (1644–1718), who in the middle of yet another war between England and France published *An Essay Towards the Present Peace of Europe* (1693), in which he proposed the creation of a European diet or parliament that could be used for dispute resolution. He suggested that quarrels might be settled by a three-quarters majority vote, something like the qualified majority voting system used today (see page 99). This would be weighted according to the economic power of the various countries: Germany would have 12 votes, France 10, England 6 and so on (Heater, 1992, pp. 53–6; Salmon and Nicoll, 1997, pp. 3–6). In 1717 the Abbé de Saint-Pierre (1658–1743) published his three-volume *Project for Settling an Everlasting Peace in Europe*, in which he argued for free trade and a European Senate. (His ideas were later to inspire Schiller to write 'Ode to Joy' which – sung to Beethoven's Ninth Symphony – has become the European anthem (Heater, 1992, p. 85).)

Several prominent thinkers and philosophers subsequently explored the theme of peace through unity. For example Jean-Jacques Rousseau wrote in favour of a European federation; Jeremy Bentham, in *A Plan for An Universal and Perpetual Peace* (1789), wrote of his ideas for a European assembly and a common army; Immanual Kant's *Thoughts on Perpetual Peace* (1795) included suggestions for the achievement of world peace; and the Comte de Saint-Simon, in response to the Napoleonic wars, published a pamphlet in 1814 titled *The Reorganization of the European Community,* in which he argued the need for a federal Europe with common institutions, but within which national independence would be maintained and respected.

For political figures, the desire to overcome Europe's political divisions usually led them to the narrow view that conquest was the best response, but found themselves foiled by the sheer size of the task and the resistance of key actors to changes in the balance of power. The attempts by Charlemagne, Philip II of Spain and the Habsburgs to establish a European hegemony all failed, argues Urwin (1995, p. 2), because of the 'complex fragmented mosaic of the continent . . . [and] the inadequate technical resources of the would-be conquerors to establish and maintain effective control by force over large areas of territory against the wishes of the local populations'.

The first attempt to achieve unity by force in modern times was made by Napoleon, who brought what are now France, Belgium, the Netherlands, Luxembourg and parts of Germany and Italy under his direct rule. He saw himself as the 'intermediary' between the old order and the new, and hoped for a European association with a common body of law, a common court of appeal, a single currency and a uniform system of weights and measures. In contrast to Napoleon's idealistic notion of unity, and despite rapid economic, social and technological change, nineteenth-century Europe was dominated by nationalist ideas, which emerged during the French Revolution and led most notably to the unification of Italy in the 1860s and Germany in 1871. Nationalism led to rivalry among European states, both within Europe and further afield in the competition among those states for colonies.

The concept of a United States of Europe continued to be promoted by nineteenth-century intellectuals such as Victor Hugo, who in 1848 declared that the nations of Europe, 'without losing [their] distinctive qualities or . . . glorious individuality, will merge closely into a higher unity and will form the fraternity of Europe . . . Two huge groups will be seen, the United States of America and the United States of Europe, holding out their hands to one another across the ocean.' However, political leaders did not embrace such ideas, and a combination of nationalism and competition for colonial possessions led to increased militarization and the outbreak in 1914 of the Great War, in which all the competing tensions within Europe finally boiled over. One of the results of the war was chaos in much of central Europe, and the peace arranged under the 1919 Treaty of Versailles avoided as many questions and problems as it addressed.

Before, during and after the war, philosophers and political leaders continued to put their minds to the question of how to encourage Europeans to rise above nationalism and consider themselves part of a broader culture, thereby helping them to address and remove the causes of conflict and allowing Europe to defend itself against external threats. Dubois, Penn, Saint-Simon and others had already explored such ideas but they had all been writing in a vacuum of public interest. The horrors of the First World War now created an audience that was more receptive to the idea of European integration, and discussions involved not just intellectuals but political leaders as well. The most enthusiastic proponents tended to be smaller states that were tired of being caught up in big power rivalry, and several made practical moves towards economic cooperation. For example, Belgium and Luxembourg created a limited economic union in 1922, and in 1930 joined several Scandinavian states in an agreement to limit tariffs.

One of the best-known of the intellectual contributors to the debate about European unity was Count Richard Coudenhove-Kalergi, who proposed a Pan-European Union (Box 2.1). He failed to generate a mass following, but his ideas attracted the interest of a number of leading figures in the arts, such as Richard Strauss and Ortega y Gasset, and several current or future political leaders, including Georges Pompidou, Thomas Masaryk, Konrad Adenauer, Winston Churchill and two French prime ministers, Édouard Herriot and Aristide Briand (1862–1932). Immediately after the war, the prevailing view in France was that European cooperation was an impossible dream and that the best hope for peace lay in French strength and German weakness (Bugge, 1995, p. 102). Herriot was one of those who disagreed, and in 1924 he called for the creation of a 'United States of Europe', to grow out of the postwar cooperation promoted by the League of Nations.

For his part, Briand called for a European confederation working within the League of Nations, and in May 1930 distributed a memorandum to governments outlining his ideas (Salmon and Nicoll, 1997, pp. 9–14). In it he wrote of the need for 'a permanent regime of solidarity based on international agreements for the rational organization of Europe'. He used such terms as 'common market' and 'European Union', and even listed specific policy needs, such as the development of trans-European transport networks, and anticipated what would later become the regional and social policies of the EU. Although he is often described in France as one of the founding fathers of European integration, his memorandum was sidelined by the gathering tensions that led to the Second World War.

All prospect of discussions of this kind leading to European unity was swept violently aside by the rise of Nazi Germany, which was intent on correcting the 'wrongs' of the Versailles treaty and creating a German 'living space'. Adolf Hitler spoke of a 'European house', but only in terms of the importance of German rule over the continent in the face of the perceived threat from communists and 'inferior elements' within and outside Europe. Many of the nationalist tensions that had built up in Europe during the nineteenth century – and had failed to be resolved by the Great War – now boiled over once again into conflict. Hitler was able to expand his Reich to include Austria, Bohemia, Alsace-Lorraine and most of Poland, and to occupy much of the rest of continental Europe.

The ideological division of Europe after 1945 added to the pre-existing economic and social divisions, so that it became normal to think of the region as having multiple identities: the capitalist west, the socialist east, the industrial centre, the Mediterranean south and the Nordic north. However, the end of the Cold War in 1990–91 also brought an end to the ideological and social divisions that had been represented by the Berlin

Box 2.1 Paneuropa

The period of peace after the First World War saw the publication of a flood of books and articles exploring variations on the theme of European union. The most influential of these were written by Count Richard Coudenhove-Kalergi (1894–1972), the son of an Austrian diplomat and his Japanese wife, and founder in 1922 of the Pan-European Union.

The problems facing Europe after the war convinced Coudenhove-Kalergi that the only workable guarantee of peace was political union, and he outlined his ideas in a book titled *Paneuropa,* published in 1923. He argued that while Europe's global supremacy was over, the internal decline of Europe could be avoided if its political system was modernized, with a new emphasis on large-scale cooperation. Changes in Europe could not happen in isolation from those in the rest of the world, however, and Coudenhove-Kalergi felt that the best hope of world peace lay in the creation of five 'global power fields':

- the Americas (excluding Canada)
- the USSR
- Eastern Asia (China and Japan)
- Paneuropa (which would include continental Europe's colonies in Africa and southeast Asia)
- Britain and its empire (including Canada, Australia, southern Africa, the Middle East and India).

He excluded the USSR from Europe because it was too diverse and did not have the democratic traditions necessary for the development of Paneuropa. He was uncomfortable about excluding Britain, but did so because he felt it was so powerful as to be a political continent in its own right. It could serve as a mediator with the United States, however, and could become part of Paneuropa if it lost its empire.

Coudenhove-Kalergi argued that an arms race among European states would be destructive and keep Europe in a permanent state of crisis. Instead, he proposed a four-stage process for the achievement of European union: a conference of representatives from the 26 European states, the agreement of treaties for the settlement of European disputes, the development of a customs union, and the drafting of a federal European constitution. He also suggested that English should become the common second language for Europe, since he felt that it was becoming the dominant global language.

wall and the iron curtain, and as the differences between east and west began to decline it became more normal to think of the region as a whole.

Europeans still make many distinctions among themselves. Eastern Europe is still working to rid itself of the heritage of state socialism, and Germans still distinguish between those from the east and those from the west. Cultural and economic differences also continue to influence perceptions of Europe: the Mediterranean states to the south are distinctive from the maritime states to the west or the Scandinavian states to the north. However, compared with just a generation ago, the differences that separate Europeans have become much less distinct and much less obvious. Language differences still stand as a potent reminder of cultural divisions, but the increased mobility of Europeans, a communications revolution that has made Europe a smaller place, and the growth in trade that has put a greater variety of European products on the shelves of shops across the region have helped build a sense among Europeans that there is less to distinguish them from one another than they once thought.

Where is Europe?

Even as Europeans move along the path of economic, social and political integration, the definition of Europe remains ambiguous, for several reasons. First, few of the EU's member states are culturally homogeneous, and there is no such thing as a European race. The constant reordering of territorial lines over the centuries has created a situation in which every European state has national minorities, and several of those minorities – notably the Basques and the Irish – are divided by national frontiers. Many states have also seen large influxes of immigrants in the last forty years, including Algerians to France, Turks to Germany and Indians to Britain. Not only is there nothing like a dominant culture, but most Europeans rightly shudder at the thought of their separate identities being subordinated to some kind of homogenized Euroculture.

Second, residents of the EU speak at least 36 languages (Keegan and Kettle, 1993, p. 92), which are vigorously defended as symbols of national identities and act as a constant reminder of the differences among Europeans; one of the factors that eased the development of the United States was the existence of a common language. Multilingualism also means that all official EU documents are translated into the 11 official languages of the member states, although the work of EU institutions is increasingly carried out in English and French. Supported by its rapid spread as the language of global commerce and diplomacy, the dominance of English grows, and it is slowly becoming the language of Europe. This worries the French in particular and other Europeans to some extent, but it is probably irresistible and will at least give Europeans a way of talking to each other, and perhaps help reduce the cultural differences that divide them.

Third, the histories of European states overlapped for centuries as they colonized, went to war or formed alliances with each other. However, those overlaps often emphasized their differences rather than giving them the sense of a shared past, and European integration grew in part out of the reactive idea of ending the conflicts that arose from those differences. Historical divisions were further emphasized by the colonial interests of some European states, which encouraged them to develop competing sets of external priorities at the expense of cultivating closer ties with their neighbours. Even today, Britain, France, Spain and Portugal have close ties with their former colonies, while Germany – for different reasons – has interests in eastern Europe.

Finally, and most fundamentally, the confusion over the definition of Europe arises out of uncertainty about its political and geographical boundaries. Every other continent is defined by its coastline, but while the western, northern and southern boundaries of Europe are marked by the Atlantic, the Arctic and the Mediterranean, respectively, it has no clear eastern boundary. Strictly speaking it is not even a continent (usually defined as a large, unbroken land mass), but is part of the Asian continent. However it has been seen as distinct from Asia for the last 2000 years or more, even if no-one can really agree on where Europe ends and Asia begins.

The eastern boundary of Europe is usually defined as running down the Ural Mountains, across the Caspian Sea, and along the Caucasus Mountains, but these are merely geographical features that have been adopted despite political realities. The Urals, for example, were nominated as a boundary by an eighteenth-century Russian cartographer, Vasily Tatishchev, simply so that Russia could claim to be an Asian as well as a European power. If we continue to accept the Urals as a boundary, then six former Soviet republics – Belarus, Ukraine, Moldova and the three Baltic states – are part of Europe. The three Baltic republics have historically been bound to Europe, and have been moving into the western European orbit since the break-up of the USSR, but questions remain about the orientation of Belarus, Ukraine and Moldova.

The biggest problem with the Urals is that they do not mark the frontier between two states, but are deep in the heart of Russia. Russians have sometimes been defined – and have seen themselves – as European, but Russia west of the Urals was long known as Eurasia because of the distinctions imposed on the region by Europeans, and Russia today sees its political and economic interests as being significantly different from those of Europe. The most obvious problem with defining Russia as European is that three-quarters of its land area lies east of the Urals and more than forty ethnic minorities live within Russia, most of whom are unquestionably non-European.

In central Europe, changes in the balance of power long meant that the Poles, the Czechs and the Slovaks were caught in the crossfire of great-power competition, which is why this region was known as the 'lands between'. The Slavs in particular became divided between those who accepted Catholicism, Greek Orthodoxy or Islam, which resulted in cultural heterogeneity in spite of the greater linguistic homogeneity among Slavs than among the peoples of western Europe (Delanty, 1995, p. 54). The west looked on this area as a buffer zone against Russia, a perception that was helped by the failure of its people to form lasting states identified with dominant ethnic groups. During the Cold War the distinctiveness of eastern Europe was emphasized by the ideological divisions between east and west, despite the historical ties that meant Poland was closer to western Europe than to Russia.

For their part, the Balkans occupy an ambiguous position between Europe and Asia, being a geographical part of the former but historically drawn towards the latter. They were long regarded as an extension of Asia Minor, and until relatively recently were still described by Europeans as the Near East (Hobsbawm, 1991, p. 17). The Balkans have long been regarded as a zone of transition between two 'civilizations', whether the term is applied to religions (the boundary between Islam, Catholicism and Eastern Orthodoxy) or to political communities (the boundary between the eastern and western Roman empires, between the Habsburg and Ottoman empires, and more recently between Slavic-Russian, western and eastern influences).

Historical maps of the Balkans show how affiliations have constantly changed: they have come under the Macedonians, the Romans, the eastern Roman empire, Slavic tribes, Christianity, the Kingdom of Hungary, the Venetians and – from the sixteenth century until 1918 – the Ottoman Turks. Except during the Tito regime (1945–80), the region has never come close to being united, and the allegiance of its inhabitants has always been divided. These changes created what Delanty (1995, pp. 51–2) describes as 'frontier societies in the intermediary lands' between great powers. The Slavs continue to have affiliations with Russia, which is part of the reason why NATO was wary about becoming too deeply involved in the conflicts in Bosnia and Kosovo.

Finally there is the question of Turkey, which most Europeans see as part of Asia Minor and part of the Islamic sphere of influence. However, we usually think of Europe and Asia as meeting at the Bosphorus, which means that about 4 per cent of Turkey lies in Europe. So is Turkey a European state? It has applied for EU membership, but the EU has so far refused to open negotiations, expressing concern about Turkey's poverty, its large population and its mixed record on human rights. However, questions about the southeastern limits of Europe have not prevented the EU from negotiating membership with Cyprus, which is further from Brussels than most of Turkey and is divided into Greek and Turkish zones.

The Cold War has not been over for very long, and most of us still find it difficult to ignore the political, economic and social distinctions that divided the countries on either side of the iron curtain; try as they might, most older Europeans still look on Hungary and Poland as being somehow different from Belgium and France. A further distinction has been added since the 1970s by the accelerating closeness among EU member states, which has divided Europe into countries that are members of the EU and those that are not. There is little question, however, that Europe is closer than it has ever been to being considered a region with common interests and a common identity.

Europe today

If its borders with Turkey and Russia are taken as its eastern limits, then Europe today consists of 38 countries: the 15 members of the EU, 3 other western European states (Switzerland, Norway and Iceland), 12 eastern European states, 6 former Soviet republics and 2 Mediterranean states (Malta and Cyprus). It is one of the wealthiest regions of the world: its 582 million people make up nearly ten per cent of the world's population and live on just over four per cent of the world's land area, but they generate about 31 per cent of the world's economic wealth. Nearly all of that wealth is concentrated in western Europe: the 15 EU members, together with Switzerland, Norway and Iceland, generate nearly $8.5 trillion (€9.7 trillion) in gross domestic product (GDP), while in 1999 the 18 eastern European states and former Soviet republics had a combined GDP that was less than that of Spain (Table 2.1).

While there is a large measure of political, economic and social cohesion in western Europe, there are also significant differences and these have had an impact on the process of integration. The leaders of the EU member states, for example, do not always meet as equals: their powers are based on different political and administrative foundations, and they face different sets of economic and social problems that sometimes oblige or encourage them to take conflicting positions at the negotiating table.

Table 2.1 Demographic, economic and political indicators

	Area (000 sq. km)	Population (million)	Gross domestic product (billion $)	Per capita gross national income ($)	Political system	Admin. system
European Union (15):						
Germany	357	82.1	2 112	25 620	Rep. PD	Federal
UK	245	59.5	1 441	23 590	CM. PD	Unitary
France	552	58.6	1 432	24 170	Rep. P/P	Unitary
Italy	301	57.6	1 171	20 170	Rep. PD	Unitary
Spain	506	39.4	596	14 800	CM. PD	Unitary
Netherlands	41	15.8	394	25 140	CM. PD	Unitary
Belgium	33	10.2	248	24 650	CM. PD	Federal
Sweden	450	8.9	239	26 750	CM. PD	Unitary
Austria	84	8.1	208	25 430	Rep. P/P	Federal
Denmark	43	5.3	174	32 050	CM. PD	Unitary
Finland	338	5.2	130	24 730	Rep. P/P	Unitary
Greece	132	10.5	125	12 110	Rep. PD	Unitary
Portugal	92	10.0	114	11 030	Rep. P/P	Unitary
Ireland	70	3.7	93	21 470	Rep. PD	Unitary
Luxembourg	2	0.4	20**	n/a	CM. PD	Unitary
Sub-total	3 246	375.3	8 497			
Other Europe (5):						
Switzerland	41	7.1	259	38 380	Rep.	Federal
Norway	324	4.5	153	33 470	CM. PD	Unitary

Cyprus*	9	0.8	9**	n/a	Rep. P/P	Divided
Iceland	103	0.3	8**	n/a	Rep. P/P	Unitary
Malta*	0.3	0.4	5**	n/a	Rep. PD	Unitary
Sub-total	477	13.1	434			
Eastern Europe (18):						
Poland*	323	38.7	155	4 070	Rep. P/P	Unitary
Czech Republic*	79	10.3	53	5 020	Rep. PD	Unitary
Hungary*	93	10.1	48	4 640	Rep. PD	Unitary
Ukraine	604	50.0	39	840	Rep. P/P	Unitary
Romania*	238	22.5	34	1 470	Rep. P/P	Unitary
Belarus	208	10.0	27	2 620	Rep. P/P	Unitary
Slovakia*	49	5.4	20	3 770	Rep. PD	Unitary
Croatia	57	4.5	20	4 530	Rep. P/P	Unitary
Slovenia*	20	2.0	20	10 000	Rep. PD	Unitary
Yugoslavia	102	10.6	15**	–	Rep. PD	Unitary
Bulgaria*	111	8.2	12	1 410	Rep. PD	Unitary
Lithuania*	65	3.7	11	2 640	Rep. P/P	Unitary
Latvia*	65	2.4	6	2 430	Rep. PD	Unitary
Estonia*	45	1.4	5	3 400	Rep. PD	Unitary
Bosnia-Herzegovina	51	3.9	4	1 210	Rep. PD	Unitary
Albania	29	3.4	4	930	Rep. PD	Unitary
Macedonia	26	2.0	3	1 660	Rep. P/P	Unitary
Moldova	34	4.3	1	410	Rep. P/P	Unitary
Sub-total	2 199	193.4	477			
Europe total	5 922	581.8	9 408			

Table 2.1 continued overleaf

Table 2.1   *continued*

	Area (000 sq. km)	Population (million)	Gross domestic product (billion $)	Per capita gross national income ($)	Political system	Admin. system
Other (7):						
United States	9 364	278.2	9 152	31 910	Rep. Pres.	Federal
Japan	378	126.6	4 347	32 030	Imp. PD	Unitary
China	9 598	1 253.6	989	780	Rep. SS	Unitary
Canada	9 971	30.5	635	20 140	CM. PD	Federal
Russia	17 075	146.2	401	2 250	Rep. P/P	Federal
Australia	7 741	19.0	397	20 950	CM. PD	Federal
Turkey*	775	64.4	186	2 900	Rep. PD	Unitary
World	133 567	5 978.0	29 995	5 020		

* States that have applied for EU membership.

** Estimates

Key: Rep. = republic, PD = parliamentary democracy, Pres. = presidential, CM = constitutional monarchy, Imp. = imperial, P/P = presidential/parliamentary, SS = state socialist.

Source: World Development Indicators database, World Bank Web site, http://www.worldbank.com. All figures are for 1999.

Political structure

Most European countries have political systems based on variations on the theme of parliamentary government, with either a monarch or a president as figurehead, and executive power vested in an elected prime minister who is the leader of the largest political party (or coalition) in the national legislature. One of the legacies of monarchies in most European societies is the distinction between the head of state and the head of government, which stands in contrast to the fusion of these two positions in the US system. Heads of state take several different forms:

- Eight European countries still have monarchies: Belgium, Denmark, Luxembourg, the Netherlands, Norway, Spain, Sweden and the UK. However, these are all constitutional monarchies, meaning that the monarchs have negligible political power and government is carried out in their name (they reign, but they do not rule). All are limited to ceremonial roles, and are afforded little opportunity to advise or influence the elected heads of government.

- Most other European states have a figurehead president who has similar powers and a similar standing to that of a monarch, but instead of inheriting the job by an accident of birth, they are either appointed or elected to their position for a fixed term. In several countries – including Germany, Italy and Switzerland – the president is elected by the legislature; elsewhere he or she is elected directly by the people, but is not expected to be a political figure. The only slight exception is in Finland, where the president has a central role in foreign policy and can become involved in domestic policy if the situation allows.

- Several countries have a dual executive, or a mixed presidential/ parliamentary system of government: they include Belarus, Finland, France, Iceland, Poland, Portugal, and Ukraine. Executive power is vested in the president, who is directly elected by the people, but legislative power is vested in the legislature, overseen by a prime minister and a council of ministers. If the president's party dominates the legislature, the president has substantial powers over appointments and over the legislative programme – most notably, the president appoints the prime minister and the council of ministers, and also sets the political agenda. If the president's party is in a minority, however, the prime minister and council of ministers come from a different party, base their power on their support in the legislature and are much less obliged to the president.

Non-executive presidents and monarchs have the advantage of being able to act as symbols of national unity. They can provide stability and continuity, especially in the case of monarchs, who often outlast a succession of prime ministers – by 2002, for example, Britain's Queen Elizabeth had worked with eleven prime ministers, and Sweden's King Carl Gustav with eight. In Italy various presidents have played a crucial role in helping offset the disruptive effects of the frequent collapse of governments, and holders of that office have been known to become involved in public debates; President Cossiaga, for example, came out in support of electoral reform in the wake of the financial scandals of the early 1990s and the subsequent collapse of credibility of Italian political parties.

Presidents in countries with dual executives have a significantly different position within their domestic political structures, which gives them a different status at meetings with other European leaders. As noted above, when a president's party dominates the legislature, that president has considerable powers over the legislative programme and is in a strong position when it comes to negotiating international agreements. However, in the case of France, recent elections have resulted in presidents having to work with opposition party prime ministers. This was the case for President Chirac after the 1997 National Assembly elections; with the socialists winning the majority of votes, domestic affairs were taken over by Prime Minister Lionel Jospin, and Chirac could do little more than immerse himself in foreign affairs. Even there he found himself disadvantaged in his discussions with other EU leaders because he could not rely on the backing of the National Assembly.

Executive power in most European states is vested in a head of government: the prime minister, or the chancellor in Germany and Austria. In contrast to the fixed term imposed on legislators in the United States, prime ministers and legislators in Europe are elected for a maximum term – usually four or five years (three years in Sweden) – and the leader has the power to call elections at any time within that term. The main power of prime ministers is vested in their virtual monopoly over appointments to senior government positions, and the fact that they can normally rely on parliamentary majorities that are strong enough to ensure the success of their legislative programmes. This is certainly true of prime ministers in states that regularly return majority governments, but much less true of those with coalition governments, such as Germany and Italy. While the former have substantial political powers, the latter must base their programmes on consensus and bipartisanship, and are driven by the need to achieve compromises that keep all the party groups within their coalition happy.

Almost all European legislatures are based on the parliamentary model, in which the government consists of a prime minister and cabinet that is answerable to – and usually part of – the elected legislative body. By definition, a legislature is where laws are introduced, discussed, amended if necessary, and either accepted or rejected. Most European parliaments have two chambers, a lower and more powerful chamber that is directly elected by the people, and an upper and usually less important chamber whose members may be elected directly or indirectly, or appointed. Austria, Germany and the Netherlands have upper chambers whose members are elected or appointed by the state or local governments. Several smaller European states, including Denmark, Finland, Norway, Portugal and Sweden, have only one chamber.

Europeans have a wide variety of political parties from which to choose at elections, with every part of the ideological spectrum represented. On the left, communists have seen their support declining significantly in recent years, and now receive far fewer votes than they did in the heyday of Eurocommunism in the 1970s. The strongest and most enduring of the left-wing ideologies is social democracy, which now forms the foundation of political parties in almost every EU member state. A more conservative form of socialism, social democracy incorporates a belief in the welfare state and some degree of government ownership of services with a support for self-reliance and moderate positions on social issues.

The ideological right is dominated by Christian democratic parties, which are active in most of the EU member states. More concerned than secular conservative parties about social issues, and more willing to support welfare as a means of avoiding social conflict, Christian democratic parties have been particularly influential in Germany, France and Italy, where they have adopted more liberal positions than British and Irish conservatives. One of the effects of the European Parliamentary elections (see Chapter 4) has been to encourage social democrats and conservatives to form trans-European blocs, and while they do not as yet run on a European platform, these two blocs have consistently been the biggest in the European Parliament.

A recent phenomenon in national European politics has been the rise of political parties representing more focused sectors of society: these include greens, subnational and regionalist parties, and nationalist parties of the far right. Greens have done particularly well in Belgium, Germany, and some of the Scandinavian states, their views representing a backlash against unsustainable consumerism and economic development. Regional parties, while still small, have evolved in economically or culturally divided EU member states such as Belgium, Britain and Italy. The far right, building on xenophobia and opposition to immigration, has had its biggest impact in Austria, Belgium, France and Italy.

Electoral systems are far from standardized in Europe. Although most countries offer their voters proportional representation (PR), several different forms of PR are practised. The most common is the straight party list system, in which the country is divided into districts with multiple representatives, all parties field a list of candidates in each district, and the votes are shared out among the candidates according to the proportion of votes they receive. This system is practised in Spain, Portugal, the Benelux countries, and the five Nordic states. The most notable exception to the PR rule is Britain, which has a plurality or majority system (sometimes known as 'first past the post'), in which candidates from different parties compete against each other and the person who wins the most votes wins the seat, irrespective of whether or not they win a majority of votes. The Blair administration has introduced PR for European elections and elections to regional assemblies, and has debated the possibility of introducing PR for general elections.

The plurality system has two advantages: it usually results in one party winning a clear majority (and so contributes to governmental stability), and it assigns a single member of the legislature to each electoral district, allowing constituents to develop political and psychological links with one representative. However, the system tends to be unfair in that the proportion of seats won by competing parties is often very different from the proportion of votes cast; parties that have solid blocs of support around a country turn those into legislative seats, while parties whose support is strong but more thinly spread often come second, and win fewer seats. This was particularly obvious in the 2001 British elections, when the governing Labour party won 41 per cent of the votes, but nearly 63 per cent of the seats in the House of Commons, while the opposition Conservatives won 32 per cent of the votes, but only 25 per cent of the seats.

PR is more representative of voter preferences, but voters are represented by a group of legislators rather than just one. More problematically, the system also results in more parties being able to win seats in the legislature, making it less likely that any one party will win a majority. The result is usually a coalition government, with two or more political parties reaching an agreement to govern together. This often means that they have to compromise their policy goals in order to maintain the coalition, and they may only have a small majority, thereby creating instability. The most extreme case of such instability is Italy, which has had nearly 60 governments since 1945, some of which have lasted only a matter of weeks before collapsing. In order to promote stability, Italy changed its electoral system in 1993 from one based exclusively on PR to one using a combination of PR and winner take all.

The result of this variety of political structures is that the power of the individual leaders of the member states is often based on different foundations, which may affect their ability to negotiate with their counterparts. For example, British prime ministers who head a strong majority in their respective legislatures are able to adopt a relatively uncompromising position in intra-EU negotiations, while French presidents without a legislative majority, or Italian or Danish prime ministers who lead a finely balanced coalition government, may be in a weak negotiating position and more inclined to follow than to lead.

Administrative structure

Government in western Europe tends to be highly centralized. All but four European states (Germany, Austria, Belgium and Switzerland) are unitary systems, meaning that all significant power is focused at the national level. Local units of government exist, but have relatively few independent powers or rights, and must generally follow the lead set by the national government.

The practical meaning of 'unitary' is debatable; local government in Sweden and Denmark has more functions than do Swiss cantons, and the balance continues to change as administration in Switzerland becomes more centralized (Gallagher *et al.*, 1992, p. 130). In practice, unitary administration means that a state has two or even three levels of government, with the national government being responsible for foreign and defence policy, managing the national economy, welfare policy, transport, environmental management, industrial development policy and other matters that are considered as best dealt with from a national perspective. Meanwhile a network of local units of government – which come under labels as varied as municipality, commune, county, parish, district, borough, province, department or region – are usually responsible for overseeing public services such as land use planning, policing, local transport, schooling, public housing, refuse collection, road maintenance and social services.

For their part, Austria, Belgium, Germany and Switzerland are federations in which national government coexists with local units of government having their own independent powers and responsibilities, and powers are more decentralized. Federalism usually works best in large countries where strong local government makes sense simply for reasons of convenience, or in countries that have significant social divisions and where decentralization gives different groups more power over their own affairs. The United States is often taken as the model of federalism, an arrangement that was used as a means of bringing the original 13 colonies together under a joint system of government.

Federalism in Switzerland is rooted in differences in language and religion, so that the populations of individual cantons speak French, German or Italian, and are either mostly Protestant or mostly Catholic (Gallagher *et al.*, 1992, p. 137). In contrast, federalism in Germany was imposed by the occupying powers after the Second World War as a means of decentralizing the German state, and several of the *Länder* created under the new system had no historical traditions. Federalism is sometimes proposed as a possible answer for the problems of culturally or historically divided societies such as Britain, which is already experiencing federalizing tendencies as Scotland, Wales and Northern Ireland develop their own regional assemblies.

As noted in Chapter 1, federalism at the European level has become controversial in recent years, being regularly used by Eurosceptics as a red flag with which to warn against the loss of powers by EU member states. They often talk of the possibility of a federal government in Brussels, associating the term with such notions as 'big government' and 'loss of sovereignty'. The Thatcher and Major governments in Britain were particularly leery of the idea. In 1988 Margaret Thatcher made her views clear in one of her most oft-quoted statements: 'We have not successfully rolled back the frontiers of the state in Britain, only to see them re-imposed at a European level, with a European super-state exercising a new dominance from Brussels'. For John Major, federalism became a critical issue during the debate over the Maastricht treaty. The draft included the objective of achieving a federal Europe, but British opposition led to the removal of all references to the idea, and the treaty was eventually described as 'a new stage in the process of creating an ever closer union among the peoples of Europe'.

However it is questionable whether most Europeans really understand how federalism works, since so few of them have experienced it firsthand at the national level. It is also questionable whether a federal Europe – should it ever be created – would have the same characteristics as a federal Austria or Germany. There is no one fixed definition of a federal system; in some cases (such as India and Russia) national government is relatively strong, in others (such as Switzerland) it is relatively weak, and in almost all cases the balance of power between national and local government changes according to economic and political realities; this has certainly been the case in the United States, where there has long been a debate about which level has the advantage in that balance. The seeds of a federal European government have been planted, but whether they will eventually flower or instead remain a much looser confederal arrangement remains to be seen.

Economic structure

All western European states are predominantly free-market capitalist systems, meaning that most economic activity is driven – and prices set – by supply and demand, and governments limit their intervention in the marketplace. This has been particularly true since the 1980s, when the Thatcher government privatized many state-owned industries and services, and several continental European states followed suit. The size of the public sector in most countries declined markedly, and free market enterprise and competition grew. (Of course, there is no such thing in practice as a purely capitalist system – governments always intervene in some way in the market, for example through regulation, price controls, or rules on competition.)

Western European states are also predominantly postindustrial, meaning that their economies have gone through a transition from agriculture to industry to a heavy reliance on services. The latter are economic activities that do not produce tangible commodities, for example the retail sector, food services, banking, insurance and other financial activities. Typically, services in a postindustrial state account for about 65–70 per cent of gross domestic product (GDP), industry for about 25–30 per cent and agriculture for the balance. The poorer European states tend to have the largest agricultural sectors: while 18–23 per cent of Greek men and women work in agriculture and 12–15 per cent of Irish men and women, only 1–5 per cent of Britons, Danes, Dutch, Germans, and Swedes are similarly engaged.

While the national economic systems of Europe are similar in principle, levels of national economic development are not, and the balance of power is tilted in favour of the big four western European states: Germany, Britain, France, and Italy account for just over two-thirds of the population of the European Union (and 44 per cent of the population of Europe), for nearly three-quarters of the GDP of the EU (and 65 per cent of the GDP of Europe) and for most of Europe's industrial production and trade.

All of western Europe has experienced substantial economic growth since 1945, and prosperity has begun slowly to spread to eastern Europe in recent years, but the levels of growth and prosperity have always differed from one region to another (Box 2.2). Broadly speaking there is an economic heartland in the centre of Europe, running from northern Italy across Switzerland to the Benelux countries and neighbouring parts of France and Germany, and continuing across the Channel from London to the edge of the English midlands. This is the area where most industry and energy production is focused, with the greatest concentration of population, the highest levels of GDP and the fewest people working in agriculture.

More generally, Europe has pockets of economic dynamism and underdevelopment. The highest levels of activity are found in the economic heartland, particularly in the Rhineland, around northern Italian cities and in and around Paris, Rotterdam and London. These have neighbouring zones of balanced economic development, with a combination of prosperous agriculture, moderate urban growth, light industry and services. Balanced against these areas are the depressed industrial regions of Europe, such as the Ruhr, the English east midlands and south Wales. Finally, the

Box 2.2 The quality of life in Europe

Assessed by almost any objective measure of the quality of life, Western Europeans are among the most privileged people in the world. The average European has access to an advanced system of education and health care, an extensive and generous welfare system, a vibrant consumer society and a sophisticated transport and communications system. An African infant is 21 times more likely to die at birth than a European infant, the average European can expect to live to about 77, which is 24 years longer than the average African and 18 years longer than the average Indian. Europeans enjoy almost universal literacy, employed Europeans enjoy more paid holiday leave and leisure time than almost anyone else, and the provision of shelter and nutrition is more than adequate.

Much can be attributed to the philosophy adopted by most European governments after the Second World War that the state should provide a wide range of basic social services, creating a safety net through which even the poorest and the most underprivileged would not be allowed to slip. Hence every EU member state has some form of state education and national health care, and the provision of care for children and the aged has increased as the number of lone parent families and retirees has grown. Most European states even do well in comparison with the United States, which has the most technologically advanced health care in the world but lacks a national health service, and is one of the richest economies in the world yet still has 15 per cent of its people living in poverty.

Not all of Europe's welfare policies have succeeded, and it is one of the great ironies of life in modern industrialized democracies that considerable want continues to exist in the midst of plenty. Poverty has not gone away and in several places has worsened, creating considerable differences across Europe. For example, while the number of children living in poverty stands at 4–10 per cent in Sweden, Germany, and the Netherlands, it is as high as 16–18 per cent in Britain and Italy. However this is still much better than in the United States, where the figure is nearly 30 per cent (statistics quoted in Bradford, 1998, p. 265).

periphery of Europe tends to be the most underdeveloped, either because it has lacked adequate investment, because it is remote and sparsely populated or – in the case of most of eastern Europe – because it is less industrialized and still suffering the effects of Soviet-style central planning.

The single market programme has exacerbated the problem by promoting cross-frontier competition, allowing industry and business to move to the areas of maximum efficiency and greatest profits, and promoting the movement of workers. At the same time, though, EU regional policies have helped provide more investment for poorer regions (see Chapter 5), and social policies have helped place workers on a more equal footing (see Chapter 6). The single market has also helped promote trans-European corporate mergers and joint ventures, improving economies of scale so that the biggest European corporations are now able to compete more effectively with those from the United States and Japan.

Economic differences are reflected in population numbers (Figure 2.1). Western Europe is one of the most densely populated regions of the world: overall population density is about 115 people per square kilometre compared with 30/sq. km in the United States, and 9/sq. km in Russia. Within the EU, population density varies from nearly 470/sq. km in the Netherlands to about 20/sq. km in Finland and Sweden, the spread reflecting environmental factors and different levels of industrialization. The most densely populated parts of Europe are also among the wealthiest: northern Italy, western Germany, the Benelux countries, and southeastern England. The most sparsely populated include the poorest or the coldest: much of eastern Europe, central Spain, northwest Scotland, Iceland and northern Scandinavia.

Figure 2.1   *Population indicators*

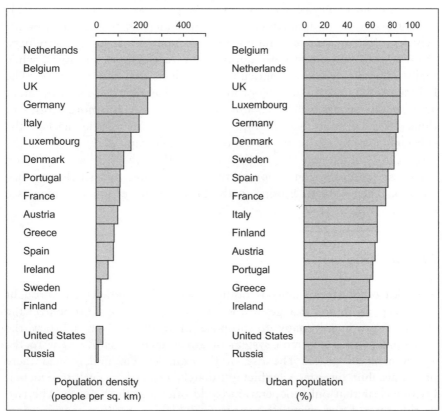

Source: World Development Indicators database, World Bank Web site, http://www.worldbank.com. All figures are for 1999.

Not surprisingly, the greatest population growth is taking place in and around the major centres of industry and services, and new residential and leisure areas. Capital cities have seen growth since the mid-nineteenth century, their attraction lying in their role as administrative, cultural, service and prestige centres, their central position in national transport networks, and their pools of skilled labour and large marketplaces (Minshull and Dawson, 1996, p. 209). Regions of postwar industrial redevelopment, such as the Rhine valley in Germany and the West Midlands in Britain, have also seen sustained population growth. Meanwhile rural and peripheral regions and declining industrial areas have undergone steady depopulation. These trends have made Europe one of the most urbanized parts of the world. While only 77 per cent of Americans live in towns or cities, the level of urbanization in European states is often well over 85 per cent, with Belgium coming highest at 97 per cent and Ireland lowest at 59 per cent.

The European Union has become the world's biggest trading power, and its exports and imports have grown rapidly since 1945, thanks in large part to the growth of intra-European trade. Worldwide exports from the EU consist mainly of manufactured goods, machinery, machine tools, motor vehicles, electronics, telecommunications equipment, aerospace products, chemicals, clothing, consumer durables and agricultural products, while major imports include oil, agricultural products and raw materials. The EU member states still actively protect their sovereignty in many different areas, but when it comes to economic issues it has become more realistic to think of them collectively – the completion of the single market, the substantial easing of the movement of people and capital, the power of the European Commission to negotiate on behalf of the EU as a whole on trade issues and the conversion in 12 member states to a single currency have all taken western Europe to the brink of full economic union (see Chapter 7).

Conclusions

The idea of European unity is nothing new. The conflicts that brought instability, death and changes to the balance of power in Europe over the centuries prompted many to propose unification – or at least the development of a common system of government – as a means to the achievement of peace. The rise of the state system undermined these proposals, but interstate conflict ultimately reached a level at which it became clear that only cooperation could offer a path to peace. The two world wars of the twentieth century – which in many ways began as European civil wars – emphatically underlined the dangers of nationalism and of the continued promotion of state interests at the expense of regional interests.

The new thinking has dramatically altered the idea of Europe over the past two generations. The eastern and southeastern borders of Europe may have maintained their historical tradition of change, but in the postindustrial and democratic west, the nature of the internal relationship among the states that make up Europe has changed out of all recognition. For the first time, the concept of European unity has found a widespread audience. The audience may not always have been enthusiastic, but there has been a generational shift since 1945 as those who witnessed the horrors of the Second World War are superseded by those who have known nothing but a general peace in the region. Where intellectuals and philosophers once argued in isolation that the surest path to peace in Europe was cooperation, or even integration, the costs of nationalism are now more broadly appreciated, ensuring a wider and deeper consideration of the idea of regional unity.

Europeans still have much that divides them, and those differences are immediately apparent to anyone who travels across the region. There are different languages, cultural traditions, legal, education and health care systems, social priorities, cuisines, modes of entertainment, patterns of etiquette, styles of dressing, ways of planning and building cities, ways of spending leisure time, attitudes towards the countryside, and even sides of the road on which to drive. Europeans also have differences in the way they govern themselves, and in what they have been able to achieve with their economies and social welfare systems.

Increasingly, however, Europeans have more in common. The economic and social integration that has taken place under the auspices of the European Union and its precursors since the early 1950s has brought the needs and priorities of Europeans closer into alignment. It has also encouraged the rest of the world to see Europeans less as citizens of separate states and more as citizens of the same economic bloc, if not yet the same political bloc. Not only has there been integration from the Mediterranean to the Arctic Circle, but the 'lands between' – which spent the Cold War as part of the Soviet bloc and part of the buffer created by the Soviet Union to protect its western frontier – are now becoming part of greater Europe for the first time in their history. The result has been a fundamental redefinition of the idea of Europe.

In the next chapter we will look at the specific steps taken by western European governments to build the European Union, the underlying motives of integration, and the debates involved in the process.

Chapter 3

The Evolution of the EU

Domestic and international background
First steps towards integration (1945–58)
Deepening and widening (1958–86)
Economic and social integration (1979–92)
From Community to Union (1992–)
Conclusions

We must build a kind of United States of Europe.
Winston Churchill, Zurich, 1946

The idea of 'Europe' has been with us for centuries, but tangible efforts to promote voluntary European unity date back barely fifty years. It was only after the Second World War that all the theories about the possible benefits of European integration were finally tested in practice. There were several false starts, but the most critical first step was taken on 9 May 1950, at a press conference held at the French Foreign Ministry in Paris. To the attendant journalists, French foreign minister Robert Schuman announced a plan he had agreed with French businessman Jean Monnet and West German chancellor Konrad Adenauer under which the coal and steel industries of France and Germany would be brought together under the administration of a single joint authority.

Other countries were invited to take part, but only Italy and the three Benelux countries expressed interest. Nevertheless, this modest experiment involving six western European states would lead in stages to the European Union as we know it today. The original priorities were threefold: postwar economic construction, the wish to prevent European nationalism leading once again to conflict, and the need for security in the face of the threats posed by the Cold War. At the core of this thinking was concern about the traditional hostility between Germany and France, and the argument that if these two could cooperate they might provide the foundation for broader European integration.

The six members of the European Coal and Steel Community, which was founded in 1952, went on to create the European Economic Community in 1958, with a more ambitious set of goals. These included the development of a common agricultural policy, agreement on a common external tariff for all goods coming into the Community, and the development of a single market, within which there would be free movement of people, goods, money and services. Membership expanded in 1973 with the accession of Britain, Ireland and Denmark, followed in the 1980s by Greece, Portugal and Spain.

Economic problems and disagreements about what needed to be done to remove the internal barriers to trade threatened to undermine development of the single market, but a new impetus was provided in 1986 with agreement of the Single European Act, which set a five-year deadline for completing all the remaining tasks. The single market is now in place, membership of the EU has grown to 15 countries and more than 375 million people, negotiations are under way aimed at extending membership into eastern Europe, and March 2002 saw the most ambitious – and most controversial – step in the short history of European integration: final adoption of a single currency. The achievements have been remarkable, but many Europeans are still ambivalent about the European Union, and question the ultimate objectives of integration. And while membership has grown, doubts remain about the many items of unfinished business on the European agenda.

This chapter provides a brief history of European integration since the Second World War, describing the key steps that have been taken during the evolution of the EU, and their underlying motives. It moves from the Treaty of Paris to the Treaties of Rome, on to the construction of the single market and early attempts to bring about economic union and common social and foreign policies, and ends with the treaties of Maastricht, Amsterdam, and Nice, and the state of progress on the euro and eastern enlargement. The European Union is a work in progress, however, so there are many changes yet to come.

Domestic and international background

The European Union was born out of the ruins of the Second World War. Before the war, Europe had dominated global trade, banking and finance, its empires had stretched across the world and its military superiority had been unquestioned. However, Europeans had often gone to war with each other, and their conflicts undermined the prosperity that cooperation might have brought. Many thought that the Great War of 1914–18 might finally convince Europeans of the futility and brutality of war, but it was to take yet another conflagration finally to convince them that they needed to fundamentally rethink how they related to each other if a lasting peace was to be achieved.

The Second World War resulted in the death of more than 40 million people and caused widespread devastation. Cities lay in ruins, agricultural production was halved, food was rationed and communications were disrupted by the destruction of bridges, railways and harbours. While the physical damage caused by the First World War had been relatively restricted, every country involved in this latest conflict sustained heavy casualties and physical damage. The war also dealt a severe blow to European power and influence, clearing the way for the emergence of the United States and the Soviet Union as superpowers, and creating a nervous new balance in the distribution of political influence in the world.

Against this background a number of European leaders revived the argument that European states should set aside their differences and build bridges of cooperation aimed at removing the causes of war, and perhaps even leading to European economic and political union. The argument had a new significance given the scale of the postwar reconstruction effort, but Europeans had different opinions about its merits.

- France was destabilized by the national trauma of wartime collaboration and the structural weaknesses of the government of the Fourth Republic (created in 1946), and was to suffer further blows to its national pride with the defeat of French forces in Indochina in 1954 and the Suez crisis in 1956. Three times in less than a century it had gone to war with Germany, and three times had suffered substantial losses; there was no certainty that the defeat of Nazism meant the final removal of the German threat.

- Germany had become introverted, not only because of the extent of wartime destruction, but also because of shame over its role in starting and fighting the war. It was occupied by four allied powers, whose disagreements led to the division of Germany into a socialist eastern sector and three capitalist western sectors. The conservative Christian Democratic government of Konrad Adenauer set about aligning West Germany with the Western alliance and rebuilding West German respectability, goals which fitted well with the idea of regional economic integration.

- Austria was also divided into separate zones of occupation, but had been relatively undamaged by the war and was able to return to its constitution of 1920, and quickly to hold democratic elections. Although it declared itself neutral in 1955, its economic interests pulled it increasingly towards economic integration with its western neighbours (Schultz, 1992).

- Like Germany, Italy emerged from the war both introverted and devastated. It was less successful than Germany in creating political stability and suffered regular changes of government. For the administration of pro-European prime minister Alcide de Gasperi (1945–53), European integration offered a means of fostering peace and helping Italy to deal with its internal economic problems, notably unemployment and the underdevelopment of the south.

- Its resistance to Nazism had strengthened Britain's sense of national identity. It was politically stable and wealthier and more powerful than France and Germany, but many of its major cities had been bombed, its exports had been cut by two-thirds and its national wealth by 75 per cent. Voters looking for change elected a socialist Labour government in 1945, which embarked on a popular programme of nationalization and welfare provision, and signalled the end of Britain's imperial status by granting independence to India and Pakistan in 1947. However, cooperation with Europe was far from British minds, few Britons even thinking of themselves as European.

- Ireland had remained neutral during the war but was economically tied to Britain, so its attitude towards regional cooperation was highly influenced by Britain's stance.

- The three Benelux countries – Belgium, the Netherlands and Luxembourg – had all been occupied by the Germans, and remained concerned after the war about their inability to protect themselves. Agreement was reached in 1944 among the three governments-in-exile to promote trilateral economic cooperation after the war, and the creation in 1948 of the Benelux customs union led to the abolition of internal customs controls and the agreement of a joint external tariff. While all three countries kept many protectionist measures, their governments went on to agree the Benelux Economic Union in 1958, emphasizing their integrationist credentials.

- The five Nordic states (Denmark, Finland, Iceland, Norway and Sweden) began their postwar cooperation with the creation in 1946 of the Committee on Legislative Cooperation, which was charged with ensuring that new national laws were in line with one another and encouraging a common Nordic position at international conferences. In 1952 Denmark, Iceland, Norway and Sweden formed the Nordic Council, which worked to promote the abolition of passport controls, the free movement of workers and the development of joint ventures. The development of the Council was helped by the fact that its member states had small populations, were relatively wealthy and homogeneous, had few major social problems and were governed by socialist or social democratic governments. Finland joined in 1956.

- Spain and Portugal were exceptions to the prevailing rule of democratic stability in western Europe, and were both poor and politically marginalized. Spain had been ruled since 1939 by Francisco Franco, and Portugal since 1928 by Antonio Salazar; neither man was in favour of cooperating with neighbouring countries after the war, and both states remained on the margins of the international community for many years.

- Greece enjoyed economic growth after the war thanks to US financial and military assistance, but remained poor and experienced protracted domestic political tensions that led to military dictatorship in 1967–74.

While their domestic priorities were occasionally different, west European governments were compelled to realize that changes taking place at the global level demanded new thinking. In July 1944, representatives from 44 countries – including the United States and all the allied European states – had met at Bretton Woods in New Hampshire to make plans for the postwar global economy. All agreed to an Anglo-American proposal to promote free trade, non-discrimination and stable exchange rates, and supported the view that Europe's economies should be rebuilt and placed on a more stable footing.

Because wartime resistance had been allied with left-wing political ideas, there was a political shift to the left after the war, with socialist and social democratic parties winning power in several European countries. Many of the new governments launched programmes of social welfare and nationalization, emphasizing central economic planning. Fundamental to this approach were the theories of the British economist John Maynard Keynes, who argued for some government control over some aspects of the economy in order to control the cycle of booms and busts. Keynesianism became the basis of postwar economic reconstruction and west European governments increasingly intervened in their economies to control inflation and rebuild industry and agriculture. However, it soon became clear that substantial capital investment was needed if Europe was to rebuild itself. The readiest source of such capital was the United States, which saw European reconstruction as essential to its own economic and security interests, and made a large investment in the future of Europe through the Marshall Plan (Box 3.1).

As one of the two new postwar superpowers, the United States also found itself playing the role of global policeman, its primary goal being to defend western Europe (and ultimately itself) from the Soviet threat. Its assumptions that Europe had enough people, money and resources to recover from the war, and that the allies would continue to work together, both proved wrong (Urwin, 1995, pp. 13–14). Furthermore, its European allies were divided over the extent to which they felt they could rely on the United States to defend them, and the doubters began to think in terms of greater European cooperation.

Most immediately, the western allies were undecided about what to do with Germany. In June 1948 they moulded their three zones into a new

Box 3.1 The Marshall Plan, 1948–51

US policy after 1945 was to withdraw its military forces as quickly as possible from Europe. However, it soon became clear that Stalin had plans to expand the Soviet sphere of influence, and the US State Department began to realize that it had underestimated the extent of Europe's economic destruction; despite a boom in the late 1940s, sustained growth was not forthcoming. When an economically exhausted Britain ended its financial aid to Greece and Turkey in 1947, President Truman argued the need for the United States to fill the vacuum in order to curb communist influence in the region.

US policymakers also felt that European markets needed to be rebuilt and integrated into a multilateral system of world trade, and that economic and political reconstruction would help forestall Soviet aggression and the rise of domestic communist parties (Hogan, 1987, pp. 26–7). Thus Secretary of State George Marshall argued that the United States should provide Europe with assistance to fight 'hunger, poverty, desperation and chaos'. The original April 1947 State Department proposal for the plan made clear that one of its ultimate goals was the creation of a western European federation (quoted in Gillingham, 1991, pp. 118–19).

The European Recovery Programme (otherwise known as the Marshall Plan) provided just over $12.5 billion in aid to Europe between 1948 and 1951 (Milward, 1984, p. 94), the disbursement of which was coordinated by the Organization for European Economic Cooperation (OEEC), a new body set up in April 1948 with headquarters in Paris. Governed by a Council of Ministers made up of one representative from each member state, the OEEC's goals included the reduction of tariffs and other barriers to trade, and consideration of the possibility of a free trade area or customs union among its members. Opposition from several European governments (notably Britain, France and Norway) ensured that the OEEC remained a forum for intergovernmental consultation rather than becoming a supranational body with powers of its own (Wexler, 1983, p. 209; Milward, 1984, pp. 209–10).

Although the effects of the Marshall Plan are still debated, there is little question that it helped underpin economic and political recovery in Europe, and helped bind more closely the economic and political interests of the United States and western Europe. It was a profitable investment for the United States, but it also had considerable influence on the idea of European integration – as western Europe's first venture in economic cooperation, it encouraged Europeans to work together and highlighted the mutual dependence among their economies (Urwin, 1995, pp. 20–2). It also helped liberalize intra-European trade, and helped ensure that economic integration would be focused on western Europe.

West German state with a new currency. The Soviets responded with a blockade around West Berlin, prompting a massive western airlift to supply the beleaguered city. The US Congress was resistant to direct American commitments or entanglements in Europe, but saw the need to counterbalance the Soviets and to ensure the peaceful cooperation of West Germany. In 1949 the North Atlantic Treaty was signed, by which the United States agreed to help its European allies to 'restore and maintain the security of the North Atlantic area'. Canada too signed, along with Britain, France, Italy, the Benelux countries, Denmark, Iceland, Norway and Portugal. The pact was later given more substance with the creation of the North Atlantic Treaty Organization (NATO), headquartered in Paris until it was moved to Brussels in 1966. The United States was now committed to the security of western Europe.

The NATO members agreed that an attack on one of them would be considered an attack on all of them, but each agreed only to respond with 'such actions as it deems necessary'. The Europeans attempted to take their own defence a step further in 1952 and proposed the creation of a European Defence Community, but this was prevented by political opposition in Britain and France (see below). Nonetheless Britain was anxious to encourage some kind of military cooperation, and invited France, West Germany, Italy and the Benelux states to become founding members of the Western European Union (WEU), under which members agreed to give all possible military and other aid to any member that was attacked. However, the WEU went beyond purely defensive concerns, and the agreement signed by the seven founding members in Paris in October 1954 included the aim 'to promote the unity and to encourage the progressive integration of Europe'. Within days of the launch of the WEU in May 1955 and the coincidental admission of West Germany into NATO, the Soviet bloc created the Warsaw Pact. The lines of the Cold War were now defined, and its implications were illustrated all too clearly by events in Hungary in 1956.

In October the government of Imre Nagy announced the end of one-party rule, the evacuation of Russian troops from Hungary, and Hungary's withdrawal from the Warsaw Pact. Just as Britain and France were invading Egypt to retake the Suez Canal following its nationalization in July 1956 by Gamal Abdel Nasser, the Soviets responded to the Hungarian decision by sending in tanks. The United States wanted to criticize the Soviet use of force and boast to the emerging Third World about the moral superiority of the West, but obviously could not while British and French paratroopers were storming the Suez Canal. Britain and France were ostracized in the UN Security Council, British Prime Minister Anthony Eden resigned, and the attempt to regain the Suez Canal was quickly abandoned.

The consequences of France's problems in Indochina, the Suez crisis and the Hungarian uprising were profound: Britain and France began to reduce the size of their armed forces, finally recognizing that they were no longer world powers capable of independent action in the Middle East, or perhaps anywhere; both embarked on a concerted programme of decolonization; Britain looked increasingly to Europe for its economic and security interests; and it became obvious to Europeans that the United States was the dominant partner in the North Atlantic alliance, a fact that particularly concerned the French.

First steps towards integration (1945–58)

The priority for European leaders after the Second World War was to create conditions that would prevent Europeans from ever going to war with each other again. For many, the major threats to peace and security were nationalism and the nation-state, both of which had been discredited by the war. For many, Germany was the core problem – peace was impossible, it was argued, unless Germany could be contained and its power diverted to constructive rather than destructive ends. It had to be allowed to rebuild its economic base and its political system in ways that would not threaten European security.

Meanwhile, the growing hostility between the United States and the Soviet Union led Europeans to worry that they were becoming pawns in the Cold War. There was clearly a need to protect western Europe from the Soviet threat, but there was concern about the extent to which Europeans and Americans could find common ground, and the extent to which western Europe could rely on US protection. Perhaps Europe would be better advised to take care of its own security. This, however, demanded a greater sense of unity and common purpose than Europe had ever been able to achieve.

The spotlight fell particularly on Britain, which had taken the lead in fighting Nazism and was still the dominant European power. In 1942–43, Winston Churchill had suggested the development of 'a United States of Europe' operating under 'a Council of Europe' with reduced trade barriers, free movement of people, a common military and a High Court to adjudicate disputes (quoted in Palmer, 1968, p. 111). He made the same suggestion in a speech at the University of Zurich in 1946, but it was clear that Churchill felt this new entity should be based around France and Germany and would not necessarily include Britain – before the war he had argued that Britain was 'with Europe but not of it. We are interested and associated, but not absorbed' (Zurcher, 1958, p. 6).

National pro-European groups decided to organize a conference aimed at publicizing the cause of regional unity. The Congress of Europe, held in The Hague in May 1948, was attended by delegates from 16 states and observers from the United States and Canada. Many ambitious ideas were discussed, but the most tangible outcome was the Council of Europe, founded with the signing in London in May 1949 of a statute by ten European states. The statute noted the need for 'closer unity between all the like-minded countries of Europe' and listed the Council's aims, including 'common action in economic, social, cultural, scientific, legal and administrative matters', but not defence.

The Council, which was headquartered in Strasbourg, had a governing Committee of Ministers, on which each state had one vote, and a 147-member Consultative Assembly made up of representatives nominated from national legislatures. Although membership of the Council expanded, it never became anything more than a loose intergovernmental organization. It made progress on human rights, cultural issues and even limited economic cooperation, but it was not the kind of body that European federalists wanted.

While the OEEC and the Council of Europe encouraged Europeans to think and work together, opposition from antifederalists in Britain, Scandinavia and elsewhere ensured that neither would promote significant regional integration. Among those looking for something more substantial were the French businessman Jean Monnet (1888–1979) and Robert Schuman (1880–1963), French foreign minister from 1948 to 1953. Both were enthusiastic Europeanists, felt that practical steps needed to be taken that went beyond the broad statements of organizations such as the Council of Europe, and agreed that the logical starting point should be the resolution of the perennial problem of Franco–German relations.

By 1950 it was clear to many that West Germany had to be allowed to rebuild its industrial base if it was to play a useful role in the western alliance. One way of doing this without allowing Germany to become a threat to its neighbours was for it to rebuild under the auspices of a supranational organization, which would tie Germany into the wider process of European reconstruction. Looking for a starting point that would be meaningful but not too ambitious, Monnet focused on the coal and steel industries, which offered strong potential for common European organization, for several reasons:

- Coal and steel were the building blocks of industry, and the steel industry had a tendency to create cartels. Cooperation would eliminate waste and duplication, break down cartels, make coal and steel production more efficient and competitive, and boost industrial development.

- Because the heavy industries of the Ruhr had been the foundation of Germany's power, and France and Germany had previously fought over coal reserves in Alsace-Lorraine, creating a supranational coal and steel industry would contain German power.
- Integrating coal and steel would make sure that Germany became reliant on trade with the rest of Europe, underpinning its economic reconstruction and helping the French lose their fear of German industrial domination (Monnet, 1978, p. 292).

Monnet felt that unless France moved quickly, the United States would become the focus of a new transatlantic anti-Soviet alliance, Britain would be pulled closer to the United States, Germany's economic and military growth could not be controlled and France would be led to its 'eclipse' (ibid., p. 294). As head of the French national planning commission, he knew that effective economic planning was beyond the ability of individual states working alone. He also knew from personal experience that intergovernmental organizations had a tendency to be hamstrung by the governments of their member states, and to become bogged down in ministerial meetings. To avoid these problems he proposed a new institution independent of national governments; in other words it would be supranational rather than intergovernmental.

After discussions with Monnet and West German Chancellor Konrad Adenauer, Robert Schuman took these ideas a step further at his May 1950 press conference. In what later became known as the Schuman Declaration, he argued that Europe would not be united at once or according to a single plan, but step by step through concrete achievements. This would require the elimination of Franco–German hostility, and Schuman proposed that French and German coal and steel production be placed 'under a common High Authority, within the framework of an organization open to the participation of the other countries of Europe'. This would be 'a first step in the federation of Europe', and would make war between France and Germany 'not merely unthinkable, but materially impossible' (Schuman, quoted in Weigall and Stirk, 1992, pp. 58–9).

The proposal was revolutionary in the sense that France was offering to sacrifice a measure of national sovereignty in the interests of building a new supranational authority that might end an old rivalry and help build a new European peace (Gillingham, 1991, p. 231). Although membership of this new body was offered to all western European states, only four accepted: Italy, which wanted respectability and economic and political stability, and the Benelux countries, which were in favour because they were small and vulnerable, had twice been invaded by Germany, were heavily reliant on exports and felt that the only way they could gain a significant voice in world affairs and ensure their security was to become part of a bigger regional unit.

The other European governments had different reasons for not taking part: Spain and Portugal were dictatorships and had little interest in international cooperation; in Denmark and Norway the memories of German occupation were still too fresh; Austria, Sweden and Finland were keen on remaining neutral; Ireland was predominantly agricultural and tied economically to Britain; Britain still had extensive interests outside Europe, exported very little of its steel to western Europe, and the new Labour government had just nationalized the coal and steel industries and did not like the supranational character of Schuman's proposal.

The lines of thinking now established, the governments of the Six opened negotiations and on 18 April 1951 signed the Treaty of Paris, creating the European Coal and Steel Community (ECSC). The new organization began work in August 1952 after ratification of the terms of the treaty by each of the member states. It was governed by a nominated nine-member High Authority (with Jean Monnet as its first president), and decisions were taken by a six-member Special Council of Ministers. A nominated 78-member Common Assembly helped Monnet allay the fears of national governments regarding the surrender of powers, and disputes between states were to be settled by a seven-member Court of Justice.

The founding of the ECSC was a small step in itself, but remarkable in that it was the first time that any European government had given up significant powers to a supranational organization. It was allowed to reduce tariff barriers, abolish subsidies, fix prices and raise money by imposing levies on steel and coal production. It faced national opposition to its work, but its job was made easier by the fact that some of the groundwork had already been laid by the Benelux customs union. Although the ECSC failed to achieve many of its goals (notably the creation of a single market for coal and steel), it had ultimately been created to prove a point about the feasibility of integration, which it did.

While the ECSC was at least a limited success, two much larger, more ambitious and arguably premature experiments in integration failed dismally. The first of these was the European Defence Community (EDC), the goal of which was to promote western European cooperation on defence and bind West Germany into a European defence system. A draft treaty was signed by the six ECSC members in 1952 but it failed to be ratified, mainly because the French were nervous about the idea of German rearmament so soon after the war and did not want to give up control over their armed forces. Furthermore Britain – still the strongest European military power – was not included, and Europe could not have a workable common defence force without a common foreign policy (Urwin, 1995, p. 63).

Meanwhile, the European Political Community was intended as the first step towards a European federation. A draft plan was completed in 1953 for a European Executive Council, a Council of Ministers, a Court of Justice and a popularly elected Parliament. With the collapse of the EDC, however, all hope of a political community died, at least temporarily. The failure of these two initiatives was a sobering blow to the integrationists and sent shockwaves through the ECSC. Monnet resigned the presidency of the High Authority in 1955, disillusioned by the political resistance to its work and impatient to further the process of integration (Monnet, 1978, pp. 398–404).

While the ECSC made modest but solid achievements in its first four years, there were limits to its abilities and Europeanists felt that something more needed to be done to give momentum to the cause of integration. The six ECSC members agreed that coal and steel had been a useful testing ground, but that it was becoming increasingly difficult to develop these two sectors in isolation. A meeting of the ECSC foreign ministers at Messina in Italy in June 1955 resulted in agreement that it was time to 'relaunch' the European idea. They adopted a Benelux proposal 'to work for the establishment of a united Europe by the development of common institutions, the progressive fusion of national economies, the creation of a common market, and the progressive harmonization of their social policies' (Messina Resolution, in Weigall and Stirk, 1992, p. 94).

A committee was set up under the chairmanship of Belgian Foreign Minister Paul-Henri Spaak to look into the options. Its report led to a new round of negotiations and the signing in March 1957 of the two Treaties of Rome, one creating the European Economic Community (EEC) and the other the European Atomic Energy Community (Euratom), both of which came into force in January 1958. The EEC had a similar administrative structure to the ECSC, with a nine-member quasi-executive Commission, a Council of Ministers with powers over decision making, and a seven-member Court of Justice. A new 142-member Parliamentary Assembly was created to cover the EEC, ECSC and Euratom.

The EEC Treaty committed the Six to the creation of a common market within 12 years by gradually removing all restrictions on internal trade, setting a common external tariff for all goods coming in to the EEC, reducing barriers to the free movement of people, services and capital among the member states, developing common agricultural and transport policies, and creating a European Social Fund and a European Investment Bank. Action would be taken in areas where there was agreement, and disagreements could be set aside for future discussion. The Euratom Treaty, meanwhile, was aimed at creating a common market for atomic energy, but Euratom remained a junior actor in the process of integration and focused primarily on research.

Deepening and widening (1958-86)

By January 1958 the six founding members of the European Communities had signed three treaties, created a small network of joint institutions and set a number of ambitious goals aimed at integrating many of their economic activities. Problems were encountered along the way, but there were also many achievements:

- Although the 12-year deadline set in 1958 for the removal of barriers to a common market was not met, internal tariffs fell quickly enough to allow the Six to agree a common external tariff in July 1968, and to declare an industrial customs union.
- Bureaucratic bloat and replication were always a possibility, but although critics of European integration regularly pointed accusing fingers at the European Commission, its staff numbers remained low, and decision making was streamlined in April 1965 with the Merger Treaty, which combined into one the separate councils of ministers and commissions of the three communities. The decision making process was given both authority and direction by the formalization in 1975 of regular summits of EC leaders coming together as the European Council. The EEC was also made more democratic with the introduction in 1979 of direct elections to the European Parliament.
- Integration brought the removal of the quota restrictions that the member states had used to protect their domestic industries from competition from imported products. Intra-EEC trade between 1958 and 1965 grew three times faster than that with third countries (Urwin, 1995, p. 130), the GNP of the Six grew at an average annual rate of 5.7 per cent, per capita income and consumption grew at 4.5 per cent and the contribution of agriculture to GNP was halved (Ionescu, 1975, pp. 150–4).
- The free movement of goods across borders would be restricted as long as EEC members had non-tariff barriers such as different standards and regulations on health, safety and consumer protection. Standards were harmonized during the 1960s and 1970s, although it was not until the passage of the 1986 Single European Act that a concerted effort was made to bring all EEC members into line.
- Another priority was to lift restrictions on the free movement of workers. While some limits remained well into the 1990s, progress was made towards easing them during the 1960s and 1970s.
- Agreement on a Common Agricultural Policy (CAP) was achieved in 1968, creating a single market for agricultural products and assuring EEC farmers of guaranteed prices for their produce. CAP initially

encouraged both production and productivity, but it became the single biggest and most controversial item in the EEC budget (see Chapter 7).

- The Six worked more closely together on international trade negotiations and their joint influence was greater than it would have been if they had negotiated individually. The EEC acted as one, for example, in negotiations under the General Agreement on Tariffs and Trade (GATT), and in reaching preferential trade agreements with 18 former African colonies under the 1963 Yaoundé Convention (see Chapter 8).

Despite the achievements, the EEC was still a small, exclusive and elitist club. The most obvious absentee was Britain, which continued to view itself after the war as a world power. That notion ended with the 1956 Suez crisis, which shook the foundations of Britain's special relationship with the United States, and also made it clear that most of the key decisions on global political and economic issues were being driven by the United States and the USSR. Britain was not opposed to European cooperation, but was doubtful about the closeness of the ties proposed by Monnet and Schuman, so instead decided to champion a looser exercise in cooperation under the auspices of the European Free Trade Association (EFTA).

With a goal of free trade rather than economic and political integration, EFTA was founded in January 1960 with the signing of the Stockholm Convention by Austria, Britain, Denmark, Norway, Portugal, Sweden and Switzerland. In contrast to the contractual arrangements set up for the EEC by the Treaty of Rome, membership of EFTA was voluntary and involved no institutions beyond a Council of Ministers that met two or three times a year and a group of permanent representatives serviced by a small secretariat in Geneva.

EFTA helped cut tariffs, but achieved relatively little in the long term, mainly because several of its members did more trade with the EEC than with their EFTA partners. It soon became clear to Britain that political influence in Europe lay not with EFTA but with the EEC, that Britain risked political isolation if it stayed out of the EEC, and that the EEC was actually working – the member states had made impressive economic and political progress and British industry wanted access to the rich EEC market. In August 1961, barely 15 months after the creation of EFTA, Britain applied for EEC membership, as did Denmark and Ireland. They were joined in 1962 by Norway.

Denmark's motive was mainly agricultural: it was producing three times as much food as it needed, and the EEC represented a big market for those agricultural surpluses, as well as a boost for Danish industrial development. Ireland saw EEC membership as a way of furthering its industrial plans, reducing its reliance on agriculture, and loosening its ties with Britain. Norway realized the importance of the EEC market. With four of its members apparently trying to defect, EFTA ceased to have much purpose, so Sweden, Austria and Switzerland all applied for associate membership of the EEC; they were followed in 1962 by Portugal, Spain and Malta.

Negotiations between Britain and the EEC opened in early 1962, and appeared to be on the verge of a successful conclusion when they fell foul of Charles de Gaulle's Franco–German policy. De Gaulle had plans for an EEC built around a Franco–German axis, saw Britain as a rival to French influence in the Community, was upset that he had not been given equal status at the wartime summits of the allied powers, and resented Britain's lack of enthusiasm for the early integrationist moves of the 1950s. He also felt that British membership would give the United States too much influence in Europe.

Monnet, however, was keen on British membership, and even tried to bring Adenauer around to his point of view, but the latter shared de Gaulle's anglophobia, and agreed that development of the Franco–German axis was the key. In the space of just ten days in January 1963 de Gaulle signed a new Franco–German treaty and vetoed the British application. He further upset Britain and some of his own EEC partners by reaching the veto decision unilaterally and making the announcement at a press conference in Paris. Since Britain's application was part of a joint package with Denmark and Ireland, their applications were rejected as well.

Britain reapplied in 1967, but de Gaulle again vetoed its application. Following his resignation in 1969 Britain applied for a third time, and this time its application was accepted, along with those of Denmark, Ireland and Norway. Following membership negotiations in 1970–71, Britain, Denmark and Ireland finally joined the EEC in January 1973. Norway would have joined as well but a public referendum in September 1972 narrowly went against membership. The Six had now become the Nine.

An additional round of enlargements took place in the 1980s and pushed the borders of the EEC further south and west. Greece had made its first overtures to the EEC in the late 1950s, but had been turned down on the ground that its economy was too underdeveloped. It was given associate membership in 1961 as a prelude to full accession, which might have come sooner had it not been for the Greek military coup of April 1967. With the return to civilian government in 1974, Greece almost immediately applied for full membership, arguing that EEC membership would help underpin its attempts to rebuild democracy. The Community agreed, negotiations opened in 1976 and Greece joined in 1981.

Map 2 *Growth of the EU*

KEY

= Founder Members of ECSC, 1952

= First Enlargement 1973

= Second Enlargement 1981–86

= Third Enlargement 1995

= East Germany 1990

Spain and Portugal had both requested negotiations for associate membership in 1962, but both were dictatorships. Spain was given a preferential trade agreement in 1970 and Portugal in 1973, but it was only with the overthrow of the Caetano regime in Portugal in 1973 and the death of Franco in Spain in 1975 that EEC membership for the two states was taken seriously. Despite the relative poverty of Spain and Portugal, problems over fishing rights and concern about Spanish and Portuguese workers moving north in search of work, the EEC felt that membership would encourage democracy in the Iberian peninsula and help link the two countries more closely to NATO and western Europe. Negotiations opened in 1978–79 and both states joined in 1986, the Ten thereby becoming the Twelve.

The doubling of membership had several political and economic consequences: it increased the influence of the EEC (which was by now the biggest economic bloc in the world), it complicated the Community's decision making processes, it reduced the overall influence of France and Germany, and – by bringing in the poorer Mediterranean states – it altered the internal economic balance of the EEC. Rather than enlarging any further, it was decided to focus on deepening the relationship among the Twelve. Applications were made by Turkey (1987), Austria (1989), Cyprus and Malta (1990), and although East Germany entered through the back door with German reunification in 1990, there was to be no further enlargement until 1995.

Economic and social integration (1979–92)

By 1986 the EEC had become known simply as the European Community (EC). Its member states had a combined population of 322 million and accounted for just over one-fifth of all world trade. The EC had its own administrative structure and an independent body of law, and its citizens had direct (but limited) representation through the European Parliament.

However, progress towards integration remained uneven. The creation of a common market was one of the key goals of the Treaty of Rome, but – while the customs union was in place – barriers remained to the free movement of people and capital (including different national technical, health, and quality standards, and varying levels of indirect taxation), European businesses were not competing well on the global market, and scientists and industrialists were failing to collaborate. It was argued that there could never be a true single market without a common European currency, a controversial idea because it would mean a significant loss of national sovereignty and because – in neofunctionalist terms – it would represent a significant move towards political union. These issues had now begun to concern EC leaders, who responded with two of the most important steps in the process of integration since the treaties of Paris and Rome: the launch of the European Monetary System, and agreement of the Single European Act.

The EEC treaty had mentioned the need to 'coordinate' economic policies, but had given the Community no specific powers to ensure this, so in practice coordination had been minimal. New momentum had come in 1969 with a change of leadership in France and West Germany: president Georges Pompidou had been less averse than de Gaulle to strengthening EC ties and chancellor Willy Brandt had been in favour of monetary union. Turbulence in the international monetary system in the late 1960s gave the idea new urgency and significance, but EEC leaders disagreed about whether economic union or monetary union should come first (Urwin, 1995, p. 155).

The principle of economic and monetary union (EMU) was discussed at a 1969 summit of EEC leaders in the Hague, who agreed to control fluctuations in the value of their currencies and to make more effort to coordinate national economic policies. In August 1971, however, the Nixon administration took the United States off the gold standard, and signalled the end of the Bretton Woods system by imposing domestic wage and price controls and placing a surcharge on imports. This led to international monetary turbulence, which was exacerbated in 1973 by the Arab–Israeli war and the oil crisis. Because only West Germany, the Benelux countries and Denmark were able to keep their currencies reasonably stable, the goal of achieving EMU by 1980 was quietly abandoned.

In 1979, a new initiative was launched, known as the European Monetary System (EMS). Using an Exchange Rate Mechanism (ERM) based around an accounting tool known as the European Currency Unit (ecu) (see Chapter 7 for details), this was designed to create a zone of monetary stability within which governments took action to keep their currencies as stable as possible. The hope was that the ecu would become the normal means of settling debts among Community members, psychologically preparing them for the idea of a single currency. The EMS helped stabilize exchange rates, so in 1989 Commission President Jacques Delors decided to take EMU a step further with the elaboration of a three-stage plan aimed at fixing exchange rates and then turning the ecu into a single currency. His hopes were dashed, however, by speculation on the world's money markets, causing Britain and Italy to pull out of the ERM, and Spain, Portugal and Ireland to devalue their currencies. Ironically the crisis deterred speculation and reinforced currency stability, and EMU was back on track by 1994, but there was doubt about how soon Stage Three of the Delors plan could be reached.

Meanwhile there was concern that progress towards the single market was being handicapped by inflation and unemployment, and by the temptation of member states to protect their home industries with non-tariff barriers such as subsidies. Competition from the United States and Japan was also growing. In response, a decision was reached at the 1983 European Council meeting in Stuttgart to revive the original goal outlined in the Treaty of Rome of creating a single market. In June 1985 the Commission published the Cockfield report, listing the specific actions that would need to be taken in order to remove all remaining non-tariff barriers and create a true single market.

The Single European Act (SEA) was signed in Luxembourg in February 1986, and – after ratification by national legislatures – came into force in July 1987. It had several goals (Box 3.2), the most important of which was to complete all preparations for the single market by midnight on 31 December 1992. This involved the removal of all remaining physical barriers (such as customs and passport controls at internal borders), fiscal barriers (mainly in the form of different levels of indirect taxation) and technical barriers (such as conflicting standards, laws and qualifications). This would create 'an area without internal frontiers in which the free movement of goods, persons, services and capital is assured'. In practical terms it meant that the Commission and the Council of Ministers had to agree nearly 300 new pieces of law by 1990, which then had to be applied at the national level. In the event the deadline came and went without all the proposals being adopted. Nonetheless the single market went into force in January 1993 with the understanding that the backlog of legislation would be cleared as soon as possible.

With all this focus on economic issues, social policy was often overlooked by European leaders. The Treaty of Rome provided for the development of a Community social policy, but this was left in the hands of the member states and was very narrowly defined, emphasizing improved working conditions and standards of living for workers, equal pay for equal work among men and women, social security for migrant workers, and increased geographical and occupational mobility for workers. As the economic links among EEC member states tightened, however, so their different levels of wealth and opportunity became more obvious. Even in the mid-1960s, per capita GDP in the Community's ten richest regions was nearly four times greater than in its ten poorest regions. With the accession of Britain, Ireland and Greece the gap grew to the point where the richest regions were five times richer than the poorest (George, 1996, pp. 143–4).

Social and regional policy has since focused on promoting cohesion by helping the poorer parts of Europe, revitalizing regions affected by serious industrial decline, addressing long-term unemployment, providing youth

Box 3.2 The 1986 Single European Act

The passage of the Single European Act was widely acclaimed as the most important and successful step in the process of European integration since the Treaty of Rome. It had many important consequences:

- It created the single biggest market and trading unit in the world. Many internal passport and customs controls were eased or lifted, banks and companies could do business throughout the Community, there was little to prevent EC residents living, working, opening bank accounts and drawing their pensions anywhere in the Community, protectionism became illegal, and monopolies on everything from electricity supply to telecommunications were broken down.
- It gave Community institutions responsibility over new policy areas that had not been covered in the Treaty of Rome, such as the environment, research and development, and regional policy.
- It gave new powers to the Court of Justice, and created a Court of First Instance to hear certain kinds of case and ease the workload of the Court of Justice.
- It gave legal status to meetings of heads of government under the European Council, and gave new powers to the Council of Ministers and the European Parliament.
- It gave legal status to European Political Cooperation (foreign policy coordination) so that member states could work towards a European foreign policy and work more closely on defence and security issues.
- It made economic and monetary union an EC objective and promoted cohesion, Eurojargon for the reduction of the gap between rich and poor parts of the EC, thereby avoiding a 'two-speed Europe'.

job training and helping the development of rural areas. The Commission gives economic assistance in the form of grants from what are collectively known as structural funds. These include the European Social Fund (ESF) (which concentrates on youth unemployment and job creation), the European Regional Development Fund (set up in response to the regional disparities that grew when Britain and Ireland joined the Community), and the Cohesion Fund (which compensates the poorest EU member states for the costs of tightening environmental controls, and provides help for transport projects). The structural funds accounted for 18 per cent of EC expenditure in 1984 but by 2002 represented nearly one-third of EU spending (see Chapter 5).

The SEA made cohesion a central part of economic integration, the assumption being that although the single market would create new jobs, this would not be enough. A boost for social policy came in 1989 with the Charter of Fundamental Social Rights for Workers (the Social Charter), which promoted the free movement of workers, fair pay, better living and working conditions, freedom of association, and protection of children and adolescents. Social issues are now one of the core policy areas for the European Union, with many of the actions taken by the governments of the member states driven by the requirements of EU law. The latter has addressed issues as varied as health and safety at work, parental leave from work, public health, and programmes to help the disabled and the elderly (see p. 156 ff).

Despite the increased focus on cohesion, regional disparities remain; the gap between the highest and lowest income levels in the EU is twice that in the United States, and neither the EU nor the member states have so far been able to deal effectively with unemployment, which was more than 8 per cent in the euro zone in mid-2001 (and 9–10 per cent in France, Germany and Italy), compared with 4–5 per cent in the United States and Japan. The Treaty of Amsterdam (see below) not only incorporated the Social Charter into the treaties, but also made the promotion of high employment an EU objective.

From Community to Union (1992–)

The controversial idea of political integration was long left on the back burner because it was felt there was little hope of political union without economic union. False starts had been made with the European Political Community and an attempt in 1961 to draw up a political charter that would spell out the terms of political union (the Fouchet Plan, see Urwin, 1995, pp. 104–7). A later initiative came out of the 1970 Davignon report, which argued in favour of foreign policy coordination, quarterly meetings among the six foreign ministers, liaison among EC ambassadors in foreign capitals and common EC instructions on certain matters for those ambassadors.

Meanwhile, foreign policies were coordinated under a process known as European Political Cooperation (EPC), which had some early successes, for example the 1970 joint EC policy declaration on the Middle East and the signature of the Yaoundé Conventions on aid to poor countries. In 1975 Italian Prime Minister Aldo Moro signed the Final Act of the Conference on Security and Cooperation in Europe (held in Helsinki) 'in the name of the European Community'. EPC was eventually given legal status with the SEA. It worked well in some areas, but was more reactive than proactive and often found European governments at odds with one another. This became clear during the 1990–91 Gulf crisis set off by the Iraqi invasion of Kuwait, when the Community as a whole issued demands to the Iraqi regime, and imposed an embargo on Iraqi oil imports, but few individual member states were actively involved in the allied military response. It became clear once again in 1998 when Britain supported US threats of military action against Iraq, but found little agreement among its EU partners.

Determined to reassert French leadership in the EC, President François Mitterrand had focused on the theme of political union at the Fontaine-bleau European Council in 1984, with the result that a decision was taken in Milan in June 1985 to convene an intergovernmental conference (IGC) on political union. The outcome was the Treaty on European Union, agreed at the European Council summit in Maastricht in December 1991 and signed by the foreign and economics ministers of the Community in February 1992 (Box 3.3). The draft treaty had included the goal of federal union, but Britain had balked at this so the wording was changed to 'an ever closer union among the peoples of Europe, in which decisions are taken as closely as possible to the citizen'.

The Maastricht treaty had to be ratified by the 12 member states before it could come into force. There were lengthy political debates in Britain, France and Germany, but Maastricht received its biggest setback when it was rejected by Danish voters in a referendum in June 1992. It was only narrowly accepted by a referendum in France in September, so its content was further discussed at the European Council meeting in Edinburgh in December 1992. Following agreement that the Danes could opt out of the single currency, common defence arrangements, European citizenship and cooperation on justice and home affairs, a second referendum was held in Denmark in May 1993, and the treaty was accepted.

A major topic of political discussion in recent years has been the further enlargement of the EU. Any country wishing to join must meet at least five informal requirements: as well as being European and democratic, applicants must follow free-market economic policies, accept the terms of the treaties, and accept the *acquis communitaire* (the body of laws and policies already adopted by the EU). Deciding whether applicants meet these criteria has proved difficult, not least because of the problem of defining 'Europe', as discussed in Chapter 2.

Throughout the 1980s, discussions about enlargement focused on other western European states, if only because they came closest to meeting the criteria for membership. In order to prepare prospective members, negotiations began in 1990 on the creation of a European Economic Area (EEA), under which the terms of the SEA would be extended to the seven EFTA members, in return for which they would accept the rules of the single market. The EEA came into force in January 1994, but had already begun to lose relevance because Austria, Sweden, Norway and Finland had applied for EC membership. Negotiations with these four applicants were completed in early 1994, each held a national referendum, and all but Norway (where the vote once again went against membership) joined the

Box 3.3 The 1992 Treaty on European Union

Like the Single European Act before it, the Treaty on European Union – usually known as the Maastricht treaty – made some substantial changes to the contract among the member states of the EU:

- Reflecting the lengths to which the member states will occasionally go to reach compromises, a peculiar arrangement was agreed under Maastricht by which – instead of new powers being given to the European Community – three 'pillars' were created, and the whole structure was given the new label 'European Union'. The first pillar consisted of the three pre-existing communities (economic, coal and steel, and atomic energy), and the second and third pillars consisted of two areas in which there was to be more formal intergovernmental cooperation: a Common Foreign and Security Policy (CFSP), and home affairs and justice. Final responsibility for the CFSP remained with the individual governments rather than being handed over to the EU.
- A timetable was agreed for the creation of a single European currency by January 1999, confirming the essence of the plan outlined by Jacques Delors in 1989.
- EU responsibility was extended into new policy areas such as consumer protection, public health policy, transport, education and (except in Britain) social policy.
- There was greater intergovernmental cooperation on immigration and asylum, a European police intelligence agency (Europol) was created to combat organized crime and drug trafficking, a new Committee of the Regions was set up, and regional funds for poorer EU states were increased.
- New rights were provided for European citizens and an ambiguous European Union 'citizenship' was created; this meant, for example, the right of citizens to live wherever they liked in the EU, and to stand or vote in local and European elections.
- New powers were given to the European Parliament, including a 'codecision procedure' under which certain kinds of legislation are subject to a third reading in the European Parliament before they can be adopted by the Council of Ministers.

EU in January 1995. This left just Norway, Switzerland, Iceland and Liechtenstein in EFTA.

- Switzerland, which had considered applying for EC membership in 1992, rejected the EEA and in 1995 found itself completely surrounded by the EU. Demands for the Swiss to open their highways to EU trucks and intra-EU trade increased the pressure for EU membership, but further discussion ended – at least temporarily – in March 2001 when a national referendum went heavily against EU membership, by 77 per cent to 23 per cent.
- Iceland, with a population of just 300 000, relies largely on the export of fish and does more than half its trade with the EU, and so will find the logic of joining the EU increasingly difficult to resist.
- With a population of just 30 000, Liechtenstein is little more than an enclave of Switzerland and is likely to follow the Swiss lead.

Looking further east, Turkey has been anxious to join for some time and applied for membership in 1987. While its eligibility has been confirmed and it has been in a customs union with the EU since 1996, Turkey is populous (64 million people), poor and predominantly Islamic. In addition to the troubling economic and social questions thus raised, Turkey's human rights record is poor and its application has been opposed by Greece. It was angered by the decision of the European Council in December 1997 not to include it in the next round of enlargement negotiations, particularly as the EU said yes to Cyprus, which has been divided since 1975 into Turkish and Greek zones.

The most likely prospects for medium-term accession are central and eastern European states that turned to free market policies after the collapse of the Soviet bloc in 1991. Negotiations opened in the spring of 1998 with the Czech Republic, Estonia, Hungary, Poland and Slovenia (and with Cyprus). Looking still further east, accession by the other Baltic states (Latvia and Lithuania) and three former Soviet republics (Ukraine, Belarus and Moldova) cannot be discounted, but will depend on the resolution of questions about their relationship with Russia and how quickly they make the transition to free market policies. Latvia, Lithuania, Slovakia, Bulgaria and Romania have all applied – the first three have reasonably strong credentials but the last two are unlikely to be considered seriously until later (see Box 8.3, p. 213).

In June 1997 the EU leaders signed the Treaty of Amsterdam, a new set of revisions to the founding treaties of the EU. The treaty fell far short of its original goal of achieving political union to accompany the economic and monetary union promoted by the SEA and Maastricht, and the 15 leaders were unable to agree anything more than modest changes to the structure of EU institutions in preparation for enlargement. However,

Map 3   *Potential new members of the EU*

policies on asylum, visas, external border controls, immigration, employment, social policy, health protection, consumer protection, and the
environment were developed, cooperation between national police forces
(and the work of Europol) was strengthened, and improvements were
made to the arrangements for EU foreign policy, including agreement that
a single commissioner would be the EU representative on external
relations. There was also agreement on instituting a single European
currency in January 1999, and enlarging the EU to the east. Finally,

Amsterdam provided an opportunity to assess the progress made since the signing of the Treaty of Paris.

First, it was almost universally agreed that the single market programme had been a great success. Not all of the legislation needed to remove the final barriers to trade had been implemented, but the EU had become one of the two biggest markets in the world and intra-EU trade and competition had grown rapidly.

Second, the EU still had no joint foreign or defence policy, although it had made progress in some areas. It was a major actor on the world stage in terms of aid to eastern Europe, had signed preferential trade agreements with 71 African, Caribbean and Pacific countries, and was helping to build a Mediterranean free trade area (to be completed by 2010 and encompassing nearly 700 million people). However, the 15 member states still pursued many of their own interests and take different positions on foreign policy problems.

Third, there was no common policy on immigration, visas and asylum, although progress on the removal of border controls continued. In 1985 France, Germany and the Benelux states signed the Schengen Agreement, under which all border controls were to be removed. All EU member states except Britain and Ireland have since joined, along with two non-members: Iceland and Norway. The terms of the agreement allow the signatories to implement controls at any time and not all have introduced truly passport-free travel, but it marked a substantial step towards the final removal of border controls.

Finally – and most critically of all – progress continued on the creation of a single European currency. A decision was taken in 1995 to call it the euro, and the timetable agreed under Maastricht required participating states to fix their exchange rates in January 1999. At a special EU summit in May 1998 it was decided that all but Greece met the conditions necessary to join the euro, but public and political opinion in the member states was divided on which should or would fix their exchange rates. While inflation rates were low in member states in 1998, their unemployment rates were not, and the rate of industrial growth was slowing in several. There was also considerable public resistance to the idea of the single currency in several countries, notably Britain and Germany. In the event, all but Denmark, Sweden and the UK adopted the euro, banknotes and coins began circulating in January 2002, and the 12 members of the euro zone abolished their national currencies in March.

The deepening of European integration – and the future widening of membership of the European Union – has increased the pressure for changes in the structure of EU institutions. They still show many of the signs of the arrangements made when the European Community was an exclusive club of six countries. With membership now up to 15, and shortly to grow to 20 or more, the calculations used for the distribution of votes and seats in those institutions – and the nature of the relationship among the member states – are in need of revision. Such changes were on the agenda of negotiations which led to the writing and the signature in December 2000 of the Treaty of Nice, the most recent set of revisions to the Treaty of Rome. Unfortunately the new treaty dealt more with numbers (votes in the Council of Ministers, seats in the European Parliament, and so on) than with a redefinition of the tasks and character of the EU institutions. A new set of negotiations was beginning as this book went to press, aimed at debating a possible new constitution for the EU.

Conclusions

Europe has travelled a long road in the past fifty years. Just after the Second World War, most European states were physically devastated, the suspicions and hostilities that had led to two world wars in the space of a generation still lingered, and western Europe found itself being pulled into a military and economic vacuum as power and influence moved outwards to the United States and the Soviet Union. The balance of power changed as an exhausted Britain and France dismantled their empires and reduced their militaries, while West Germany rapidly rebuilt and became the dominant force in European politics. Intent on avoiding future wars, and concerned about being caught in big power rivalry, European leaders began considering new levels of regional cooperation, pooling the interests of western European states and helping give the region new confidence and influence.

Beginning with the limited experiment of integrating their coal and steel industries and building on an economic foundation and security shield underwritten by the United States, six European states quickly agreed a common agricultural policy, a customs union and the beginnings of a common market. The accession of new members in the 1970s and 1980s greatly increased the size of the Community's population and market, pushing its borders further to the west and to the east. The global economic instability that followed the end of the Bretton Woods system and the energy crises of the 1970s served to emphasize the need for western European countries to cooperate if they were to have more control over their own future rather than simply to respond to external events.

After several years of relative lethargy the European experiment was given new impetus by completion of the single market, and then by the controversial decision to stabilize exchange rates as a prelude to the abolition of national currencies and the adoption of a single European currency. At the same time, the European Union increasingly shows a united face to the rest of the world, with more cooperation on foreign and trade policy, and the seeds of a European defence capacity. The effects of integration have been felt in a growing number of policy areas, including agriculture, competition, transport, the environment, energy, telecommunications, research and development, working conditions, culture, consumer affairs, education and employment.

The next step of note will be expansion into eastern Europe. More than twenty countries with a combined population of 206 million people could conceivably qualify for EU membership over the long term, beginning with several of the more successful converts to democracy and capitalism, which are likely to join by 2005. Expansion will not only change the balance of power once again, further reducing the long-dominant role in western European affairs of the French–German nexus, but promises to alter fundamentally the social, political and economic landscape for eastern Europe. The prefixes 'western' and 'eastern' in relation to Europe may become increasingly irrelevant.

At the core of all these developments has been a set of five major institutions, supported by a growing body of specialized agencies. The next chapter focuses on the structures and powers of those institutions, which have taken on the characteristics of a new level of authority to which the member states and their citizens are subject.

Chapter 4

The Institutions of the EU

A constitution for Europe
The European Commission
The Council of Ministers
The European Council
The European Parliament
The European Court of Justice
Conclusions

> . . . *the Union must start adapting its institutions and establishing more coherence in its policies so that it is easier to see what it does and what it stands for.*
>
> European Commission White Paper, 2001

As the European Union has grown, so have the powers and the reach of its institutions. Unfortunately, the changes made to the treaties over the years have created a governing structure that is complex, confusing, and still under development. Those changes have come mainly as a response to short-term needs and political compromises, and there is little sense of what the 'government' of the EU will eventually become. The treaties of Amsterdam and Nice were to have included major innovations, but they ended up providing little more than some light tinkering, so more changes are inevitable as membership of the EU expands to eastern Europe over the next few years, and as the balance of power among the member states changes.

The EU institutions cannot easily be compared with the governing bodies of the member states. The College of Commissioners is something like a cabinet of ministers, but not quite. The European Parliament has some of the powers of a legislature, but not all. The European Commission is a bureaucracy, but it is also much more. The European Council and the Council of Ministers are like nothing found in most national governments. The Court of Justice is the only institution to directly parallel those found at the national level – it has most of the features of a typical constitutional court. To complicate matters, the institutions do not amount to a 'government' in the conventional sense of the word, because the member states still hold most of the decision making powers, and are responsible for implementing EU policies on the ground.   *sum*

In summary, the five major institutions work as follows: the European Commission develops proposals for new laws and policies, on which final decisions are taken by the Council of Ministers and the European Parliament. Once a decision is made, the European Commission is responsible for overseeing the implementation of laws and policies by the member states. Meanwhile, the Court of Justice works to ensure that laws and policies meet the terms and spirit of the treaties, while the European Council brings the leaders of the member states together at periodic summit meetings to guide the overall direction of European integration.
                                                          some
This brief outline says nothing about the many subtle nuances of European decision making, nor does it convey the many informal aspects of EU government: the different levels of influence exerted by member states; the political and economic pressures that drive the decisions of the member states; the key role played by interest groups, corporations, staff in the Commission, specialized working groups in the Council of Ministers, and the permanent representatives of the member states; and all the muddling through and incremental change that often characterizes policy making in the EU, as in conventional systems of government.

This chapter looks at the major institutions of the EU, describing how they are structured, showing how they fit in to the policy process, and explaining how they relate to each other and to the member states. It paints a picture of a system that is often complicated, occasionally clumsy, and regularly misunderstood. It argues that the EU institutions are caught in a web of competing national interests, and that the conflicting forces of intergovernmentalism and supranationalism are pulling each of them in different directions, but that they are still – to all intents and purposes – a confederal administration of the European Union.

A constitution for Europe

Oddly enough for a body that has so much influence over the lives of so many people, the European Union does not have a constitution. It has a collection of treaties which have many of the same effects as a constitution, and studies of EU law often talk about constitution-building and the 'constitutionalization' of the EU legal order (see Mancini, 1991; Dehousse, 1998, Chapter 2; Shaw, 2000, Chapter 3), but the reluctance of many European leaders to give up control and to admit that the EU is a new level

Figure 4.1　*The European policy process*

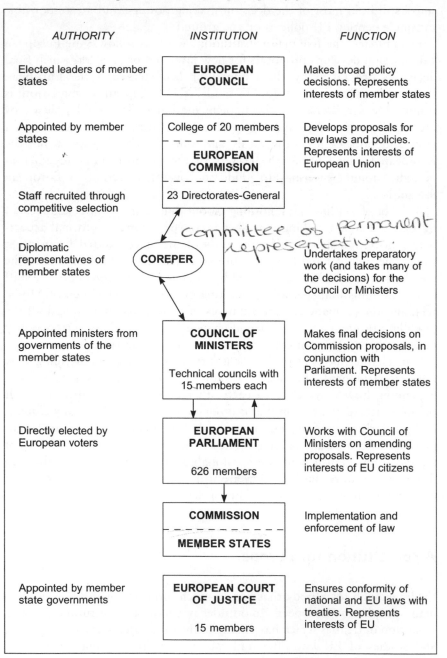

of government has meant that the treaties have never been formally recognized in political discussions as a constitution, nor treated as such.

A constitution is typically a written document that describes the structure of a system of government, outlines the powers of the different governing institutions, describes limits on those powers, and lists the rights of citizens relative to government. It is usually fairly short, provisions are made by which it can be amended, and a constitutional court exists with the duty of interpreting the constitution by measuring the laws and actions of government against the content and principles of the constitution.

The treaties – eight of them and counting – are usually described in a *Treaties* way that implies that there are eight separate documents that outline the powers of the EU. In fact, there is only one document, because the last seven have been revisions of the rules as much as additions to the rules. The European Court of Justice has helped make the treaties more like a constitution, but rather than clarifying matters, each new treaty has tended to add new complications, making the rules of the EU even more difficult to follow and understand.

When American leaders decided to create the United States of America, they drew up a constitution that had four important features. First, it was a contract between people and government, outlining their relative roles, powers and rights. Second, it was short and succinct, meaning that it could easily be read and understood by almost anyone. Third, it was ambiguous and provided few details on the specific powers of government, thereby allowing room for evolutionary change. Finally, there was provision for amendments to be made, but – by happy accident – loopholes ensured that the most important changes to the constitution were to come as a result of judicial interpretations provided by the US Supreme Court and new laws passed by the US Congress. These have changed many of the details of the structure of government, allowing the constitution to keep up with prevailing political, economic and social values.

The European 'constitution' has none of these advantages. Instead of being a contract between people and government, it is a contract among governments. Instead of being short, it is long, rambling and dull, often confusing even the legal experts. Its density has combined with its lack of stirring declarations to discourage Europeans from reading it or learning its key points, making the idea of European integration even more alien to them than it already is. Instead of being ambiguous, the obsession of European leaders with making sure that there is minimal room for misunderstanding has produced treaty revisions that go into migrainous detail on the specific powers of EU institutions, the policy responsibilities of the EU, and the rights of citizens. And instead of being changed only by formal amendments, by judicial interpretation, or by changes in EU law, it is regularly given wholesale revisions as a result of new treaties.

Constitutional experts have called for the key points in the treaties to be rewritten as a Basic Treaty of the European Union, an idea to which the European Commission has responded favourably (*The Economist*, 22 July 2000, pp. 48–9). This would demand the convening of a constitutional conference, which would set off a heated and lengthy debate over what the EU is and what it should be. However, such a conference would also help focus the minds of Europeans and their leaders on what they expect of the EU. A 'constitutional convention' was due to be launched in March 2002, leading to a year-long debate aimed at developing suggestions for how to reform the EU. Its success, however, depended upon national leaders rising above the petty and trivial and taking the broad view. How long it will take for the institutional structure of the EU to achieve any kind of permanence and become more real to its citizens remains to be seen.

The European Commission

The process by which laws and policies are made in the EU begins with the European Commission, the executive–bureaucratic arm of the EU. It is responsible for developing proposals for new laws and policies, for overseeing the execution of those laws and policies once they are adopted, and for promoting the general interests of European integration. Head-quartered in Brussels, its staff work in multiple buildings around the city, and in regional cities around the EU and national capitals around the world. It is the most supranational of the EU institutions, and has not only encouraged member states to harmonize their laws, regulations and standards in the interests of removing barriers to trade, but has been the source of some of the most important policy initiatives of the last forty years, including the single market programme and the development of the euro.

Eurosceptics like to scorn the Commission, arguing that it is big, expensive and powerful, that it meddles in the internal affairs of member states, that its leaders are not elected, and that it has too little public accountability. But the criticism is often misplaced and misguided:

- Commission leaders are not elected, it is true, but to have them elected would be to give them the kind of independence that national governments fear.
- It sometimes appears secretive and anonymous – also true – but its record is no worse than that of national bureaucracies, and in some ways is better.

Box 4.1 European Union law

The key difference between the EU and any other 'international organization' is that the EU has built a body of law which is applicable in all its member states, which supersedes national law in areas where the EU has 'competence', and which is backed up by rulings from the Court of Justice. The creation of this body of law has involved the voluntary surrender of powers by the member states in a broad range of policy areas, and the development of a new level of legal authority to which the member states are subject.

The foundation of the EU legal order is provided by the eight treaties: Paris, the two treaties of Rome, the Merger Treaty, the Single European Act, Maastricht, Amsterdam, and Nice. These are the primary rules, out of which have come thousands of secondary rules, which take five main forms:

- *Regulations* are the most powerful, and the most like conventional acts of a national legislature. They are directly applicable in that they do not need to be turned into national law, they are binding in their entirety, and they take immediate effect on a specified date. Usually fairly narrow in intent, regulations are often designed to amend or adjust an existing law.
- *Directives* are binding in terms of goals, but it is left up to the member states to decide what action they need to take to achieve those goals. For example, a 1988 directive on pollution from large industrial plants set targets for the reduction of emissions (how much, and by when), but left it up to the member states to decide individually how to meet those targets. Directives usually include a date by which national action must be taken, and member states must tell the Commission what they are doing.
- *Decisions* are also binding, but are usually fairly specific in their intent, and aimed at one or more member states, at institutions, or even at individuals. Some are aimed at making changes in the powers of EU institutions, some are directed towards internal administrative matters, and others are issued when the Commission has to adjudicate disputes between member states or corporations.
- *Recommendations* and *Opinions* have no binding force. They are sometimes used to test reaction to a new EU policy, but they are used mainly to persuade or to provide interpretation on the application of regulations, directives and decisions.

Until the early 1990s the EU was adopting a staggering 6000–7000 laws every year, but the number has since fallen to about 1500–1800. The fall-off was due in part to a deliberate policy by the Santer Commission to focus more on the implementation of existing laws, and in part to the completion of the single market programme.

- It is small given the size of its task (it has just over 20 000 staff, making it smaller than many national government ministries) and its administrative budget accounts for less than five per cent of the EU total.
- Most importantly, the Commission is not a decision making body, but simply carries out the wishes of the member states, and makes sure that the general goals of integration are converted into specific actions. Real decision making power still rests with the Council of Ministers, which is firmly under the control of the governments of the member states.

The Commission is headed by a 20-member College of Commissioners, which serves a five-year term and functions as something like a European cabinet, making the final decisions on which proposals for new laws and policies to send on to the Council, and taking collective responsibility for their decisions. One of the 20 is appointed president, and each Commissioner has a portfolio for which he/she is responsible (see Table 4.1), the subjects of the portfolios reflecting the policy responsibilities of the EU. The 20 posts are distributed among the EU member states, with the five biggest countries (Germany, Britain, France, Italy and Spain) having two each, and the rest one each. This will be changed in 2005, when each member state will be limited to one Commissioner. Once the EU has 27 member states, the European Council will decide how many Commissioners there will be (no more than 27), and will agree how they will be rotated among the member states.

Commissioners are appointed by their national governments, but they are not national representatives, and they must swear an oath of office saying that they will renounce any defence of national interests. There are no formal rules on appointments, but nominees are discussed with the nominee for president, and must be acceptable to other governments and to the European Parliament (for details on the process, see Nugent, 2001, pp. 82–8). As the powers of the Commission have increased, and the EU has become a more significant political force, postings to the Commission have become more desirable and more important, and Commissioners are becoming both younger and more technocratic.

The dominant figure in the Commission is the president, the person who comes closest to being the leader of the EU. The word 'leader' should be treated with some caution, though, because the president does not have the same political status as a head of government, and the Commission is ultimately the servant of the member states. However, the president has considerable authority within the Commission: he can influence the appointment of other Commissioners, has sole power over distributing portfolios, sets the agenda for the Commission, can launch major new policy initiatives, can take over new responsibilities for himself, chairs meetings of the College, and represents the Commission in dealings with

Table 4.1   *The European Commissioners, January 2002*

Name	Country	Key portfolios
Romano Prodi	Italy	President
Neil Kinnock	UK	Vice-president, institutional reform
Loyola de Palacio	Spain	Vice-president, relations with EP, transport and energy
Michel Barnier	France	Regional policy
Frits Bolkestein	Netherlands	Internal market
Philippe Busquin	Belgium	Research
David Byrne	Ireland	Health, consumer protection
Anna Diamantopoulou	Greece	Employment and social affairs
Franz Fischler	Austria	Agriculture
Pascal Lamy	France	Trade
Erkki Liikanen	Finland	Enterprise, information society
Mario Monti	Italy	Competition
Poul Nielson	Denmark	Development, humanitarian aid
Chris Patten	UK	External relations
Viviane Reding	Luxembourg	Education and culture
Michaele Schreyer	Germany	Budget
Pedro Solbes Mira	Spain	Economic and financial affairs
Günther Verheugen	Germany	Enlargement
Antonio Vitorino	Portugal	Justice and home affairs
Margot Wallström	Sweden	Environment

other EU institutions and national governments. From 2005, the president will be able to reshuffle portfolios midterm (with College approval), giving him even more influence over the Commission.

As with all such positions, the powers of the office depend to some extent on the personality of the officeholder. Following several early presidents who did not make much of an impression on the European public, the administration of former French economics minister Jacques Delors in 1985–94 changed everything. Delors centralized authority, had

Table 4.2   *Presidents of the European Commission*

1958–67	Walter Hallstein (West Germany)
1967–70	Jean Rey (Belgium)
1970–72	Franco Maria Malfatti (Italy)
1972	Sicco Mansholt (Netherlands) (interim)
1973–76	Francois-Xavier Ortoli (France)
1977–80	Roy Jenkins (Britain)
1981–84	Gaston Thorn (Luxembourg)
1985–94	Jacques Delors (France)
1995–99	Jacques Santer (Luxembourg)
1999	Mario Monti (Spain) (interim)
1999–*2004*	Romano Prodi (Italy)
2004 – ?	*José Manuel Barroso (Portugal)*

firm ideas about a strong, federal Europe asserting itself internationally, and used this vision to push the EU in many new directions; his name is associated particularly with the single market and single currency programmes. He was succeeded in January 1995 by Jacques Santer, former prime minister of Luxembourg, who avoided bold new initiatives, and focused instead on improving the implementation of existing laws and policies. The Santer College resigned *en masse* in January 1999 following allegations of nepotism and incompetence against some of its members. Santer was replaced by former Italian prime minister Romano Prodi, who was charged with reforming the Commission, overseeing the transition to the euro, and preparing for expansion into eastern Europe.

There are few formal rules regarding how the president is appointed. It has become normal for the leaders of the member states to decide the appointment at the European Council held in the June before the term of the incumbent Commission ends, settling on someone acceptable to all of them and to the European Parliament. Appointed for renewable five-year terms, the president will usually be someone with a strong political reputation, a strong character, and proven leadership abilities.

Below the College, the Commission is divided into 23 directorates-general (DGs), which are equivalent to national government ministries. Every DG is responsible for a particular policy area, has its own director-general, and is tied to a Commissioner. Some DGs are bigger, wealthier, busier, and more important than others, the ranking being a reflection of the extent to which the EU is active in different policy areas. Hence those dealing with external affairs, industry, and agriculture are more powerful and more prominent, while those dealing with fisheries, energy and education are smaller and less influential.

Table 4.3 *Directorates-general of the European Commission*

Agriculture	Financial Control
Budget	Fisheries
Competition	Health and Consumer Protection
Development	Information Society
Economic and Financial Affairs	Internal Market
Education and Culture	Justice and Home Affairs
Employment and Social Affairs	Personnel and Administration
Energy and Transport	Regional Policy
Enlargement	Research
Enterprise	Taxation and Customs Union
Environment	Trade
External Relations	

The general task of the Commission is to ensure that EU policies are advanced in light of the treaties (for details, see Edwards and Spence, 1997, Chapter 1). It does this in five ways.

- *Powers of initiation.* The Commission makes sure that the principles of the treaties are turned into laws and policies. It has a monopoly over drafting new laws, and can draw up proposals for new policy areas, as it did with the Single European Act and the Delors package for economic and monetary union. Proposals can come from a Commissioner or a staff member of one of the DGs, may be a response to a ruling by the Court of Justice, or may flow out of the requirements of the treaties. Member state governments, interest groups, and even private corporations can all exert direct or indirect pressure on the Commission, and the last two decades have also seen more policy suggestions coming from the European Council.

  A new piece of EU legislation will begin life as a draft written by middle-ranking officials in one of the DGs. It will then work its way up through the different levels of the DG, being discussed with outside parties (such as interest groups or corporations) and with other DGs, being amended along the way. The draft will finally reach the College of Commissioners, which can accept a proposal, reject it, send it back down the line for redrafting, or defer making a decision. Once accepted, it will be sent to the European Parliament for an opinion, and to the Council of Ministers for a decision. This process can take anything from months to years, and Commission staff will be involved at every stage.

- *Powers of implementation.* Once a law or policy is accepted, the Commission is responsible for making sure that it is implemented by the member states. It has no power to do this directly, but instead works through national bureaucracies, using its power to collect information from member states, to take to the Court of Justice any member state, corporation, or individual that does not conform to the spirit of the treaties or follow subsequent EU law, and to impose sanctions or fines if a law is not being implemented.

  The Commission has its own monitoring teams, but they do not have the personnel to police every member state, so it usually has to rely on reports from member states, or whistle-blowing by governments, individuals, corporations or interest groups. The Commission adds to the pressure by publicizing the progress on implementation, hoping to embarrass the laggards into action. Until 1993, compliance was based on goodwill and an agreement to 'play the game'; Maastricht gave the Commission new powers to take a state to the Court of Justice, which can then impose a fine. Most cases of non-compliance come not so much out of a deliberate avoidance by a member state as out of differences over interpretation or differences in the levels of efficiency of national bureaucracies.

- *Acting as the conscience of the EU.* The Commission is expected to rise above competing national interests and to represent and promote the general interest of the EU, however that is defined. It is also expected to help smooth the flow of decision making by mediating disagreements between or among member states and other EU institutions.

- *Management of EU finances.* The Commission makes sure that all EU revenues are collected, plays a key role in drafting and guiding the annual budget through the Council of Ministers and Parliament, and administers EU expenditure, especially under the Common Agricultural Policy and the structural funds.

- *External relations.* The Commission has been given the authority by the member states to represent the EU in dealings with international organizations such as the United Nations and the World Trade Organization. It is also a key point of contact between the EU and the rest of the world; more than 160 governments have opened diplomatic missions in Brussels accredited to the EU, while the EU has opened more than 130 offices in other parts of the world, staffed by Commission employees. The Commission also vets applications for full or associate membership from non-member states; it looks into all the implications and reports back to the Council. If the Council decides to open negotiations with an applicant, the Commission oversees the process.

The Commission has been a productive source of initiatives for new laws and policies, and is much more accessible and open than, say, the Council of Ministers. It has been at the core of European integration since the beginning, and while it has not always made the best use of the resources it has available, its staff on the whole are professional and hard-working, and the critical charges made against the Commission by the Eurosceptic media are often unfair and misinformed.

The Council of Ministers

The Council of Ministers is the major decision making branch of the EU, the primary champion of national interests, and arguably the most powerful of the EU institutions. Yet it is the institution about which most Europeans know the least: its meetings are held in secret, it attracts very little media coverage, and it has been the subject of much less academic study than the Commission or Parliament. When Europeans think about the activities of the EU, they tend to first think of (and blame) the Commission, forgetting that the Council of Ministers actually makes the final decisions. In many ways, its powers make the Council more like the legislature of the EU than the European Parliament, although new powers for Parliament in recent years have made the two bodies into 'co-legislatures'.

Once the Commission has proposed a new law or policy, it is discussed and amended by the Council of Ministers and the European Parliament, and the Council is then responsible for final acceptance or rejection. Headquartered in the Justus Lipsius Building in Brussels, the Council of the European Union is one of the most intergovernmental of EU institutions. It consists of national government ministers, and its membership changes according to the topic under discussion; hence employment ministers will meet to deal with employment issues, transport ministers to discuss new proposals for transport policy and law, and so on.

The Council of Ministers is made up of nearly two dozen so-called technical councils. The most important of these is the General Affairs Council (GAC), which brings together the EU foreign ministers to deal broadly with internal and external relations, and to discuss politically sensitive policies and proposals for new laws. Economics and finance ministers meet together as Ecofin, agriculture ministers as the Agriculture Council, and beside them are councils dealing with issues such as the environment, research, fisheries and education.

Each council normally consists of the appropriate set of national government ministers, together with the relevant European Commissioner, whose presence is designed to make sure that the Council does not lose sight of broader EU interests. How often each council meets depends on the importance of its area. The GAC, Ecofin and the Agriculture Council meet monthly because of the amount of work on their agendas, but the councils dealing with other issues meet perhaps only 2–4 times each year. Most meetings last no more than one or two days, and are held in Brussels.

Between meetings of ministers, national interests in the Council are protected and promoted by permanent representations, or national delegations of about 30–40 professional diplomats, which are much like embassies to the EU. The heads of delegations – the Permanent Representatives – meet every week in the powerful Committee of Permanent Representatives (COREPER), whose critical role in EU policy-making is routinely overlooked. COREPER acts as a link between Brussels and the member states, conveys the views of the national governments, and keeps capitals in touch with developments in Brussels. Most importantly, it makes decisions. It prepares Council agendas, oversees the committees and working parties set up to sift through proposals, decides which proposals go to which council, and makes many of the decisions about which proposals will be accepted and which will be left for debate by ministers. In many cases, the hard decisions have already been made before the ministers meet.

Direction is given to the deliberations of the Council and COREPER by the presidency of the Council of Ministers, which is held not by a person, but by a member state. Every EU member state has a turn at holding the presidency for a spell of six months, the baton being passed in January and July each year. The state holding the presidency has several responsibilities:

- It sets the agenda for European Council meetings, and for the EU as a whole.
- It arranges and chairs meetings of the Council of Ministers and COREPER, and oversees Council relations with other EU institutions.
- It mediates and bargains, and promotes co-operation among member states. The success of a presidency is measured according to the extent to which the incumbent member state is able to encourage compromise and agreement among the EU members, as well as by what is delayed, opposed, or promoted (Brewin and McAllister, 1991).
- It runs EU foreign policy for six months, acts as the main voice of the EU on the global stage, coordinates member state positions at international conferences and negotiations in which the EU is involved, and (along with the president of the Commission) represents the EU at meetings with the president of the United States, and at the annual meetings of the G8 group of industrialized countries.
- It chairs at least one meeting of the European Council.

Box 4.2 Specialized EU institutions

As the work of the EU has grown, so has the number of specialized agencies created to deal with specific aspects of its work. They now include the following:

- *Committee of the Regions (Brussels)*. Created in 1994, this allows representatives of local units of government to meet and discuss matters relating to regional and local issues. Most of its 222 members are elected local government officials.
- *Court of Auditors (Luxembourg)*. Created in 1977, this is the EU's financial watchdog. It has 15 auditors appointed for six-year renewable terms, who carry out annual audits of the accounts of EU institutions.
- *Economic and Social Committee (Brussels)*. Created in 1958, this allows employers, workers and other sectional interests to meet and express their views. Most of its 222 members come from industry, agriculture, and the professions.
- *European Agency for the Evaluation of Medicinal Products (EMEA) (London)*. Created in 1995, the Agency harmonizes the work of national drug regulatory bodies, helps reduce costs that drug companies incur by having to win separate approvals from each member state, and helps overcome the protectionist tendencies of states unwilling to approve new drugs that might compete with those already produced by domestic drug companies.
- *European Central Bank (Frankfurt)*. Created in 1998 to replace the European Monetary Institute set up in 1994, the main job of the Bank is to ensure monetary stability by setting interest rates in the euro zone (see Box 7.3, p. 188).
- *European Environmental Agency (Copenhagen)*. Created in 1993, the Agency collects information from the member states and neighbouring non-EU states, which is used to help develop environmental protection policies, and to measure the results.
- *European Investment Bank (Luxembourg)*. An autonomous institution created in 1958 to encourage 'balanced and steady development' by granting loans and giving guarantees, the Bank's projects help poorer regions, support the modernization and improved competitiveness of industry, and must be of common interest to several member states or to the EU as a whole. Its single biggest project was the Channel tunnel. It is managed by a Board of Governors consisting of the finance ministers of the member states.
- *European Police Office (Europol) (The Hague)*. Created in 1999, Europol promotes police cooperation within the EU by managing a system of information exchange targeted against terrorism, drug-trafficking, and other serious forms of international crime.

There are several advantages to the rotating presidency. For example, it allows the leaders of the member states to convene meetings and launch initiatives on issues of national interest, to bring those issues to the top of the EU agenda, and – if they do a good job – to earn prestige and credibility. It also allows the leaders of smaller states to negotiate directly with other world leaders and helps the process of European integration by making the EU more real to the citizens of the country holding the presidency; six months is usually long enough to make an impression, but is also short enough to make sure that every member state is periodically at the helm.

There are also several disadvantages to the presidency. As the European Union has grown, so has the workload of the presidency, and some of the smaller states have found themselves struggling to provide the necessary leadership. As membership of the EU expands in the next few years, the cycle of the presidency will lengthen. With 15 member states, each has a turn at the helm only once every 7½ years; with 20 member states this will become once every ten years. Enlargement will also see countries joining the EU that are either poor, small, or unused to playing a leading role at international conferences. Inevitably, the structure of the presidency will have to be rethought.

The work of the presidency and the Council is supported by a secretariat general based in Brussels, headed by a Secretary General appointed for a five-year term. The secretariat drafts agendas, keeps records, and provides the activities of the Council with some continuity. It does this by working closely with the permanent representatives, and by briefing every Council meeting on the status of each of the items on the agenda.

Once the European Commission has proposed a new law, it is sent to Parliament and the Council of Ministers for debate and for a final decision on adoption or rejection. The more complex proposals will usually go first to one or more specialist Council working parties, which will look over the proposal in detail, identifying points of agreement and disagreement, and responding to suggestions for amendments made by Parliament (for more detail, see Hayes-Renshaw and Wallace, 1997). The proposal will then go to COREPER, which looks at the political implications, and tries to clear as many of the remaining problems as it can, ensuring that the meeting of ministers is as quick and as painless as possible. The proposal then moves on to the relevant Council for a final decision. Ministers prefer to reach a consensus whenever they can, and to avoid a formal vote. Even when a vote is called, the countries in the minority may simply acquiesce (Dinan, 1999, pp. 262–3). If an issue goes to a vote, however, ministers have three options:

- *Unanimity*. This was once needed where a new policy was being introduced or an existing policy framework was being amended. Its use has been increasingly restricted, though, and it is now needed only if the Council is looking at a new law in selected policy areas, including foreign and security policy, asylum, immigration, economic policy, and taxation. The use of unanimity gives each member state the power of veto, but the Amsterdam treaty introduced a 'constructive abstention' procedure by which a member state would not be obliged to apply a particular decision, but would recognize that the EU was committed.

- A *simple majority*. This is used mainly if the Council is dealing with a procedural issue or working under treaty articles, but as the SEA and Maastricht broadened the number of issues and areas in which a qualified majority vote could be used, the use of majority voting declined.
- A *qualified majority*. This is needed for almost every other kind of decision where ministers have failed to reach a consensus. Instead of each minister having one vote, each is given several votes roughly in proportion to the population of his/her member state (see Table 4.4). To be successful, a proposal must win 62 out of a possible 87 votes, but it can also be defeated by a *blocking minority* of 26 votes. Under changes agreed by the Treaty of Nice, the figures will change with effect from January 2005 as new member states join the EU. The number of votes that each existing member has now will change, each new member state will be given a predetermined number of votes, and two new conditions will apply: for a proposal to be accepted, the majority of member states must approve, and the states in favour must represent at least 62 per cent of the EU population.

Because the Council of Ministers is a meeting place for national interests, the keys to understanding how it works are terms such as compromise, bargaining, and diplomacy. The ministers are often leading political figures at home, so they are motivated by national political interests. They are also ideologically driven, and their authority will depend to some extent on the stability of the governing party or coalition at home. All these factors combine to pull ministers in many different directions, and to deny the Council the kind of structural regularity enjoyed by the Commission.

The European Council

The European Council is often described as an extension of the Council of Ministers, but it is actually very different both in terms of its powers and its composition. More a process or a forum than a formal institution, it consists of the heads of government of the EU member states, their foreign

Table 4.4   *Qualified majority voting in the Council of Ministers*

Member state	Current number of votes	Current number of citizens per vote (millions)	Reallocation of votes under Treaty of Nice	Number of citizens per vote (millions)
Germany	10	8.21	29	2.83
UK	10	5.95	29	2.05
France	10	5.86	29	2.02
Italy	10	5.76	29	1.99
Spain	8	4.92	27	1.46
Netherlands	5	3.16	13	1.22
Greece	5	2.10	12	0.88
Belgium	5	2.04	12	0.85
Portugal	5	2.00	12	0.83
Sweden	4	2.22	10	0.89
Austria	4	2.02	10	0.81
Denmark	3	1.77	7	0.76
Finland	3	1.73	7	0.74
Ireland	3	1.23	7	0.53
Luxembourg	2	0.20	4	0.10
Total	87	4.31*	237	1.58*
Qualified majority	62			
Blocking minority	26			

* Average

Votes for new member states will be as follows: Poland 27, Romania 14, Czech Republic 12, Hungary 12, Bulgaria 10, Lithuania 7, Slovakia 7, Latvia 4, Estonia 4, Slovenia 4, Cyprus 4, Malta 3.

ministers, and the president and vice-presidents of the Commission. This group meets at least twice each year at two-day summits, and provides strategic policy direction for the EU. The Council is something like a steering committee or a board of directors; it discusses the broad issues and goals of the EU, leaving it to the other EU institutions to work out the details.

The Council was created in 1974 in response to a feeling among some European leaders that the Community needed better leadership, and a body that could take a more long-term view of where the Community was headed. It immediately became an informal part of the Community decision making structure, although its existence was only finally given legal recognition with the Single European Act. Maastricht elaborated on its role, but did not provide much clarity beyond noting that the Council would 'provide the Union with the necessary impetus for its development and shall define the general political guidelines thereof'.

The Council has been an important force for integration, with many of the most important initiatives of recent years coming out of Council discussions – these have included the launch of the European Monetary System in 1978, and the discussions that led to the Maastricht, Amsterdam and Nice treaties. Council summits have also issued major declarations on international crises, reached key decisions on institutional changes (such as the 1974 decision to begin direct elections to the European Parliament), and given new clarity to EU foreign policy. But the Council has also had its failures, including its inability to speed up agricultural or budgetary reform, or to agree common EU responses to crises in Iraq and the Balkans.

Its members have always kept the exact role of the European Council deliberately ambiguous. An attempt to define that role came at the Stuttgart European Council in 1983 and the agreement of the 'Solemn Declaration on European Union'. Combining this with earlier declarations produces the following list of very general goals:

- to exchange views and reach a consensus.
- to give political impetus to the development of the EU.
- to begin cooperation in new policy areas.
- to provide general political guidelines for the EU.
- to guarantee policy consistency.
- to reach common positions on foreign policy issues.

More specifically, the European Council makes the key decisions on the overall direction of political and economic integration, internal economic issues, foreign policy issues, budget disputes, treaty revisions, new member applications, and institutional reforms (such as the changes that were made under the Treaty of Nice). The summits achieve all this through a combination of brain-storming, intensive bilateral and multilateral discussions, and bargaining. The mechanics of decision making depend on a combination of the quality of organization and preparation, the leadership skills of the presidency (which convenes and chairs each summit), and the ideological and personal agendas of individual leaders. The interpersonal dynamics of the participants is also important: the political significance of the Franco-German axis has always been critical, for example, and has been given additional influence by the good personal relations that have usually existed between the leaders of the two states. Leaders who have been in office a long time or who have a solid base of political support at home will be in a very different negotiating position from those who do not.

Regular summits of the Council are held in June and December every year, with additional meetings held whenever necessary. The meetings are hosted by the country holding the presidency of the Council of Ministers, and until recently took place either in the capital of that country, or in a regional city or town, such as Cardiff, Bonn or Gotebörg; they are now all held in Brussels. Organization is left largely to the leadership of the member state holding the presidency, which usually sees the summits as an opportunity to showcase the priorities of that member state. The agenda is driven in part by the ongoing priorities of the EU, but also by the particular priorities of the member state. The goal is to agree a set of Conclusions of the Presidency, an advanced draft of which is usually awaiting the leaders at the beginning of the summit, and provides the focus for discussions.

Officially, the Council has no set agenda, but there has to be some direction, so it is usual for senior officials from the country holding the presidency to work with the Council of Ministers to develop an agenda. The items on the agenda depend on circumstances; national delegations normally have issues they want to raise, there must be some continuity from previous summits, and leaders will often have to deal with a breaking problem or an emergency that needs a decision. Some issues (especially economic issues) are routinely discussed at every summit. The Commission may also promote issues it would like to see discussed, and an active presidency might use the summit to bring items of national or regional interest to the attention of the heads of government.

Preparations for each summit begin as soon as a member state takes over the presidency in January or July. Monthly meetings of the foreign ministers try to resolve potential disagreements, and as the date for the summit approaches, the prime minister and foreign minister of the state holding the presidency become increasingly involved. About ten days before the summit, the foreign ministers meet to finalize the agenda and to iron out any remaining problems and disputes. The more agreements they can broker in advance, the less likely the summit itself will end in failure (Johnston, 1994, pp. 27–31). Some summits are routine, and result in general agreement among leaders; others see deep differences in opinion, with some member states perhaps refusing to agree a common set of conclusions.

The summits themselves usually run over a period of two days, beginning with informal discussions over breakfast, and moving into details at plenary sessions held in the morning, afternoon, and – if necessary – evening. Overnight, officials from the presidency and the Secretariat of the Council of Ministers will work on the draft Conclusions, which will be discussed at another plenary on the morning of the second day, and – if necessary – at a final session in the afternoon. The summit then normally ends with the public release of the Conclusions.

In order to keep them manageable, plenaries are usually restricted to the leaders of the member states, their foreign ministers and two officials from the Commission, including the President. With no more than one adviser per country, interpreters, two officials from the presidency, one from the Council of Ministers secretariat, and three from the Commission, there are no more than 60 people in the room. The Council tries to take its decisions on the basis of unanimity, or at least of consensus, but the occasional lack of unanimity may force a formal vote, and some member states may want to attach conditions or reservations to the conclusions. As well as the formal plenary sessions, summits usually break out into subsidiary meetings, including those between foreign ministers, and regular bilateral meetings between prime ministers over breakfast or coffee.

The summits are always major media events, and are surrounded by extensive security, a need that became particularly obvious with the street demonstrations against globalization during the June 2001 summit in Goteborg, Sweden. Enormous symbolism is attached to the outcomes of the summits, which are measured according to the extent to which they represent breakthroughs, or show EU leaders to be bogged down in disagreement. Failure and success reflect not only on the presidency, but on the whole process of European integration. The media attention devoted to summits is often enough in itself to concentrate the minds of participants and to encourage them to agree, although this did not apply to the December 2000 summit in Nice; intended to finalize the details of the Treaty of Nice, it was widely seen as less than successful because of the disappointing nature of the treaty.

Because the European Council obviously has more power over decision making than any other EU institution, it has tended to take power away from those institutions. It can, in effect, set the agenda for the Commission, override decisions reached by the Council of Ministers, and largely ignore Parliament altogether. Any hopes that the Commission might have once had that it could develop an independent sphere of action and power has largely disappeared with the rise of the European Council. Certainty about the present and potential future role of the Council is clouded by its ambiguities, and opinion remains divided over whether it is an integrative or a disintegrative body (Johnston, 1994, pp. 41–8).

The European Parliament

The European Parliament (EP) has long been a junior member in the EU decision making system. By definition, a legislature is an institution in which proposals for new laws are introduced, discussed, amended and

Table 4.5   Seats in the European Parliament, 2002

	PPE-DE	PSE	ELDR	Greens	GUE	UEN	TDI	EDD	NI	Total	Reallocation of seats under Nice
Germany	53	35	–	5	6	–	–	–	–	99	99
France	21	22	–	9	11	6	5	6	7	87	72
Italy	34	16	8	2	6	9	12	–	–	87	72
UK	36	30	11	6	–	–	–	3	1	87	72
Spain	28	24	3	4	4	–	–	–	1	64	50
Netherlands	9	6	8	4	1	–	–	3	–	31	25
Belgium	6	5	5	7	–	–	2	–	–	25	22
Greece	9	9	–	–	7	–	–	–	–	25	22
Portugal	9	12	–	–	2	2	–	–	–	25	22
Sweden	7	6	4	2	3	–	–	–	–	22	18
Austria	7	7	–	2	–	–	–	–	5	21	17
Denmark	1	3	6	–	1	1	–	4	–	16	13
Finland	5	3	5	2	1	–	–	–	–	16	13
Ireland	5	1	1	2	–	6	–	–	–	15	12
Luxembourg	2	2	1	1	–	–	–	–	–	6	6
EU	232	181	52	46	42	24	19	16	14	626	535

Notes:
PPE-DE   European People's Party and European Democrats
PSE   Party of European Socialists
ELDR   European Liberal, Democratic and Reform Party
Greens   Greens/European Free Alliance
GUE   European United Left/Nordic Green Left
UEN   Europe of the Nations
TDI   Independents
EDD   Europe of Democracies and Diversities
NI   Non-attached

Seats for new member states will be as follows: Poland 50, Romania 33, Czech Republic 20, Hungary 20, Bulgaria 17, Slovakia 13, Lithuania 12, Latvia 8, Slovenia 7, Estonia 6, Cyprus 6, Malta 5.

voted upon. However, the EP cannot introduce laws or raise revenues (these are powers of the Commission), and it shares the powers of amendment and decision with the Council of Ministers. Parliament also has a credibility problem: it is the most democratic of EU institutions, because it the only one that is directly elected by voters in the member states, but few EU citizens know what it does, and they have not yet developed the same kinds of psychological ties to the EP as they have to their national legislatures.

However, Parliament has shrewdly used its powers to play a more active role in running the EU, and has been entrepreneurial in suggesting new laws and policies to the Commission. It has also used arguments about democratic accountability to force the other institutions to take it more seriously. Where it once mainly reacted to Commission proposals and Council votes, it has become much more aggressive in launching its own initiatives and making the other institutions pay more attention to its opinions. It has won more powers to amend laws and to check the activities of the other institutions, with the result that it now has equal standing with the Council of Ministers on deciding which proposals for new laws will be enacted and which will not.

\ The European Parliament is the only directly elected international legislature in the world. It has a single chamber, and the 626 Members of the European Parliament (MEPs) are elected by universal suffrage by all eligible voters in the EU for fixed, renewable five-year terms. The number of seats is divided up among the member states very roughly on the basis of population, so that Germany has 99 while Luxembourg has just six (Table 4.5). This formula means that bigger countries are under-represented and the smaller countries over-represented; thus, roughly speaking, Britain, France and Italy have one MEP per 670 000 citizens, while Denmark and Finland have one MEP per 330 000 citizens. Under the terms of Nice, the allocations will change with enlargement, all existing states except Germany and Luxembourg will lose seats, and the total number will be capped at 732.

Absurdly, Parliament's buildings are divided among three cities: while the administrative headquarters are in Luxembourg, and parliamentary committees meet in Brussels for about 2–3 weeks every month (except August), the Parliamentary chamber is situated in Strasbourg, and MEPs are expected to meet there in plenary sessions (meetings of the whole) for about 3–4 days each month except August. Since committees are where most of the real bargaining and revising takes place, and since 'additional' plenaries can be held in Brussels, few MEPs actually attend the Strasbourg plenaries, preferring to spend most of their time in Brussels. All attempts to move Parliament to Brussels have been blocked by the French government, which stubbornly insists that Strasbourg remain the site for plenary sessions. This not only undermines the credibility of the EP, but inflates its budget.

The EP is chaired by a president, who presides over debates during plenary sessions, decides which proposals go to which committees, and represents Parliament in relations with other institutions. The president must be an MEP, and is elected by other MEPs for 2 ½-year renewable terms (half the life of a Parliamentary term). The president would probably come out of the majority party group if there were one, but since no one party has ever had a majority, he/she is chosen as a result of inter-party bargaining. To help with the work of dealing with many different party groups in Parliament, the president works with the chairs of the different party groups in the Conference of Presidents, which draws up the agenda for plenary sessions and oversees the work of parliamentary committees.

Like most national legislatures, the EP has standing and ad hoc committees which meet in Brussels to consider legislation relevant to their area or to carry out parliamentary inquiries. The committees have their own hierarchy, which reflects the varying levels of Parliamentary influence over different policy areas: among the most powerful are those dealing with the environment and the budget. Seats on committees are distributed on the basis of a mixture of the balance of party groups, the seniority of MEPs, and national interests. For example, there are more Irish and Danish MEPs on the agriculture committee than on committees dealing with foreign and defence matters.

Elections to the European Parliament are held on a fixed five-year rotation, and all MEPs stand for re-election at the same time. Every member state uses multi-member districts and variations on the theme of proportional representation (PR), either treating their entire territory as a single electoral district or dividing it up into several large Euro-constituencies. Seats are then divided among parties according to their share of the vote. France, for example, has 87 seats, so if French party A wins 50 per cent of the vote, it will be given 50 per cent of the French seats (44), and if Party B wins 40 per cent of the vote, it will be given 40 per cent of the seats (35), and so on.

As noted in Chapter 2, PR has the advantage of reflecting more accurately the proportion of the vote given to different parties, but it also results in many small parties being elected to Parliament, spreading the distribution of seats so thinly that no one party has enough to form a majority. While this encourages legislators from different parties to work together and reach compromises, it also makes it more difficult to get anything done. Also, PR leads to voters being represented by a group of MEPs of different parties, and constituents may never get to know or develop ties with a particular MEP.

Box 4.3 Parties in the European Parliament

MEPs are not national representatives, so they do not sit in national blocks. Instead, they come together in cross-national ideological groups with roughly similar goals and values. European elections bring as many as 50–60 different parties to the EP, many of which consist of as few as 1–2 members; since there is little they can achieve alone, it is in their interests to build alliances with other parties. Some of these have been marriages of convenience, and while there is still much changeability in the EP, groups have built more consistency and focus with time (for details, see Hix and Lord, 1997).

Moving from left to right on the ideological spectrum, the major party groups in 2002 were as follows:

- *European United Left (GUE).* Mainly French, Greek and German leftists.
- *Party of European Socialists (PSE).* For a long time the biggest group in Parliament, with a few ex-communists on the left but dominated by more moderate social democrats. It has members from every EU country, with Germany, Britain, Spain and France sending the biggest contingents.
- *Liberal, Democrat and Reform Group (ELDR).* Contains members from every country except Germany, Greece, France, Austria and Portugal, but is difficult to pinpoint in ideological terms. Most of its members sit in or around the centre.
- *Greens/European Free Alliance.* Contains members from every country except Belgium, Ireland, Luxembourg, Austria and Britain, and has seen substantial growth in recent years, making it the fourth biggest party group in the EP.
- *European People's Party and European Democrats (EPP-DE).* Long the second largest group in Parliament, the EPP became the biggest after the 1999 elections. Right of centre, it contains MEPs from every EU member state, with the delegations from Germany, Britain, Italy and Spain being the largest.

Voters must be 18 years of age, and citizens of one of the EU member states. Some member states restricted voting to their own citizens, but changes introduced by Maastricht allowed any citizen of a member state living in another member state to vote or stand for election to the EP where they live. Turnout at European elections is lower than turnout at national elections in the member states, and the average has fallen steadily from more than 67 per cent in the 1979 elections to 49 per cent in 1999. Britain achieved the dubious distinction in 1999 of having the lowest national voter turnout ever: just 24 per cent. Among the explanations:

- European elections are still a relative novelty.
- Few European voters know what Parliament does.
- There is no change of government at stake.
- EP party groups do not co-ordinate election campaigns across all the member states.
- The media still tend to play down the significance of European elections.
- Eurosceptic voters may be disinclined to take part.
- European elections are still approached by most voters as a poll on their national governments rather than an opportunity to influence EU policies, about which many voters are still confused and uncertain.

Although it cannot introduce legislation, Parliament's powers to influence and amend EU law have grown. As well as the advisory and supervisory powers set out in the treaties, Parliament has several essentially negative powers: the Commission tries to anticipate the EP's position while drawing up a proposal, Parliament can delay or kill a proposal by sitting on it, and it also has the power to dismiss the Commission (for details, see Westlake, 1994, Chapter 3). Unfortunately, the concern of member states with preserving their powers over decision making in the Council of Ministers has created a complex legislative process:

- By the Treaty of Rome, Parliament was given a *consultation procedure* under which it was allowed to give a nonbinding opinion to the Council of Ministers before the latter adopted a new law in selected areas, such as aspects of transport policy, citizenship issues, the EC budget, and amendments to the treaties. The Council could then ask the Commission to amend the draft, but the Commission had no obligation to respond.
- The SEA introduced a *cooperation procedure* which gave Parliament the right to a second reading for certain laws being considered by the Council of Ministers, notably those relating to aspects of economic and monetary policy.
- Maastricht created a *codecision procedure* under which Parliament was given the right to a third reading on bills in selected areas, thereby sharing powers with the Council in these areas. Maastricht also extended Parliament's powers over foreign policy issues by obliging the Presidency of the European Council to consult with the EP on the development of a common foreign and security policy.
- Under the *assent procedure*, Parliament has equal power with the Council over decisions on allowing new members to join the EU, giving other countries associate status, and on the EU's international agreements; decisions on all these must win the support of a parliamentary majority.

The Treaty of Amsterdam significantly increased the powers of Parliament by abolishing the cooperation procedure on everything except certain issues related to economic and monetary union (over which the member states wanted to retain control), and increasing the number of areas to which the codecision procedure applied from 15 to 38; these now include public health, movement of workers, vocational training, the structural funds, transport policy, education, customs cooperation, consumer protection, and the environment.

In addition to these legislative powers, Parliament also has joint powers with the Council of Ministers over fixing the EU budget, so that the two institutions between them constitute the 'budgetary authority' of the EU – they meet biannually to adopt a draft and to discuss amendments. The EP can ask for changes to the budget, ask for new appropriations for areas not covered (but cannot make decisions on how to raise money), and ultimately – with a two-thirds majority – can reject the budget.

Finally, Parliament has several supervisory powers over other EU institutions, including the right to debate the annual programme of the Commission, to put written or oral questions to the Commission, and to approve the appointment of the College of Commissioners. The most potentially disruptive of Parliament's powers is its ability – with a two-thirds majority – to force the resignation of the entire College of Commissioners through a vote of censure. While this power has never been used, Parliament came close in January 1999 after charges of mismanagement and nepotism were directed at two members of the College. Instead of firing the entire College, the EP opted for an investigation into the charges. Anticipating a vote of censure, the Santer Commission resigned just before the findings of the investigation were published in March.

The European Court of Justice

The Court of Justice is the most underrated (and perhaps the most overworked) of the five major institutions of the EU. While the Commission and the Council of Ministers attract most of the media and public attention, and become embroiled in the biggest political controversies, the Court has quietly gone about its business of clarifying the meaning of European law. Its activities have been critical to the progress of European integration, and its role just as significant as that of the Commission or Parliament, yet few Europeans know what it does.

The job of the Court is to make sure that national and European laws – and international agreements being considered by the European Union – meet the terms and the spirit of the treaties, and that EU law is equally, fairly, and consistently applied throughout the member states. It does this by ruling on the 'constitutionality' of all EU law, giving opinions to national courts in cases where there are questions about the meaning of EU law, and making judgements in disputes involving EU institutions, member states, individuals, and corporations. In so doing, the Court gives the EU authority and makes sure that its decisions and policies are consistent and fit with the agreements inherent in the treaties.

EU law takes precedence over the national laws of member states where the two come into conflict, but only in areas of EU 'competence': where the EU is active and where the member states have given up powers to the EU. Hence the Court does not have powers over criminal law or family law, but has instead made most of its decisions on the kind of economic issues in which the EU has been most actively involved. It has had less to do with policy areas where the EU has been less active, such as education and health.

Based in the Palais de Justice, part of a cluster of EU institutions which make up the Centre Européen on a plateau above the city of Luxembourg, the Court is the supreme legal body of the EU, and the final court of appeal on all EU laws. It made its most basic contribution to the process of integration in 1963 and 1964 when it declared that the Treaty of Rome was not just a treaty, but was a constitutional instrument that imposed direct and common obligations on member states, and took precedence over national law.

The Court also established important additional precedents through decisions such as *Costa v ENEL 1964*, which confirmed the primacy of EU law, and the Cassis de Dijon case of 1979, which greatly simplified completion of the single market by establishing the principle of mutual recognition: a product made and sold legally in one member state cannot be barred from another (see Chapter 7). Other Court rulings have helped increase the powers of Parliament, strengthened individual rights, promoted the free movement of workers, reduced gender discrimination, and helped the Commission break down the barriers to competition.

The Court of Justice has 15 judges, each appointed for a six-year renewable term of office. In order to keep the work of the Court running smoothly, the terms are staggered, so about half the judges come up for renewal every three years. The judges are theoretically appointed by common agreement among the governments of the member states, so there is no national quota. However, because every member state has the right to make one nomination, all 15 are effectively national appointees. The persistence of the quota emphasizes once again the role of national interests in EU decision making.

Apart from being acceptable to all the other member states, judges must be independent, must be legally competent, and must avoid promoting the national interests of their home states. Some judges have come to the Court with experience as government ministers, some have held elective office, and others have had careers as lawyers or as academics; whatever they have done in their previous lives, they are not allowed to hold administrative or political office while they are on the Court. They can resign from the Court, but they can only be removed by the other judges (not by member states or other EU institutions), and then only by unanimous agreement that they are no longer doing their job adequately.

The judges elect one of their own to be president by majority vote for a three-year renewable term. The president presides over Court meetings, is responsible for distributing cases among the judges and deciding the dates for hearings, and has considerable influence over the political direction of the Court. Despite his critical role in furthering European integration, the president – Gil Carlos Rodríguez Iglesias of Spain in 2002 – never becomes a major public figure in the same mould as the president of the Commission.

To speed up its work, the Court is divided into chambers of between 3 and 6 judges, which make the final decisions on cases unless a member state or an institution asks for a hearing before the full Court. (Under changes introduced by Nice, hearings before the full Court will be replaced by hearings before a Grand Chamber of 13 judges.) To further ease the workload, the judges are assisted by nine advocates general, advisers who review each of the cases as they come in and deliver a preliminary opinion on what action should be taken and on which EU law applies. The judges are not required to agree with the opinion, or even to refer to it, but it gives them a point of reference from which to reach a decision. Although advocates general are again appointed in theory by common accord, one is appointed by each of the Big Five member states, and the other four are appointed by the smaller states. One of the advocates general is appointed First Advocate General on a one-year rotation.

The Court of Justice has become busier as the reach of the European Union has widened and deepened. Whereas in the 1960s it heard about 50 cases per year and made about 15–20 judgements, today it hears 370–400 cases per year, and makes about 200–300 judgements. As the volume of work grew during the 1970s and 1980s, it was taking the Court up to two years to reach a decision on more complex cases. To move matters along, agreement was reached in 1989 to create a subsidiary Court of First Instance, whose job is to be the first point of decision on less complicated cases. If cases are lost at this level, the parties involved may appeal to the Court of Justice. There are 15 judges on the Court – one from each member state – and it uses the same basic procedures as the Court of Justice.

The work of the Court falls under two main headings:

- *Direct Actions*. These are cases (all heard by the Court of First Instance) where an individual, company, member state, or EU institution brings proceedings against an EU institution or a member state. For example, a member state might have failed to meet its obligations under EU law, so a case can be brought by the Commission or by another member state. The Commission has often taken member states to Court charging that they have not met their single market obligations. Private companies can also bring actions if they think a member state is discriminating against their products.

  Direct actions can also be brought against the Commission or the Council to make sure that EU laws conform to the treaties, and to attempt to cancel those that do not. The defendant is almost always the Commission or the Council because proceedings are usually brought against an act they have adopted. Others can be brought against an EU institution that has failed to act in accordance with the terms of the treaties. The European Parliament brought one such action against the Council of Ministers in 1983 (Case 13/83), charging that the Council had failed to agree a Common Transport Policy, as required under the Treaty of Rome. The Court ruled that while there was an obligation on the Council, no timetable had been agreed, so it was up to the member states to decide how to proceed.

- *Preliminary rulings*. These make up the most important part of the Court's work, are now heard exclusively by the Court of Justice, and account for about 25–30 per cent of the cases it considers. If a matter of EU law arises in a national court case, the national court can ask for a ruling from the European Court on the interpretation or validity of that law. Members of EU institutions can also ask for preliminary rulings, but most are made on behalf of a national court, and are binding on the court in the case concerned.

Unlike all the other EU institutions, where English is becoming the working language, the Court works mainly in French, although a case can be heard in any of 12 languages (the 11 official languages and Irish), at the request of the plaintiff or defendant. Court proceedings usually begin with a written application, describing the dispute and the grounds on which the application is based. The President assigns the case to a chamber, and the defendant is given one month to lodge a statement of defence, the plaintiff a month to reply, and the defendant a further month to reply to the plaintiff. The case is then argued by the parties at a public hearing before a chamber of judges, or – with the most important cases – before the full Court. Once the hearing is over, the judges retire to deliberate, and – having reached a conclusion – return to Court to deliver their judgement.

Court decisions are supposed to be unanimous, but votes are usually taken by a simple majority. All decisions are secret, so it is never publicly known who – if anyone – dissented. The Court has no direct powers to enforce its judgements, so implementation is left mainly to national courts or the governments of the member states, with the Commission keeping a close watch. Maastricht gave the Court of Justice new powers by allowing it to impose fines, but the question of how the fines would be collected was left open, and the implications of this new power are still unclear.

Conclusions

The European Union has built a substantial family of administrative bodies over the last few decades. Among them, they are responsible for making general and detailed policy decisions, developing and adopting laws, overseeing the implementation of laws and policies by the member states, ensuring that those laws and policies meet the spirit and the letter of the treaties, and overseeing activities in a variety of areas, from environmental management to transport, consumer protection, drug regulation and police cooperation.

Although European leaders have never said as much, these institutions amount to a confederal government of Europe. They fit the standard definition of confederalism: a general system of government co-existing with local units of government, each with shared and independent powers, but with the balance in favour of the local units (in this case, the member states). Except for the European Parliament, EU citizens do not have a direct relationship with any of the EU institutions, instead relating to them through their national governments.

Despite concerns in some of the member states about the federalization of Europe, the institutions still lack many of the features of a conventional federal government. For example, there is no European army or air force, no elected European president, no European tax system, no European foreign and defence policy, and no single postal system. Furthermore, the focus of decision making still rests with the European Council and the Council of Ministers, both of which are intergovernmental rather than supranational. Finally, the European Union is still ultimately a voluntary arrangement, and lacks the powers to force its member states to implement European law and policy. The withdrawal of one of its members would not be regarded as secession.

Nonetheless, while debates rage about the finer points of the decisions reached by the EU institutions, the national governments of the member states have transferred significant powers to these institutions. Particularly since the passage of the Single European Act, the activities of the

Commission, the Council of Ministers, Parliament and the Court of Justice have had a more direct impact on the lives of Europeans, and government in Europe is no longer just about what happens in national capitals and regional cities, but also about what happens in Brussels, Luxembourg and Strasbourg.

The relationships among the five major institutions, and between them and the governments of the member states, is constantly changing as the balance of power is adjusted and fine-tuned. Out of a combination of internal convenience and external pressure is emerging a new layer of government that is winning more powers as the member states cautiously transfer sovereignty from the local and national levels to the regional level. In the two chapters that follow, we will see what this has meant for the member states and for the citizens of Europe.

Chapter 5

The EU and the Member States

The changing powers of the member states
Reducing regional differences
Improving environmental quality
An emerging European civil society
The changing character of the EU
Conclusions

> *Forget geography, forget culture. The thing called 'Europe' . . . is about politics and economics.*
>
> The Economist, 12 February 2000

The short history of the European Union has been dominated by efforts to promote economic cooperation among its member states, and to remove the barriers to the free movement of people, money, goods and services. However, experience has shown that the economies of Europe cannot be fully integrated unless the member states also address disparities in wealth and unemployment, varying standards and regulations, different approaches to administration, and conflicting policies on issues such as consumer safety, environmental protection, transport and working conditions. As the member states have attended to these matters, so the relationships among them have changed, and they have found themselves subject to complex integrative pressures.

These pressures have been both formal and informal. William Wallace defines formal integration as the deliberate actions taken by authoritative policy makers to create and adjust rules, to establish and work through common institutions, to regulate, encourage or inhibit social and economic flows, and to pursue common policies. He defines informal integration as patterns of interaction that develop without the intervention of deliberate government decisions, following the dynamic of markets, technology, communications and social exchange, or the influence of mass movements. Wallace also distinguishes between proactive and responsive integration, the former having deliberate and explicit political aims, while the latter reacts to economic and social change (Wallace, 1990, pp. 54–5).

If all EU member states had the same political, economic and social structures, the same levels of wealth and productivity, and the same sets of standards and regulations, integration would be relatively straightforward and would lean towards the formal and the proactive. However, the member states have different structures, policies, values and levels of wealth, and so approach integration from different perspectives. Concerned with avoiding a 'two-speed' or even a 'multispeed' Europe (where member states have moved at different speeds on building cooperation in different policy areas), national leaders have often had to react to the unforeseen effects of integration, and so have found themselves being driven by informal pressures. For example, while they have devoted much time and effort to harmonizing standards, laws and regulations, the complexities of integration have compelled them in some areas simply to agree to proceed through 'mutual recognition' (if something is good enough for one state, it is good enough for them all).

The list of the effects of integration on the EU member states is lengthy and complex. In order to illustrate these effects, this chapter looks first at some of the constitutional and legal issues raised by integration, and at what integration has meant for the relationship among the member states. To show how some of the changes have come, it then focuses on two policy areas that exemplify some of the pressures behind integration: regional policy and environmental policy. In the case of the former, member states have responded to the economic disparities in Europe by shifting resources and funds from wealthier to poorer regions. In the case of the latter, they have responded to the barriers posed to the single market by differences in environmental quality and standards, and have developed a substantial body of common policy and law.

The changing powers of the member states

Human society is in a constant state of flux, and western Europe is no exception. Political, economic and social relationships among Europeans have undergone continuous change, generated in large part by changes in communications and economic activity. While subsistence economies revolved around the village and the tribal community, trade led to the development of roads and towns, and the expansion of political authority in the Middle Ages. As European society shifted from an agricultural to an industrial base in the eighteenth and nineteenth centuries, a combination of technological change and improvements in communications once again redefined political and social relationships.

Western Europe emerged from the Second World War with its place in the world substantially altered. While it had held the balance of global political, military and economic power until 1939, it now found itself squeezed militarily between the two superpowers and saw the focus of economic power shifting to new centres, notably the United States and

Japan. As discussed in Chapter 3, the need to save Europe from itself combined with the need to build economic and military security in the postwar world to encourage western European elites to call for a new sense of regional community, and for cooperation rather than competition.

As late as the 1960s and 1970s, western European states still related to each other as sovereign states with strong and independent national identities. They had considerable freedom over the making of law, and travellers were reminded of the differences between countries when they crossed national borders and had to show their passports. Controls and limits were placed on the movement of people, money, goods and services, and citizens of one state who travelled to another felt very much that they were 'going abroad'. The nation-state was dominant, and was the focus of mass public loyalty and the source of primary political and administrative authority. Italians were clearly Italians, the Dutch were clearly Dutch, and Swedes were clearly Swedes – at least this is what Europeans were encouraged to think.

The situation today is quite different, and the relationship between the EU and its member states has undergone a metamorphosis. There has been a transfer of authority from the member states to the European Union, and an agreement to share or pool the exercise of power over selected policy areas. The member states have remained the essential building blocks in this process, but they have moved far beyond the simple cooperation normally associated with conventional international organizations, and have built a new layer of institutions underwritten by a common body of laws. Whether the member states have actually *surrendered* authority, however, and thereby created a superstate with its own sovereign powers, is a debatable and contentious point (see Box 1.2, page 10).

Developments since the Treaty of Rome have led to a transfer of authority over selected policy areas from the member states to the institutions of the EU, and national leaders now reach most decisions in these areas through negotiation with their counterparts in the other member states. Debates on the effects and the meaning of the treaties have combined with day-to-day discussions within the Commission and the Council of Ministers to encourage national leaders to work towards multinational compromises, and towards a European consensus. As this has happened, it has become increasingly difficult for leaders to define and pursue 'national interests', because these interests have been subsumed under European interests. At the same time, ordinary Europeans are reminded much less than before of their national differences, and the borders that once divided the member states have become so porous that they have almost disappeared.

Spillover of different kinds has led to the development of complex networks of cooperation at almost every level: trade, transport, communications, labour relations, policing, agriculture, research and development, financial services, the environment and so on. The result, argues Wallace (1996, p. 452), has been that governments have had to decide 'which issues they choose to define as key to the preservation of sovereignty, autonomy, or national idiosyncrasy, conscious of the political costs of defining too many issues in the symbolic terminology of high politics'.

The question of the transfer of powers – or at least of the most appropriate level at which to make decisions – has been at the heart of an ongoing debate about subsidiarity, the principle that decisions should be taken at the lowest level possible for effective action. It was first raised in the European context in 1975 when the European Commission – in its response to the Tindemans report (see Chapter 6) – argued that the Community should be given responsibility only for those matters that the member states were no longer capable of dealing with efficiently. There was little further discussion until the mid-1980s, when member states opposed to increasing the power of the Commission began quoting the principle. It was finally brought into the mainstream of discussions about the EU by Article 3b of Maastricht:

> In areas which do not fall within its exclusive competence, the Community shall take action, in accordance with the principle of subsidiarity, only if and in so far as the objectives of the proposed action cannot be sufficiently achieved by the Member States and can therefore, by reason of the scale or effects of the proposed action, be better achieved by the Community.

There are at least three problems with the concept of subsidiarity. First, it cannot be used to reduce EU powers in areas that have already been defined as being within its 'competence'. Second, there are no absolutes in the debate about whether or not an action can be better achieved by the member states acting alone or the EU acting as a whole. Third, subsidiarity is aimed at limiting the powers of the EU through a political–judicial discussion about 'competence' rather than through a clarification of the relative powers of European citizens, member states and EU institutions.

European integration has been accompanied by growth in the body of European law and a reduction in the ability of national governments independently to make policy and law, according to national interests and priorities. Simultaneously, national legislatures have become weaker and more marginalized in a process that has been described (pejoratively) as 'creeping federalism'. National legislatures once had almost complete authority to make laws as their members saw fit, within the limitations created by constitutions, public opinion, the powers of other government institutions and the international community. They now find themselves focusing increasingly on those policy areas in which the EU is not yet very active, and reacting in other areas to the requirements of EU law and the pressures of regional integration.

In order to understand the relative powers of the EU and the member states, it is important to remember two key points. First, the EU is a voluntary arrangement and there is nothing in theory to prevent a member state from leaving. If a region of a nation-state were to declare its independence without first reaching some kind of agreement with the central government, it would be regarded as secession, and would probably lead to war; this is what happened, for example, with the attempted secession by the Confederacy from the United States in 1861, Biafra from Nigeria in 1967 and Chechnya from Russia in 1994–95. In contrast, membership of the EU is reversible, and several anti-European movements within the member states have called for their country to leave the EU. While this is legally permissible, however, it is practically unlikely, because the economic ties among the member states would probably make it more costly to leave than to stay in.

Second, the old 'Community method' by which all the member states were obliged to proceed at the same pace and adopt and implement the same laws and policies, has been replaced in recent years by what has been variously known as Europe *à la carte*, a Europe of 'variable geometry', or 'enhanced cooperation'. This is Eurojargon for an arrangement that allows different member states to adopt different elements of European policy. For example, Britain was allowed to opt out of the Social Charter (see Chapter 6), only twelve member states made the switch to the single currency in 2002, not all member states have removed border controls as planned under the Schengen Agreement, and traditionally neutral states such as Ireland and Finland have decided not to participate in any common European defence policy. The Treaty of Amsterdam imposed conditions that limited the scope of the application of 'enhanced cooperation', while Nice required a minimum of eight member states to take part, removed the right of each member state to veto the plan, and provided for the possibility of enhanced cooperation in foreign policy.

Under the circumstances it is debatable just how responsibilities are now divided up between the EU and the member states (see Table 5.1). Almost all policy areas are now influenced by decisions taken both at the level of the EU and of the member states, but both parties have different levels of influence, driven by a combination of formal agreements and the effects of spillover. In the realm of 'high politics' (a concept rarely defined, but usually taken to mean the universal, the persistent, or the most pressing concerns of government), the member states now have much less freedom of movement than before on many economic matters, such as trade, financial services, company law and banking (see Chapter 7). The adoption of the euro has ensured that there are now few elements of economic policy that are not primarily driven by Europe rather than by the member states, at least within the euro zone.

In contrast, the EU still has some way to go before it can claim a common foreign policy, and the member states still have much individual freedom in their relationships outside Europe and in the way they define and express their defence interests (see Chapter 8). The EU is slowly becoming a more distinctive actor on the world stage, most notably on trade issues and development aid to poorer countries, but non-European governments must still approach each of the member states individually on issues such as security threats in the Middle East, nuclear testing, relations with former colonies and so on.

In the realm of 'low politics' (matters that are both more sectional and further down the agendas of most governments) there are still distinctions between issues that come under EU jurisdiction, are shared by the EU and the member states, and are the preserve of member states, but these distinctions have become less clear with time. There is little question that agricultural policy is now almost entirely determined at the European level, the loosening of internal border controls has been accompanied by a tightening of external controls that has seen more pan-European cooperation, and environmental quality standards are now set almost entirely by EU law. Decisions on social matters such as employment and residence are increasingly being made at the European level as personal mobility moves up the policy agenda. Member states still make most of their own decisions on internal transport, but are working together on the development of trans-European highways and railways, and on the administration of airline systems and air transport. They still have national policies on investment in poorer rural areas and urban regeneration, but these are increasingly influenced by European regional policy.

Not only has there been a transfer of powers from the member states to the EU, but the member states now have a very different legal relationship with each other. In the 1960s national frontiers were potent reminders of the independence of the states, and of the political, cultural, economic and social barriers that divided Europeans. Today they are much less obvious, and among the Schengen states they are almost invisible. The differences among member states today are determined less by lines on a map and questions of law and jurisdiction, and more by differences in language or culture. The number of policy areas over which the governments of member states have real independence has declined, and the legal ties that bind their states have tightened.

There have also been important psychological changes in the relationship among the member states. There are still many reminders of the

Table 5.1   *The division of policy responsibilities*

Areas in which the balance lies with the EU	Areas in which authority is shared	Areas in which the balance lies with the member states
agriculture	culture	broadcasting
competition	employment	citizenship
consumer protection	energy	criminal justice
cross-border banking	export promotion	defence
cross-border crime	foreign relations	education
customs	information networks	elections
environment	overseas aid	health care
EU transport	regional development	land use
networks	small and medium	local transport
fiscal policy	enterprises	policing
(euro zone)	social issues	postal services
fisheries	vocational training	tax policy
immigration		
trade		
working conditions		

differences among Europeans – most obviously language – but those differences have become more blurred as Europeans have become more mobile. Nationalism remains an issue, especially among minorities and those most actively opposed to integration, but increased individual mobility has allowed Europeans not just to visit other member states on holiday, but to live in – and even 'emigrate' to – those states. Europeans are slowly transferring their loyalty from individual states to a more broadly defined European identity, and are thinking of themselves less as Germans or Belgians or Swedes and more as Europeans.

Critics of integration have long argued that one of the greatest dangers posed by integration is the homogenization that comes as member states lose their individuality in the move towards Europe-wide standards and regulations. They argue that authority is shifting from national governments mandated by the people towards a European supergovernment that lacks such a mandate. However, while much still needs to be done to strengthen the ties between the EU and its citizens (see Chapter 6), it is unlikely that economic integration will lead to cultural integration. If anything it is more likely to lead to a reassertion of cultural differences as Europeans grow to understand and appreciate the variety of the regions in which they live (Box 5.1).

Indeed it is often argued that a Europe of the regions may come to rival or even replace a Europe of the states. In the interest of correcting economic imbalances, and prompted by growing demands for greater decentralization, European states began to regionalize their administrative systems in the 1960s, and as a result regions have emerged as important actors in politics and policy (Keating and Hooghe, 1996). Regions have come to see the EU as an important source of investment and of support for minority cultures, and in some cases this has given more confidence to nationalist movements (such as those in Scotland and Catalonia,) as they feel less dependent on the support of the state governments. The logical conclusion is that forces of this kind will lead to Europe integrating and decentralizing at the same time, with the member states as we know them today squeezed in the middle.

Reducing regional differences

The European Union contains many different shades of economic and social development. It is home to some of the wealthiest cities in the world, but the rich do not have to look far to find decaying industrial areas, underdeveloped rural areas, pockets of poverty and high unemployment, and regions heavily dependent on low-profit agriculture or fisheries. Not only are there economic and social disparities within most of its member states, but levels of economic and social development vary from one member state to another.

The standard measure of economic wealth is gross domestic product (GDP), which is the total value of all goods and services produced by a country. For member states as a whole, per capita GDP varies from a high in Luxembourg (220 per cent of the EU average) and Denmark (141 per cent) to a low in Greece and Portugal (both with about half the EU average). By region, rates in 1997 varied from a high in inner London (233 per cent of the EU average) and Hamburg (197 per cent) to a low in Ipeiros, Greece (43 per cent) and the Azores, Portugal (51 per cent). Of the EU's 211 regions, 50 fell below 75 per cent of the EU average (Eurostat, February 2000). The disparities are further highlighted by unemployment rates, which in mid-2001 ranged from as low as 2 per cent (the Netherlands) to as high as 13 per cent (Spain).

The wealthiest parts of the EU are in the north-central area, particularly in and around the 'golden triangle' between London, Dortmund, Paris and Milan. The poorest parts are on the southern, western and eastern margins: Greece, southern Italy, Spain, Portugal, Ireland, Northern Ireland, western Scotland and eastern Germany. The relative poverty of these

Box 5.1 The rise of regional identity

Ironically, as the nation-states of western Europe have been busy cooperating on the construction of the European Union, so national minorities within these states have become more visible, more vocal and more demanding of greater independence. In other words, as there has been macro level integration, so there has been a micro level disintegration. Most of the debate about the implications of integration has focused on the changing relationship among member states, and between member states and the EU, but we should also be looking at how it is affecting political relationships within the member states.

We have been conditioned to think of Europe as a region divided into three dozen nation-states, but it is more realistic in cultural terms to see it as consisting of more than 100 nationalities, including Dutch and English in the maritime north, Portuguese and Cantabrians on the Atlantic coast, Alsatians and Franconians in the northwest, Bavarians, Swiss and Styrians in the Alpine regions, Castilians, Andalusians and Lugurians in the west-central Mediterranean, Serbs and Croats in the Balkans, Czechs, Slovaks and Ruthenians in the east, Poles and Lithuanians in the northern plains, and Lapps, Finns and Karelians in the northern Baltic (see Fernández-Armesto, 1997, for more details).

In some cases – such as the Cornish in England, Galicians in Spain and Lombards in Italy – these nations have been fully integrated into the larger states of which they are part. In others, integration has never been complete, secessionist movements have arisen, and there have been calls for greater self-determination and even independence. This is particularly true in Britain, where the Scots and the Welsh have had regional assemblies since 1999, and a large segment of public opinion in Scotland is in favour of independence. There are similar demands for independence or devolution from Bretons and Corsicans in France, Basques in the Spanish–French borderland, Catalans in Spain and Walloons in Belgium.

The status of national minorities has traditionally been a domestic matter for individual national governments, but European integration has helped redefine the relationship between the parts and the whole. As the member states lose their distinctive political identity, so the cultural identity of minorities is strengthened and the pressure for disintegration grows. It is possible that greater self-determination will lessen the demand among nationalists for complete independence, and that we will simply see a reassertion of cultural differences within the member states. It is also possible, however, that self-determination will lead to independence for minorities within the European Union, and a redrawing of administrative lines along cultural lines.

regions has several different sources; some are depressed agricultural areas with little industry and high unemployment, some are declining industrial areas with outdated plants, some (notably islands) are geographically isolated from the prosperity and opportunity offered by bigger markets, and most suffer relatively low levels of education and health care and have underdeveloped infrastructure, especially roads and utilities.

Wealthier member states have long had their own domestic programmes of regional economic development, aimed at encouraging new investment in poorer areas, at offsetting the effects of rural decline, and at trying to revive old industrial areas and the centres of large cities. While these programmes may help offset economic disparities *within* member states, there is a limit to how much they can deal with such disparities *among* member states. And as long as those differences exist, attempts to build a level playing field for economic activity throughout the European single market will be undermined.

Little surprise, then, that the EU has given priority to development in the poorer parts of the member states. Armstrong (1993) suggests that there are several benefits to a joint EU approach: it ensures that spending is concentrated in the areas of greatest need, it ensures coordination of the spending of the different member states, and it encourages the member states to work together on one of the most critical barriers to integration. A common regional policy also means that the member states have a vested interest in the welfare of their EU partners, helps member states deal with some of the potentially damaging effects of integration (such as loss of jobs and greater economic competition), and introduces an important psychological element: citizens of poorer regions receiving EU development spending are made more aware of the benefits of EU membership, while citizens of the wealthier states that are net contributors have a vested interest in ensuring that such spending is effective.

It would be unrealistic to hope that there will ever be completely equal conditions throughout the EU – economic inequalities are a fact of life, and cultural differences will always ensure that different communities take different approaches to common problems. The EU has recognized this, and has agreed that its regional policy should be aimed at promoting 'cohesion', defined as 'reducing disparities between the various regions' in the interests of promoting 'economic and social progress'. In order to do this, the EU has increased efforts to help bring the poorer member states closer to the level of their wealthier partners. While free marketeers have always hoped that the single market would have a 'trickle-down' effect by directing more investment towards the poorer parts of Europe, the EU has taken a more proactive approach by setting up several structural funds, or baskets of money aimed at spending in the interests of cohesion. They include the following:

- The Guidance section of the European Agricultural Guidance and Guarantee Fund (EAGGF), which is part of the Common Agricultural Policy and is aimed at the reform of farm structures and rural areas.
- The European Social Fund (ESF), which is designed to promote employment and worker mobility, combat long-term unemployment and help workers adapt to technological change. Sixty billion euros are budgeted to be spent under the fund in 2000–06. Major recipients to date have been eastern Germany, Greece, Ireland, southern Italy, Portugal and Spain.
- The European Regional Development Fund (ERDF), which is spent mainly on underdeveloped areas (particularly those affected by the decline of traditional industries such as coal, steel and textiles) and inner cities.
- The Cohesion Fund, which targets member states with a per capita GDP of less than 90 per cent of the EU average (that is, Greece, Ireland, Portugal, and Spain). It compensates these states for the additional costs incurred by the tightening of environmental regulations, and provides financial assistance for transport projects.

European regional policy dates back to the 1950s when provision was made by the European Coal and Steel Community for grants to depressed areas for industrial conversion and retraining. Funds were later provided under the Common Agricultural Policy for the upgrading of farms and farming equipment, the improvements of farming methods, and the provision of benefits to farmers. In 1969, the Commission proposed a common regional policy, including the creation of a regional development fund, but found little support among the governments of the member states.

The climate changed after the first round of enlargement in the early 1970s, when a complex pattern of political and economic interests came together to make the idea of a regional policy more palatable. Most importantly, the 'rich man's club' of the 1950s (Italy excepted) had been joined by Britain and Ireland, two countries with regional problems. Their accession not only widened the economic disparities within the EEC, but also strengthened Italy's demands for a regional policy. The Commission-sponsored Thomson Report argued in 1973 that regional imbalances were acting as a barrier to one of the goals of the Treaty of Rome ('a continuous and balanced expansion' in economic activity), threatened to undermine plans for economic and monetary union, and could even pose a threat to the common market (Commission, 1973). Agreement was reached to create a European Regional Development Fund, which was launched in 1975.

One of the problems with EU regional policy is that the definition of a 'region' and of priority areas is left to the discretion of the member states, each of which has different kinds of administrative units. These range from the *Länder* of Austria and Germany, which have powers independent of those of their national governments, to the *departements* of France and the counties of Britain, which have few independent powers and different sets of policy responsibilities. Because of these differences, member states have always had different ideas about how to justify regional spending, which has tended to be based less on real 'need' than on the relative political and economic influence member states can bring to bear on regional policy negotiations.

It has been argued that politics enters the equation in at least two ways (Coombes and Rees, 1991, pp. 209–11). First, member states have been reluctant to give the EU powers over industrial development, employment and social security because this would reduce the control they have over domestic economic policy. Second, member states have been unwilling to transfer powers without the promise of net gains to themselves. They have always looked for some kind of compensation, and have placed national interests above European interests. The structural funds have routinely been seen as a way of compensating for the uneven distribution of agricultural spending – in that sense they have become a form of institutionalized bribery.

The distribution of funds was originally based on a quota system, under which Britain, Italy and Ireland were net beneficiaries of spending under the ERDF, and the other six Community members were net contributors. Reforms in the late 1970s led to the introduction of a small 'non-quota' element (five per cent of the total could be determined by the Commission on the basis of need) and suggestions that the wealthier countries should give up their quotas altogether since they could afford their own internal development costs. More reforms in 1984 led to a tighter definition of the parts of the Community most in need of help, pushed up the non-quota segment to 20 per cent, and replaced the fixed quotas with minimum and maximum limits. Hence Germany had a limit of 3 per cent, France 10 per cent, Britain 19 per cent, Spain 24 per cent and Italy 29 per cent.

The SEA brought new attention to regional policy, introducing a new Title V on Economic and Social Cohesion, and arguing the need to 'clarify and rationalize' the use of the structural funds. Further reforms, agreed in 1988, were based on Britain's insistence on reduced CAP spending and increased spending under the structural funds to 25 per cent of the EC budget by 1993 (in the event they reached nearly 32 per cent of spending). The 1988 reforms were also aimed at improving the efficiency of regional policy by setting up Community Support Frameworks under which the Commission, the member states and the regions would work more closely together on agreeing the means to achieve regional development planning goals.

More changes to regional policy came with Maastricht, under which a Committee of the Regions was created to give regional authorities a greater say in European policy, and the Cohesion Fund was created. The latter grew out of concern that economic and monetary union might worsen regional disparities, particularly given that poorer countries were going to be handicapped by the requirement (as a prelude to the single currency – see Chapter 7) for member states to limit their budget deficits to 3 per cent of GDP.

Regional policy is today one of the most important policy concerns of the European Union. In 1975 structural fund spending accounted for less than 5 per cent of the EEC budget, but in 2002 it amounted to nearly one third of all EU spending (nearly €31 billion) and more than half of all EU citizens now benefit from projects paid for by the structural funds. A total of more than €210 billion was budgeted to be spent in the period 2000–06. The EU's regional policy has the following goals:

- Help for Objective 1 regions, defined as regions 'where development is lagging', and where per capita GDP is less than 75 per cent of the EU average. These regions also include areas with low population density (such as northern Finland and Sweden) and remote areas, such as French overseas departments. They contain just over 22 per cent of the EU population, and received nearly €21 billion in funding in 2000, or two-thirds of all spending under the structural funds. The biggest recipients are Spain, Portugal, Greece, Italy and Germany (for investment in the former East Germany), while Denmark and the Benelux countries receive no funding. Objective 1 projects are funded mainly out of the ERDF and the Cohesion Fund.
- Help for Objective 2 areas, defined as those suffering 'structural difficulties'; these include high unemployment and job losses, industrial decline, poverty, or crime, or areas heavily dependent on fishing or agriculture. They include the older industrial regions of Germany, Britain, France, and Spain, and received nearly €4 billion in 2000, mainly out of the ERDF.
- The promotion of Objective 3 programmes aimed at developing human resources. The whole of the EU is eligible, and these programmes are aimed at reducing unemployment, improving access to the labour market, and promoting equal opportunities for men and women.
- There are also a host of specialized programmes with specific objectives, some of which overlap with social policy. These include EQUAL (working against discrimination and inequality in access to work), INTERREG (promoting cooperation among border regions), LEADER+ (helping local groups to promote rural development), and URBAN (regenerating urban areas in crisis).

There is little doubt that regional policy is helping to close the gap between richer and poorer member states, and that the balance of economic power among them is changing. There is still a substantial gap in per capita GDP between the richest (Luxembourg) and the poorest (Greece), but most member states have seen their per capita GDP move towards the EU average – all but Greece, Spain and Portugal are within ten percentage points of that average. One of the biggest success stories has been Ireland, whose per capita GDP grew from 61 per cent of the EU average in 1986 to 105 per cent in 1999 (Eurostat, 2001). Changes of this kind have created new opportunities in the poorer parts of the EU that discourage the outflow of labour, generate new sources of wealth and develop new markets for the rest of Europe.

Improving environmental quality

In its early years, European integration was driven by quantity. Economic efficiency, expansion and profit were at the heart of plans for the common market, the customs union and the Common Agricultural Policy. The Treaty of Rome mentioned the need for improvements in the standard of living, but little attention was paid to the *quality* of economic development in the early years of the Community. The few pieces of environmental law that were agreed in the 1960s were prompted less by concern about environmental quality than by worries over the extent to which different national environmental standards were distorting competition and complicating progress on the common market.

By the early 1970s thinking had begun to change. There was a public reaction against what was seen as uncaring affluence, generated by a combination of improved scientific understanding, worsening air and water quality, several headline-making environmental disasters, and new affluence among the Western middle classes (see McCormick, 1995, Chapter 3 for more details). Just as the governments of the member states could not avoid being caught up in the growing demand for a response, so the improvement of environmental quality had to be pushed up the agenda of European integration. The first step was taken with the publication in 1973 of the first Environmental Action Programme. More programmes followed, emphasising the importance of environmental protection as an essential part of 'harmonious and balanced' economic growth. In 1986 the Single European Act gave the environment legal status as an EC policy concern, while subsequent institutional changes gave the European Parliament a greater role in environmental policy making, and introduced qualified majority voting on most issues related to environmental law and policy.

A multinational response to environmental problems makes sense at several levels. First, many such problems – such as air pollution – are not limited by national frontiers, and are best addressed by several governments working together. Second, individual countries working alone may not want to take action for fear of saddling themselves with costs that would undermine their economic competitiveness – they have fewer such fears when several countries are working towards the same goals at the same time. As states become more dependent on trade and foreign investment, and the barriers to trade come down, so parochial worries about loss of comparative economic advantage become less important. Third, the economic benefits of removing barriers to free trade (including different environmental standards) help offset some of the costs of taking action. Finally, rich countries can help poor countries address environmental problems through funding assistance and a sharing of technical knowledge, and over the long term will see fewer factories closing and being moved to countries with lower environmental standards.

Community policy was initially based on taking preventive action and working to make sure that divergent national policies did not act as barriers to free trade, a problem noted by the Court of Justice in 1980 when it argued that competition could be 'appreciably distorted' in the absence of common environmental regulations. States with weak pollution laws, for example, had less of a financial or regulatory burden than those with stricter ones, and might attract corporations that wanted to build new factories with a minimum of built-in environmental safeguards.

By the early 1980s the Community had switched to a focus on environmental management as the basis of economic and social development. Environmental factors were consciously considered in other policy areas, notably agriculture, industry, energy and transport, and were no longer taking second place to the goal of building a single market. The logic of this idea was taken a step further in the 1990s when the EU adopted the principle of sustainable development, agreeing that no economic development should take place without careful consideration of its potential impact on the environment.

There has been strong public support for EU activities on the environment. Eurobarometer polls have found that most Europeans rank environmental protection above finance, defence or employment as an issue of EU concern, that most feel pollution is an 'urgent and immediate problem', and that most agree that environmental protection is a policy area better addressed jointly by EU states than by member states alone. Underpinning these opinions has been the growth in support for green political parties. In the 1989 EP elections, 30 green members were returned from seven member states; in 1999, the number rose to 37, with green MEPs coming from every member state except Denmark, Greece, Portugal and Spain. By the late

---

Box 5.2 Environmental policy

The goals of EU environmental policy are outlined in the treaties and the six Environmental Action Programmes, but they are broad and generalized. They include the improvement of the quality of the environment, the protection of human health, the prudent use of natural resources, increased environmental efficiency (meaning improvements in the efficiency with which resources are used so that consumption is reduced), and the promotion of measures at the international level to deal with regional or global environmental problems.

Whatever the goals say, EU policy has so far focused on problems that are better dealt with jointly than nationally, such as the control of chemicals in the environment, the reduction of air and water pollution, the management of wastes, fisheries conservation, and the control of pesticides. The EU has also been active in areas not normally defined as 'environmental' at the national level, including noise pollution and the control of genetically modified organisms. It has been less involved in the protection of ecosystems, natural habitats and wildlife, the management of natural resources such as forests and soil, and the promotion of energy conservation and alternative sources of energy. Among the underlying principles of EU policy are the following:

- Sustainable development: renewable natural resources such as air, water, and forests should be used in such a way as to ensure their continued availability for future generations.
- Integration: environmental protection must be a component of all EU policies that might have an environmental impact. This principle applies in only three other EU policy areas: consumer protection, culture and human health.
- Prevention: the EU emphasizes action to prevent the emergence of environmental problems, rather than just responding to problems as they arise.
- Subsidiarity: the EU restricts itself to issues that are best dealt with jointly, leaving the rest to be addressed by the member states.
- Derogation: member states unable to bear the economic burden of environmental protection are given longer deadlines, lower targets or financial assistance.

1990s greens were also sitting in the national legislatures of most EU member states, and were members of coalition governments in Belgium, Finland, Germany and Italy.

A substantial body of environmental law has been agreed by the EU, covering everything from environmental impact assessment to controls on lead in fuel, sulphur dioxide and suspended particulates, lead in air, pollutants from industrial plants and large combustion plants, nitrogen dioxide, and vehicle exhaust emissions. Six action programmes have been published (the sixth covers the period 2000–2010), a plethora of green and white papers has generated discussion on a wide range of issues, and the goals of EU policy have been given new definition since 1995 by the work of the European Environment Agency (EEA), a data-gathering agency that provides information to the other EU institutions. The EEA has been involved in the publication since 1995 of a series of triennial regional assessments of the state of the European environment.

Environmental management is now one of the most important areas of policy activity for the EU, ranking only behind foreign policy cooperation, economic issues and agriculture in terms of the level of political activity involved. Environmental policy in western Europe is now made more at the EU level than at the level of the member states. In the cases of countries such as Portugal and Spain, which had done very little on the environment before joining the Community, their national laws are now almost entirely driven by the requirements of EU law.

Although there has been progress on environmental policy making, the record on implementation is not so good, and experience in this field says something more broadly about the difficulties that policy making faces at the level of the EU. The record on the environment is explained by several factors:

- a lack of financial and technical resources.
- organizational problems within EU institutions.
- the fact that most EU law has focused on developing policies rather than the means of implementing and enforcing them.
- the failure of all the parties involved in making policy to recognize the difficulty of meeting the goals they have set.
- the limited ability of the Commission to ensure that member states implement EU law.
- the long-term lack of a legal basis to EU environmental policy.

It is also explained by differences between the regulatory programmes and systems of the member states. Where Greece and Spain have had a poor record on implementation because their local government is relatively poorly organized and under-equipped, Germany and the Netherlands have a bad record because they have sophisticated systems of domestic environmental law, and lack the motivation to adapt fully their own measures to EU requirements. Meanwhile Denmark has a good record on implementation, helped by a high degree of public and official environmental awareness, effective monitoring systems and the involvement of the Danish parliament in negotiating new environmental law (Collins and Earnshaw, 1993).

It has been argued that the Commission – through the EEA – should be given the power to carry out inspections and ensure compliance by member states, but this would raise worries about loss of sovereignty and the 'interference' of the Commission in the domestic affairs of member states. Besides, effective inspections would need huge resources: even the United States Environmental Protection Agency – with a staff of 18 000 and a multibillion dollar budget – is hard-pressed to keep up with everything it is expected to do. For the foreseeable future the Commission will have to continue to rely – as it has done for many years – on whistle-blowing by environmental interest groups, and on cases being brought before national courts and the European Court of Justice.

Regional cooperation among countries promises a quicker and more effective resolution of transnational environmental problems than any other approach, at least among countries with similar political systems and similar levels of economic development. Bilateral or multilateral approaches have worked only when limited to selected issues of mutual concern, such as the management of shared rivers, lakes or oceans. Broader global approaches are handicapped by the increased likelihood of disagreement and deadlock and by the lack of competent authorities with the power to promote and enforce regulation. Given the extent to which the causes and effects of environmental problems do not respect national frontiers, the EU model may provide the only effective response to such problems, mainly because it encourages different states to cooperate rather than to adopt potentially conflicting objectives.

An emerging European civil society

The examples of regional and environmental policy show how EU member states have moved from individual to joint action in key policy areas. They have done this through a combination of strengthening pan-EU institutions and policy making, harmonizing policy goals and methods, and developing common goals and standards. However, while the member states have been the major actors in this process, it would be wrong to think that the impetus for integration was founded solely on the compromises worked out among the leaders of the member states. European integration has also led to the emergence of a European civil society, or a framework outside the formal structures of government in which people interact and associate with each other, and try to influence the work of the EU.

While national leaders have negotiated with their national interests to the fore, non-governmental organizations – or interest groups – have cut across national frontiers to promote the shared sectional interests of groups of people in multiple member states. In addition to the EU bodies that represent these interests, such as the Economic and Social Committee and the Committee of the Regions (see Box 4.2, page 97), the last 20–25 years have seen the growth of hundreds of non-governmental organizations that represent the views of a large number of groups of people with a stake in EU policy and law. Many are an outgrowth of pre-existing national groups, others have been set up specifically to respond to European issues, and many have opened offices in Brussels in order to be close to the Commission and the Council of Ministers. Studies in the 1990s indicated that there were nearly 700 groups working to influence decisions taken at the European level, about two-thirds of which had existed since 1980 or earlier. Just over 60 per cent were business groups, 21 per cent dealt with public interest issues and 16 per cent were professional organizations (Aspinwall and Greenwood, 1998).

The growth in interest group activity at the European level has paralleled the growth in the power and influence of the EU institutions, or the 'Europeanization' of policy areas that were once the reserve of national governments (Mazey and Richardson, 1996, p. 200). The groups have not always simply followed the evolution of the EU, going wherever new opportunities for influence have presented themselves, but have often been actively involved in pushing the EU in new directions. Business leaders, for example, were champions of the single market, arguing that competition among European corporations was a handicap to their ability to take on the Americans and the Japanese. At the same time, the European Commission has encouraged interest group activity; the Commission uses groups as a source of expert knowledge and to test the viability of new laws, and it also uses them to monitor the compliance records of member states; most groups are only too happy to blow the whistle on their home governments if they are not implementing EU law.

Historically, business and labour groups have been the most active, mainly because the process of integration was for so long driven by economic issues (Greenwood, 1997, p. 101). As the EU won new powers over competition policy, mergers, and the movement of workers, so business and labour groups made greater efforts to influence the Commission and the Council of Ministers. Not only are individual corporations represented either directly or through lobbying firms in Brussels, but several cross-sectoral federations have been created to represent the interests of a broader membership. These include the Union of Industrial and Employers' Confederations of Europe (UNICE, which represents 32 national business federations from 22 countries), the European Roundtable of Industrialists (which brings together the chief executives of major European corporations such as Fiat, Philips, ICI and Siemens), and the EU Committee of the American Chamber of Commerce (which represents American firms active in Europe).

Labour is also represented in Brussels, notably through groups such as the European Trade Union Confederation (ETUC), whose membership consists of a combination of European-level industry federations and national labour federations, such as Britain's TUC or Germany's DGB. Professional interests are represented by groups such as the Council of European Professional and Managerial Staff (EUROCADRES), and by associations representing everything from architects to dentists, journalists, opticians and vets. Several Brussels-based interest groups include member organizations from outside the EU, a reflection of how much the EU has come to matter to business and labour throughout Europe.

Groups representing public interests, such as consumer issues and the environment, have also become more active as the EU has become more involved in matters about which they care. Until the 1970s, environmental groups focused their attentions on national governments, because they had different priorities, and because most environmental policy in western Europe was still made at the national level. As the Community became more active in the environment in the mid-1980s, it became a more profitable target for interest group pressure. The new emphasis given to EU-level activities was reflected in the opening of offices in Brussels in the second half of the 1980s by such groups as Friends of the Earth, Greenpeace and the World Wide Fund for Nature, while many other groups employed full-time lobbyists. As environmental groups became more active, so did groups representing the industrial perspective on environmental issues, such as the European Chemical Industry Council, Eurelectric and the European Crop Protection Association.

Increased access to EU policy makers led in turn to a more systematic approach among environmental groups to Euro-lobbying, and a clear trend towards approaching domestic environmental problems as EU-wide problems. The complexity of those problems encouraged domestic groups to work more closely together and to form transnational coalitions, the best known of which is the European Environmental Bureau (EEB). Founded in 1974 with the encouragement of the Commission, the EEB is an umbrella body for national interest groups in the EU, and acts as a conduit for the representation of those groups in the EU institutions, particularly the Commission. The Bureau now claims to represent more than 130 national environmental groups with a combined membership of 23 million.

The methods that Euro-groups use are similar to those used by groups at any level: promoting public awareness in support of their cause, building membership numbers in order to increase their influence and credibility, representing the views of their members, forming networks with other interest groups, providing information to the EU institutions, meeting with EU law makers in an attempt to influence the content of law, and monitoring the implementation of EU law at the national level.

Aspinwall and Greenwood (1998) argue that the representation of interests at the European level has become more diversified and specialized, and that Euro-groups are becoming protagonists – they now try to influence policy rather than simply to monitor events, using increasingly sophisticated means to attract allegiance. Something of a symbiotic relationship has developed between the Commission and interest groups, with the former actively supporting the work of many groups and giving them access to its advisory committee meetings, and the latter doing what they can to influence the content and development of policy and legislative proposals as they work their way through the Commission.

The activities of interest groups have helped offset the problem of the democratic deficit (see Chapter 6) by offering Europeans channels outside the formal structure of EU institutions through which they can influence EU policy. They have also helped focus the attention of the members of interest groups on how the EU influences the policies that affect their lives, have helped draw them more actively into the process by which the EU makes its decisions, and have encouraged them to bypass their national governments and to focus their attention on European responses to shared and common problems.

The changing character of the EU

Changes in the relationship among the member states of the EU have complicated discussions about the character and effects of international relations, because the EU only partly fits with conventional ideas about the ways in which societies organize and govern themselves. As noted in Chapter 1, the EU is not a 'state' because it lacks many of the typical features of a state, including a strong and separate legal identity, political unity and sovereignty, powers of coercion, and significant financial independence. And while it has some of the features of an international organization, it has developed unprecedented levels of power and influence over its members. This has led some scholars to argue that the EU is not really an institution, but is better understood as an ideal, a process, a regime, or even a network that has involved not so much a transfer of powers as a pooling of sovereignty (Keohane and Hoffmann, 1991, p. 10).

Jean Monnet commented in 1975 that he saw no point in trying to imagine what political form the United States of Europe would take, and that 'the words about which people argue – federation or confederation – are inadequate and imprecise' (Monnet, 1978, p. 523). He might have been able to ignore the question thirty years ago, but if we are to understand the relationship between the EU and the member states today, and to develop a clearer sense of where European integration is headed, then we need to try and reach some kind of agreement on the nature and character of the EU. The process of integration has gone beyond the point of no return, and

European political union is now spoken of less in terms of 'if' than in terms of 'when' and 'how'. So we must think more actively about the form that 'union' might take, and what it will mean for the member states.

There have been at least three different sets of forces at work in European integration, pulling the member states in several directions:

- *Intergovernmental versus supranational.* One of the most basic questions about European integration concerns the extent to which the decisions reached by the governments of the member states are driven by the protection of national interests rather than the promotion of the interests of the EU as a whole (see Box 5.3). Are the governments of the member states trying to preserve their sovereignty by relating to each other as equals, or are they transferring sovereignty to a new supranational authority? In some respects the European Union remains a pact among independent states, but in other respects the balance of power has shifted to European institutions.

- *Independence versus dependence.* Western Europe consists of a network of legally independent states, but they are bound more closely together than some of their citizens care to admit, by history, culture and shared political and economic interests. The pressures of integration have strengthened their mutual ties, and the member states have moved along a path from independence to mutual dependence. This is particularly true in the sphere of economic policy, with the growth in investment, trade flows, and movement of workers, and the creation of pan-European industries and corporations.

- *Competition versus cooperation.* Until the Second World War the history of Europe was one of competition, conflict and changing alliances and balances of power. The balance of power continues to change today, but it does so inclusively rather than exclusively, and instead of being driven by conflict, it is driven by the need to cooperate. The competing goals of separate states have been replaced by the promotion of mutual interests, and the EU member states work increasingly closely together in a variety of policy areas.

Where the member states now sit on these three different continua is debatable, but there is little doubt that integration has moved them more towards supranationalism, dependence and cooperation. What has this meant for the member states?

First, the EU has more authority over its members than any international organization that has ever existed. It is not yet a government in itself, but is instead a melange of national governments and supranational institutions, whose links have created a confederation with federalizing tendencies. While supranationalism may describe the political process of the EU, it has been argued that the EU has always rested ultimately on a set of

Box 5.3 Intergovernmental conferences

The extent to which decision making in the EU is still intergovernmental rather than supranational is reflected in the way that many of the big decisions of recent years have come out of intergovernmental conferences (IGCs), convened outside the formal framework of the EU's institutions to allow negotiations among the governments of the member states. Even as the powers of those institutions have grown, so the IGC has become an increasingly common event on the EU calendar; there have been seven IGCs since 1950, but five of them have been held since 1985.

The first IGC was opened in May 1950, was chaired by Jean Monnet, and led to the creation of the ECSC and the signing of the Treaty of Paris. The second was opened at Messina in April 1955, and led to the creation of the EEC and Euratom and the signing of the Treaties of Rome. Perhaps because national leaders were focused on building the three Communities and the common market, because of the intergovernmental nature of Community decision making in the early years, and because of the fallout from the energy crises of the 1970s, it was to be another 27 years before another IGC was convened. Concerned about the lack of progress on integration and Europe's declining economic performance in relation to the United States and Japan, the third IGC was launched in September 1985, and by December had outlined the framework of what was eventually to become the Single European Act.

Two more IGCs met during 1991 to look at political union and monetary union, their outcome being the Treaty on European Union. A sixth IGC was launched in 1996 with institutional reform and preparations for eastward enlargement at the top of its agenda, the product of which was the Treaty of Amsterdam. Institutional reform was also on the agenda of the IGC that led to the 2000 Treaty of Nice, widely regarded as a disappointment. Hence agreement has been reached for an eighth IGC in 2004 to 'promote new forms of European governance'. The leaders of the member states will have to take a more imaginative and long-term view of European integration if this conference is not to be another disappointment.

The IGCs since 1985 have been negotiated by a combination of national government ministers and permanent representatives, and have continued to symbolize the extent to which decision making on the big initiatives of the EU still rests with the member states. While there is nothing in the founding treaties about IGCs, they have become a normal part of the calendar of European integration, and most have resulted in important decisions on the development of the EU.

intergovernmental bargains (Keohane and Hoffmann, 1991, p. 10). Opinion is divided about the extent to which it has moved beyond such bargains; realists argue that the member states are still the key actors, and that integration is driven by their decisions, while neofunctionalists argue that integration has taken on a life and momentum of its own.

Second, the EU has its own budget and bureaucracy, a large body of treaties and laws to which the member states are subject, and a court that can adjudicate disputes between member states, or between member states and the EU. But its institutions lack the power to raise taxes, have neither the power nor the personnel directly to enforce the law, and must rely almost entirely on the voluntary compliance of the member states. The most powerful of the EU institutions – the European Council, the Council of Ministers, and COREPER – are part of the structure of the European Union, but they are the meeting place for governments and do not have a life of their own above and beyond the member states. The most supranational of the institutions – the Commission, the Court of Justice, and the European Parliament – still have relatively fewer powers.

Finally, the extent to which the EU has responsibility over making public policy varies from one area to another. On agricultural and economic issues, the balance is in favour of the EU. On social and environmental issues, the trend is in favour of the EU. On matters relating to education, policing and criminal law, the balance of power still rests with the member states. Recent amendments to the treaties have resulted in the accelerated transfer (or pooling) of policy responsibility, and the introduction of the euro has meant a final, irrevocable step in the integration of fiscal policy, which will in turn provide irresistible pressure to complete the integration of other internal policy issues.

Most people like to use labels to help them understand their environment, but there are no such easy labels for the EU, or at least none on which most people can agree. Europeans are well aware of the dangers of the divisions they are leaving behind, but are much less clear about the features of the unity towards which they are moving. As Benjamin Franklin argued after trying to find a model upon which the new American republic could be based, history consists only of beacon lights 'which give warning of the course to be shunned, without pointing out that which ought to be pursued' (Franklin, in *Federalist*, 1787, no. 37).

'Boundaries are difficult to draw in a world of complex interdependence', argue Keohane and Hoffmann (1991, p. 12), 'because relationships cross boundaries and coalitional patterns vary from issue to issue, it is never possible to classify all actors neatly into mutually exclusive categories'. The EU has many intergovernmental characteristics, but over time they have given way to a growing emphasis on supranationalism. The member states are increasingly answering to a higher authority, with many of the features of confederalism and some of the features of federalism. Both these concepts take many different forms, and for Eurosceptics to talk about federalism as some kind of hell towards which Europe should not travel is too simple. The European brand of federalism already has several unique features, and once it achieves some kind of regularity, those features will look very different from most of the characteristics we usually associate with federalism.

Conclusions

While debates rage about the powers and nature of the European Union, with both support for and resistance to the expansion of EU powers and responsibilities, there is no question that its member states have lost powers to the EU and now have less political and economic independence than they did even twenty years ago. Integration has changed the relationship among EU member states at several levels: there has been a reduction in social differences, a harmonization of standards, laws and regulations, and removal of the physical and fiscal barriers that have differentiated the member states from one another. The EU record on regional and environmental policy provides an indication of the kinds of forces that are at work in this process.

Regional development has meant an attempt to help the poorer regions catch up with their richer neighbours, with the utopian goal of encouraging an equitable distribution of the benefits of regional integration. The EU has tended to equate development with growth, but whether quantity and quality go hand in hand has long been debatable. It is also debatable whether the free market can ever entirely eliminate inequalities of opportunity, which is why regional policy has been based on a kind of grand welfare system that sees the redistribution of wealth as a means of encouraging equal opportunity. It remains to be seen how long it will take to bring the different parts of the EU to the same economic level, assuming this is even possible.

In the case of the environment, there is little question that international cooperation is desirable and even inevitable. Problems such as air and water pollution ignore national boundaries, and there are repeated examples from around the world of one state being a producer and down-wind or down-stream states being recipients. As the global economy expands, the barriers posed to trade by different environmental standards add a new dimension. There will always be strong ideological disagreement about the extent to which the state should manage natural resources and regulate industry, but there is a strong internal logic to international cooperation on environmental management. There is an emerging consensus that the EU has been a positive force in environmental protection, and that European environmental problems are better dealt with at the EU level than at the national or local level.

There is also an emerging consensus that cooperation in a variety of other areas makes better sense than independent action, which can lead to unnecessary competition and duplication of effort. It is still too early to talk about a federal relationship among the member states, and between them and the EU institutions, but the trend is undoubtedly in that direction. Several levels of government are being created, all with independent powers. How far European cooperation will go depends on how we choose to define subsidiarity, but while this is moving higher up the agenda of EU negotiations, the definition of which issues are best dealt with at the level of the member state and which at the level of Europe remains fluid.

Chapter 6

The EU and its Citizens

The democratic deficit
The people's Europe
Social policy
Improving accountability
Conclusions

> *One reason for the Commission's congenital inability to make itself understood is that it is staffed by officials whose careers depend on communicating not with voters but with other officials. So desiccated jargon drives out plain language, even before it passes through the translation mill, which grinds everything into a sort of bureaucratic Esperanto.*
>
> *The Economist*, 28 July 2001

Under changes made by Maastricht, the goal of European integration is to create 'an ever closer union among the peoples of Europe, in which decisions are taken as closely as possible to the citizen'. Even the most ardent supporters of integration will admit, however, that it has been less a popular movement for change than a process begun and sustained by elites. The average European is given few opportunities to influence the work of the EU institutions, a problem that has become so serious as to earn its own label: the democratic deficit.

'What about us?' the European public might reasonably ask. 'Does anyone in Brussels or our national capitals care what we think?' It sometimes seems as though the work of the EU goes on despite public opinion, which is often confused, sometimes doubtful, and in some cases actively hostile. The channels through which Europeans can express themselves directly on the EU are few and insubstantial. Their interests are directly represented in the European Parliament, but it is one of the weaker European institutions. Voters have an indirect influence on the Council of Ministers, but ministers are accountable to national governments rather than to the electorate. The Commission and the Court of Justice promote the interests of 'Europe', but citizens have little influence on senior appointments to either body.

To make matters worse, most Europeans are perplexed by the European Union. Journalists often misrepresent the way it works, the Commission has done a bad job of explaining what it does, and most academic writing makes it sound dull and legalistic. The result is often confusion and apathy, as reflected in the poor turnout at European elections (although whether that turnout has been a cause or an effect of the elitist nature of European leadership is debatable). The European Council decided in 1984 to begin promoting 'a people's Europe' in an attempt to make Europe more 'real' to its people, and changes have been made to the treaties in order to promote 'transparency' (making the deliberations of the EU institutions more open to scrutiny), but the argument that popular enthusiasm can somehow be generated by public policy is fundamentally flawed.

The evolution of the European Union has changed the way that Europeans relate to each other, in many different ways. Some of the changes have come as a direct result of policy decisions, such as the removal of border controls and the expansion of opportunities through the single market. Other changes have been an indirect consequence, growing out of the realization among Europeans that they are involved in a joint exercise with implications for them all. Under the circumstances it is essential that more attention be paid to public opinion, that the Commission does a better job of explaining what is happening, that national leaders pay more attention to public opinion, and that citizens make more of an effort to understand what is being done in their name and play a more active role in letting their leaders know how they feel.

This chapter asks what integration has meant for Europeans, and for the nature of democracy in the European Union. It begins with an assessment of the problems arising from the democratic deficit, examining the relationship between public opinion and the decisions taken by national leaders. It then looks at some of the specific policy areas in which the EU has focused on the needs and priorities of Europeans: the People's Europe, the concept of European citizenship, cultural issues and social policy. It ends with a discussion about the kinds of changes that need to be made to bring Europe closer to its citizens.

The democratic deficit

The EU has a survey research programme known as Eurobarometer, which regularly measures public opinion on a wide variety of issues relating to European integration, ranging from views on the entire process to those on specific policies. Recent surveys have found a steady fall in levels of enthusiasm for the EU: support grew from 50 per cent in 1980 to a peak of 71 per cent in 1990, but fell in Germany after reunification, and then more widely throughout the EU in the wake of the controversy over Maastricht. By December 2000 only 50 per cent of Europeans thought that membership

Figure 6.1 *Public opinion on EU membership*

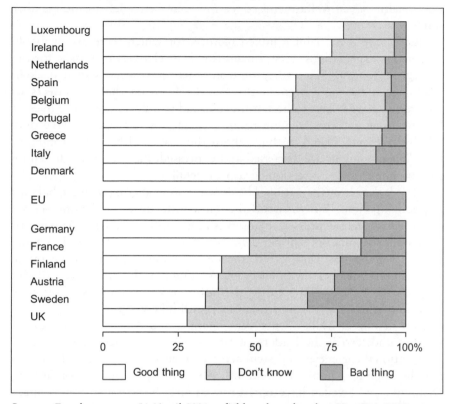

Source: Eurobarometer, 54 (April 2001 – fieldwork undertaken Nov/Dec 2000).

was a 'good thing', although only about 14 per cent thought it a 'bad thing' (Eurobarometer 54, April 2001). There has also been a decline in the number of people who think that their country has benefited from membership, from 58 per cent in 1990 to 47 per cent in 2000. Among those most enthusiastic about membership are poorer member states such as Ireland, Spain, Portugal and Greece, while the doubters include several newer and wealthier member states such as Finland, Austria, Sweden, and Britain (Figure 6.1).

When interviewees were asked which issues they felt were priorities for the EU, there was clear majority support (70–90 per cent) for EU action on maintaining peace and security in Europe, addressing unemployment and poverty, fighting organized crime and drug trafficking, protecting the environment and consumers, and guaranteeing the rights of the individual. The 2000 poll also revealed that a majority (60–70 per cent) felt that issues such as foreign policy, humanitarian aid, scientific research, the fight against poverty, regional development, and environmental protection were better addressed by joint EU action, while cultural policy, media regulation, health, social welfare and education were better left to the member states.

Figures like these paint a mixed picture, for which there are probably four major explanations. First, integration is a relatively new issue for the average European. The Treaty of Rome may have been signed back in 1957, but it has only been in the last 10–15 years that the effects of integration have begun to be felt more broadly and to impact the lives of Europeans more directly. One result is that most Europeans have only relatively recently begun to think about the costs and benefits of integration. When opinions are discussed and expressed, they are often driven by narrow interests and a tenuous grasp of detail.

Second, the actions of national leaders are often at odds with the balance of public opinion. Take the issue of enlargement, for example: only 44 per cent of EU citizens expressed themselves in favour in 2000 while 35 per cent were opposed, and only 26 per cent saw it as a priority for the EU while 62 per cent did not. Undeterred, the Commission continues to negotiate with aspirant members, with every expectation that the first wave will join by 2004–05. Policy on the euro provides another example: support may have strengthened in recent years, but is still lukewarm, with only 55 per cent in favour in 2000, 37 per cent against, and 8 per cent undecided. Equally undeterred, the leaders of twelve member states have given up their national currencies and switched to the euro, in every case failing to put the issue to a public referendum. Meanwhile, the leaders of Britain, Denmark, and Sweden have opted not to join the single currency, again without reference to national public opinion (but only 23 per cent of citizens in the three countries were in favour in 2000).

The Danish people's rejection of Maastricht in June 1992 should have been a salutary lesson; it came as a shock not just to the Danish government, but to all European governments. It was much the same with the Irish people's rejection of the Treaty of Nice in June 2001. The results raised questions about just how many other initiatives might have been rejected – or passed by small majorities – if put to national referendums in member states. For example, it is almost certain that the euro would have been rejected by German voters if put to the test in the mid-1990s, because polls found that more than 60 per cent were opposed to the idea, and unwilling to surrender the deutschemark. Given the essential role of Germany in the single currency, such a result would have dealt a crippling blow to the programme.

Third, national leaders, European institutions, the media and academic experts have done a poor job of explaining the structure and the costs and benefits of integration. To be fair, the process is enormously complex and changes constantly, and the implications of the steps taken have not always

Box 6.1 The knowledge deficit

No matter how much the European Commission tries to make Europe seem more real to its citizens, and no matter how often the European Council talks about the importance of transparency, one critical problem remains: the average European knows little about how the EU works. This has been made clear by the results of recent Eurobarometer surveys. In late 2000, for example, respondents were asked how much they felt they knew about the EU, its policies and its institutions, and to give themselves a score out of 10, with 10 meaning they knew a great deal and 1 meaning they knew little. While 8 per cent admitted they knew nothing at all, no less than 68 per cent of respondents gave themselves (failing) scores of 5 or less, and the average for the sample worked out at 4.51. Just 7 per cent gave themselves scores of 8 or higher.

Those who felt they knew the most included managers, university graduates, people who used the media regularly, and those in the age range of 25–54. Those with the lowest levels of knowledge included manual workers, retirees and people with a high school education or lower. In descending order, Austrians, Danes, Germans, Luxembourgers and the Dutch felt they knew the most, while Greeks, the Irish, Spaniards, Portuguese and Britons knew the least.

On more specific matters, more than 55 per cent of Europeans admitted they were not very well or not at all informed about the euro (although this was an improvement on the results of a 1997 survey, for which the figure was 70 per cent). Ironically, while so many plead ignorance, this did not prevent 55 per cent of respondents saying they were in favour of the single currency and 37 per cent saying they were opposed. Policy issues are not the only problem: nearly one in three Europeans have never even *heard* of the Court of Justice or the Council of Ministers, and about one in five have never heard of the European Commission or the European Central Bank. Meanwhile, reflecting popular prejudices, one in three Europeans think that the biggest item on the EU budget is the cost for officials, meetings and buildings (they actually account for just 5 per cent of EU spending, while agriculture accounts for 45 per cent). (All results from Eurobarometer 54, April 2001.)

These are not encouraging figures. It will be difficult for Europeans to develop a sense of belonging to the European Union if they continue to know so little about it, and as long as they know so little, they will not make their views known about its work. This will perpetuate the democratic deficit, and decisions will continue to be taken by a policy elite of national leaders and Eurocrats. Ironically, the lack of public knowledge persists despite attempts by the Commission to make its work more accessible through printed and audiovisual media and the internet. Unfortunately, the latter are heavy on rhetoric and light on substance.

been fully understood, even by policymakers – every new venture has produced unanticipated effects (the single market programme being a prime example) and the switch to the euro is a leap into the unknown. Nonetheless there is no constitution to which citizens can refer for clarification, the treaties confuse more than they clarify, the growing volume of information on the EU tends to focus on the minutiae of the treaties and European law, media coverage in the more Eurosceptical member states tends to mislead by emphasizing the negative at the expense of the positive, and the average European remains confused (Box 6.1).

Finally, and perhaps most fundamentally, there is the problem of the democratic deficit. This is commonly defined in terms of the unequal powers of the European Parliament relative to the other EU institutions. For example, Williams describes it (1991, p. 162) as 'the gap between the powers transferred to the Community level and the control of the elected Parliament over them', and Archer (2000, p. 58) as 'the shift in decision-making powers from the national to the EU level, without accompanying strengthening of parliamentary control of executive bodies'. Such definitions imply that the democratic deficit could be narrowed by giving Parliament greater powers, but the problem goes far beyond Parliament, and a better definition of the democratic deficit would be the gap between the powers of European institutions and the ability of European citizens to influence the work and decisions of those institutions.

The deficit takes several forms:

- The leaders of the member states, meeting as the European Council, reach decisions on important policy matters without always referring to their electorates. Less than half the 15 member states asked their citizens whether they even wanted to join the European Community or the European Union. The Maastricht treaty was negotiated largely behind closed doors, poorly explained to the European public and – despite the important changes it made to the structure and goals of the EU – was put to the test of a referendum in only three member states, one of which said no. Amsterdam and Nice were equally poorly explained, and equally poorly tested.
- Despite its powers over proposing and developing new European laws, the Commission is subject to little direct or even indirect public accountability. Appointments to the College must be approved by Parliament, but otherwise they are made without reference to the people. The president of the Commission is appointed as a result of a strange and informal little power dance among the leaders of the member states, represents the views of the EU in several international forums without a mandate from the people, and has tenure that is subject to the whims of national leaders rather than the opinions of

European citizens. Furthermore, there is little opportunity for citizens to take part in or contribute to the deliberations of the Commission, and only limited (albeit improving) opportunity for the European Parliament to hold it accountable for its initiatives and decisions.

- Meetings of the Council of Ministers and the permanent representatives in Brussels are closed, despite the fact that many of the most important decisions on the content of new laws and policies, and on their acceptance or rejection, are taken there. Ministers and representatives take the kinds of decisions that – at the national level – are taken by members of elected assemblies, who are held accountable for their actions at elections and in the court of public opinion.

- The European Parliament – the only democratically elected institution in the EU system – lacks several of the powers of a true legislature: it cannot raise revenues, introduce new laws or take the final vote on whether or not a proposal will become law, and it has only a limited ability to hold the Commission accountable for its decisions. It has worked hard to win new powers for itself, but most of the important decisions on EU law and policy are taken elsewhere.

- The Court of Justice is the institution that best champions the cause of individual Europeans, being the final court of appeal for anyone who feels they have been hurt by European law, by its non-appliance, or by contradictions between European and national law. However, Europeans have no say in appointments to the Court, nor will they until the kind of legislative confirmation that is used for courts in many member states is adopted by the EU, and nominees to the Court of Justice and the Court of First Instance are subject to investigation and confirmation by the European Parliament.

- The formal rights of Europeans relative to the EU institutions are modest: they have the right to vote in European elections, to petition Parliament or the European ombudsman (see below) if they feel their rights or interests have been violated, to gain access to the documents of EU institutions (within certain limits), and to diplomatic representation outside the EU by any member state, provided their own country has no local representation.

Worst of all, the deficit stands as a damaging psychological barrier between Europeans and the EU, preventing the development of the ties that must exist between leaders and citizens in order for a system of government to work. Under the circumstances it is hardly surprising that Europeans have so little attachment to the EU institutions. It is also hardly surprising that the anti-European media are able to generate so much public distrust and resentment towards these institutions, which can often appear distant and mysterious. This is most obvious in the case of the

Commission. Although it is a small and productive institution, and can only propose and oversee the implementation of new laws, it is often portrayed as powerful, overpaid, unaccountable and secretive. It is helped little by the fact that most of its staff occupy a series of anonymous buildings spread around the suburbs of Brussels, and that access to those buildings by ordinary Europeans is heavily restricted.

The European Commission regularly publishes policy statements known as white papers. One such paper published in 2001 addressed the issue of governance, and made some candid admissions:

> Europeans . . . increasingly distrust institutions and politics or are simply not interested in them. The problem . . . is particularly acute at the level of the European Union. Many people are losing confidence in a poorly understood and complex system to deliver the policies that they want. The Union is often seen as remote and at the same time too intrusive . . . [The EU] must start adapting its institutions and establishing more coherence in its policies so that it is easier to see what it does and what it stands for. A more coherent Union will be stronger at home and a better leader in the world . . . Reform must be started now.

The paper also defended the work of EU institutions, noting that there is a perceived inability of the EU to act effectively where a clear case exists (such as on unemployment, food safety scares, and security concerns on EU borders), that even where the EU acts effectively it does not get fair credit for its actions, that people do not see that improvements in their quality of life often come from European rather than national initiatives, that ' "Brussels" is too easily blamed by Member States for difficult decisions that they themselves have agreed or even requested', and that many Europeans 'do not know the difference between the [EU institutions, and do not] understand who takes the decisions that affect them and do not feel the Institutions act as an effective channel for their views and concerns' (European Commission, 2001, pp. 3, 7). Unfortunately, rather than making specific suggestions for change, the paper made the usual mistake of talking in generalities and employing bureaucratic notions of better involvement, more openness, greater flexibility, 'partnership arrangements', 'a more systematic dialogue', and 'policy coherence'.

While there is little question that fundamental reforms are needed to make the EU institutions more efficient, accountable and democratic, moves in this direction usually come up against the resistance of national governments: to make these institutions more democratic would be to reduce the control that national governments currently exert over them. The Treaty of Amsterdam emphasized the need to make the work of the EU comprehensible and 'transparent', but while it established the right of

Europeans to greater access to European documents, this is not the same as affording them a greater opportunity to influence the content of those documents.

Franklin (1996, p. 197) describes the lack of proper democratic accountability in the EU as 'a crisis of legitimacy'. It is unlikely that the essential psychological link between EU institutions and EU citizens will be made until such time as the European Parliament becomes a true legislature, national political parties form pan-European federations and run for election as such, and the outcome of European elections has a direct effect on the content and performance of the Commission and the Council of Ministers. But this will not happen as long as the governments of the member states feel the need to use the Council of Ministers as the guarantor of national interests.

The people's Europe

It took nearly thirty years for political leaders to begin asking their citizens what they thought about the process of integration. A report was drawn up in 1975 at the request of the European Council by Leo Tindemans, prime minister of Belgium, investigating the steps that might be taken to achieve a more integrated Europe that was 'closer' to its citizens. But nothing more was done until June 1984, when the EEC heads of government, meeting in Fontainebleau and spending most of their time agreeing reforms to the Community budget, briefly turned their attention to the idea of a 'people's Europe'. Pietro Adonnino, a former Italian MEP, was hired to chair a committee to put forward suggestions on how the EEC could be brought more closely in touch with its citizens.

The committee endorsed arrangements that had already been made for a European passport and a European flag. All national passports have since been replaced by a standardized burgundy-coloured 'European' passport bearing the words 'European Community' in the appropriate national language, and the name and coat of arms of the holder's home state. This ensures that Europeans are given equal treatment by the customs and immigration authorities of other countries, and also helps give them a sense of belonging to the EU. But these passports do not make their holders European citizens – see below.

Meanwhile the European Commission decided to declare the anniversary of the Schuman Declaration (9 May) 'Europe Day', to adopt as the official anthem of Europe Schiller's 'Ode to Joy' sung to the final movement of Beethoven's 9th Symphony, and, most importantly, to adopt as its own the flag that had been used by the Council of Europe since 1955 – a circle of twelve gold stars on a blue background. The European flag, which was designed by Paul Levy, director of information for the Council of Europe, was chosen in preference to several other designs (Bainbridge and Teasdale, 1995, pp. 188–9) and can now be seen flying on public buildings and hotels throughout the EU. (It was popularly thought that the 12 stars represented the 12 member states but the number was coincidental and the design has not been changed as membership of the EU has grown.)

The Single European Act incorporated more of the Adonnino recommendations, the most important of which was the easing of restrictions on the free movement of people. It had been understood at the time of the Treaty of Rome that an open labour market would be an essential part of a single market, but while all Community citizens were given the right to 'move and reside freely' within all the member states, this was subject to 'limitations justified on grounds of public policy, public security or public health'. Since integration in the early days was economically driven, priority was given to making it easier for people who were economically active to move from one state to another. Limits were placed on migration, initially because governments wanted to protect themselves against the possibility of a shortage of skilled workers, and then because of the lack of opportunities in the target states (Barnes and Barnes, 1995, p. 108).

Changes under the SEA have allowed EU citizens to move and live anywhere in the EU, provided they are covered by health insurance and have enough income to avoid being a 'burden' on the welfare system of the country to which they move. The governments of the member states have been anxious to control the effects of economic pressures that encourage workers to leave the poorer parts of the EU for the richer parts, thereby increasing welfare spending and making unemployment worse in those richer parts, and to control the movement of non-EU citizens, particularly Turks, North Africans, and refugees from the Balkans. At the heart of the free movement debate has been a concern about differences in welfare laws, which is why agreement of common social policies has been given high priority (see below), and why there has been a focus on meeting the needs of younger and older people.

The removal of the barriers to free movement has helped make Europeans more mobile in the last 10–15 years, and the number of non-nationals living in member states has risen. There were five million immigrants in 1950, ten million in 1970, and there are probably close to fifteen million today, although the removal of the barriers to movement has made it difficult to be sure. The flow of immigration was initially from the south to the north, and most of those moving were workers from Mediterranean states looking for higher-paying jobs, and then sending for their families to join them. Immigration flows today are more complex because there has been an increase in the movement of professionals and managers. Where Europeans once moved involuntarily for economic reasons, more are now moving voluntarily and for a variety of different reasons – they may be looking for a different environment in which to live, retiring to warmer parts of the EU, or looking for a new start in a new country.

Tourism has played an important role in encouraging movement. Where most Europeans could once afford to travel only within their own countries, the advent of cheap, mass tourism since the late 1960s has led to a marked increase in the numbers of people taking holidays in other member states. Day-trips, weekend breaks, 1–2 week stays, time shares, the purchase of holiday homes and extended visits for those who can afford the time have all combined to greatly increase the ease and comfort with which Europeans travel around the continent. Language differences still pose a psychological barrier, but the easing of restrictions on movement have combined with the introduction of the euro to make other member states seem less 'foreign' to Europeans.

All these demographic shifts have been helped by another element of the Adonnino report that was formalized by the SEA: arrangements for the mutual recognition of professional qualifications. Although the basic training for most health workers (doctors, nurses, dentists and so on) was standardized relatively early and they were quickly given the right to work in any member state, progress in other areas was slower. The initial strategy of the Commission was to work on each profession in turn, to reach agreement on the requirements, and then propose a new law. But this was time-consuming, which is why it took 17 years to harmonize the requirements for architects and 16 years for pharmacists. Progress was made in 1988 with the general systems directive, under which the member states agreed (effective 1991) to trust the adequacy of qualifications that require at least three years of professional training in other member states. The list of mutually recognized professions is growing, and now includes accountants, librarians, architects, engineers and – since 1998 – lawyers. The Commission has meanwhile published a comparative guide to national qualifications for more than 200 occupations, helping employers work out equivalencies across the member states.

An important element in worker mobility is education and youth training, in which the EU has become more involved since Maastricht by encouraging educational exchanges and addressing the critical issue of language training. The inability to speak foreign languages poses a barrier to the free movement of workers, and stands as a reminder of the differences among Europeans, so the EU has set up an array of programmes to help promote cooperation. These include ERASMUS (which encourages student and faculty exchanges among colleges and universities, and makes it easier for students to transfer credits), LINGUA (training in second and third languages), TEMPUS (which links universities in the

United States and western and eastern Europe by promoting joint research projects), COMETT (which encourages universities and industry to work together on training projects), and PETRA (which is aimed at modernizing vocational training).

The EU now has 11 official languages: Danish, Dutch, English, Finnish, French, German, Greek, Italian, Portuguese, Spanish and Swedish. Almost all EU business is conducted in English and French, although Germany is keen to make sure that German is not forgotten; one of the consequences of the eastward expansion of the EU will be an increase in the number of Europeans who speak German, which will alter the linguistic balance of power in the EU. Almost all secondary school pupils in the EU learn at least one foreign language, although some have a better record than others at becoming bilingual or multilingual. The Dutch and the Scandinavians do best, while the British do worst, having been spoiled by the growth of English as the international language of commerce and entertainment, and by the large number of continental Europeans who speak English: more than 90 per cent of secondary school pupils in Germany, Spain, the Netherlands and Denmark learn it as a second language. Meanwhile less than one in three Italian and German pupils is learning French (Eurostat, 2001).

The issue of language cuts to the core of national pride, and particularly concerns the French, who have gone to great lengths to stop the spread of 'franglais' – the use of English words in French, for example 'CD-Rom' (officially *cédérom*) and 'le fast food' (officially *prêt-à-manger*). In an attempt to prevent any one language dominating the others it has been suggested that all Europeans should learn Esperanto, an artificial international language developed in 1887, or even that Latin should be revived for the purpose. Despite the number of EU employees who work as translators, the publication of EU documents in all 11 official languages, and the attempts by France to stave off the threats posed by Anglo-American culture, it is inevitable that English – with the help of American, Japanese and German business – will continue its steady progress towards becoming the common language of Europe.

While tourism, the removal of technical barriers to movement and the promotion of language training all contribute to free movement, the treaties say nothing directly about the social and psychological barriers posed by differences in the routine of daily existence. Americans can readily travel from one state to another in search of jobs or to improve the quality of their lives, and can expect their daily routine to change little; they will find the same shops, the same banking system, the same money, the same programmes on television and so on. By contrast, Europeans not only face different languages, but must also learn new social and functional rules, including everything from new customs to new sets of road signs and

Box 6.2 Cultural policy

A common history and culture are important elements in the identity of a nation-state. Where they exist, the state tends to enjoy a high degree of legitimacy (public acceptance), which breeds stability and longevity. Where they do not exist, and where there are significant social divisions, there is more likely to be instability and a weaker sense of common identity. France is an example of a state with a high level of legitimacy, while the former Yugoslavia is an example of one without.

When Europeans think of their history and culture they are more likely to think of what divides them than of what unites them. The EU has tried to address this problem by promoting the idea of a common European culture (even though such promotion may be anathema to some – how can culture be legislated or 'promoted'?). Despite the fact that Eurobarometer polls show a majority in favour of cultural policy being left to the member states, Maastricht introduced a commitment that the EU should 'contribute to the flowering of the culture of the Member States' with a view to improving knowledge about the culture and history of Europe, conserving the European cultural heritage, and supporting and supplementing non-commercial cultural exchanges and 'artistic and literary creation'.

What this has so far meant in practice has been spending money on restoring architectural heritage, contributing to training schemes in conservation and restoration, helping to meet the costs of translating works by European authors (particularly into less widely spoken languages) and supporting cultural events. For example, the EU has funded a Youth Orchestra and a Baroque Orchestra to bring young musicians together, declared European 'Cities of Culture' (including Athens, Berlin, Bruges, and Lisbon) and established a European Cultural Month in cities in non-member states (such as Basel, Cracow, and St. Petersburg).

While the sentiments behind such projects are laudable, it is difficult to see how cultural exchanges and the development of a European cultural identity can really work unless they are driven by Europeans themselves. It is relatively easy to argue that Shakespeare, Michelangelo, Voltaire, Goethe, Charlemagne and Mozart are all part of the heritage of Europe, but it is more difficult to promote the idea of a modern pan-European popular culture. Even the most mobile of art forms – film and rock music – come up against the barrier of national preferences, and almost nothing that is not produced in English enjoys commercial success outside its home market.

traffic regulations, different processes involved in renting or buying a home, taking out car insurance or opening bank accounts, and a new selection of products on the shelves of local supermarkets. It is psychologically difficult enough for an American family to uproot itself and move hundreds of miles away, but while an Italian moving to Denmark or a Swede moving to Ireland can eventually learn how things are done locally, it involves a demanding process of acculturation. This is not the kind of problem that can be addressed by new EU laws.

The most notable of the changes introduced by Maastricht was the promotion of European citizenship, although this is not what it seems. 'Citizenship' in democracies is usually taken to mean full and responsible membership of a state, and has been described by some social scientists as including the right to equality before the law, the right to own property, the right to freedom of speech and the right to a minimum standard of economic and social welfare. However these are all rights that legal non-citizens of democracies also enjoy. What makes a citizen different from a non-citizen in practical terms is that a citizen can vote and run for elective office in his or her home state, can serve on a jury in that state, is eligible to serve in the armed forces of that state, cannot be forcibly removed from that state to another, owes allegiance to and has the right to receive protection from the state when outside its borders, is recognized as a subject of that state by other governments, and must usually obtain the permission of other governments to travel through or live in their territory.

According to Maastricht 'every person holding the nationality of a Member State shall be a citizen of the Union', but Europeans still have some way to go before they can truly be considered citizens of Europe. A step in that direction was taken with the agreement that citizens of a member state finding themselves in need in a non-European country where their home state has no diplomatic representation can receive protection from the diplomatic and consular authorities of any EU state that has a local office. Another step was taken with the easing of restrictions on voting and running for elective office, but citizens of one state living in another can only vote and stand for municipal and European Parliament elections, not for national elections.

One useful change introduced by Maastricht was the creation of a European ombudsman. If a citizen or a legal resident of any member state feels that any of the EU institutions (other than the Court of Justice and the Court of First Instance) is guilty of 'maladministration', and can make a compelling case, the European Parliament is required to ask the ombudsman to review the complaint, and if appropriate to carry out an investigation. Appointed for a five-year term that runs concurrently with the term of Parliament, the ombudsman is expected to be both impartial and independent of any government. Since the first ombudsman was appointed in 1995, the Commission has been the target of most of the complaints, which have included charges that it has failed to carry out its responsibilities as guardian of the treaties, that it lacks sufficient transparency and that it has abused its power. The number of complaints has grown over the years, which is probably less a sign that things are getting worse than a sign that more people are becoming aware of the work of the ombudsman.

Some of the Adonnino committee's recommendations have yet to be implemented, including the creation of a European lottery, the introduction of common postage stamps and the establishment of a uniform electoral procedure for European elections. The latter idea was first outlined in the Treaty of Paris, repeated in the Treaty of Rome and raised again on several subsequent occasions, but little has been achieved in practical terms. Even the definition of the word 'uniform' in this context is debatable, and while a decision was taken at the 1974 Paris summit that the goal would be met if European elections were secret, direct, based on universal suffrage and held on the same day, this has not been the end of the story.

The most obvious structural problems with European elections are (1) they are not held on the same day in all member states, (2) countries such as Germany use different electoral systems for national and European elections, and (3) the member states use different forms of proportional representation (PR). For example, while Italy, Ireland and Belgium use regional lists and divide their countries into multiple constituencies, Denmark, France, Portugal and Spain use national lists and treat their countries as one constituency. (Britain long used the same first-past-the-post system as for national and local elections, but adopted PR for EP elections in 1999 in order to fall into line with the rest of the EU.)

Dabbling with the structure of European elections does not really address the most fundamental weakness in the People's Europe programme: the absence of an electoral system that truly holds the institutions of the EU accountable to the wishes of the electorate. Elections to the European Parliament are now held on a fixed five-year rotation, but the stakes are low: the membership of neither the Commission nor the Council of Ministers changes as a result, the competing parties are still essentially national parties running on national platforms and using European elections to test their popularity at the national level, and while there are party groups within Parliament, there are still no truly pan-European political parties.

The changes that have come out of the Adonnino committee's report have had an important effect on the psychological relationship between Europeans and the EU institutions, and have helped build a European identity that has made the EU more real to Europeans. Icons are an important element of 'belonging', and the European flag has played a vital role in giving the EU a personality that goes beyond the work of its bureaucrats. Leaders have spoken of the need to promote the 'transparency' of European institutions, agreement of a uniform voting procedure is now an official EU goal and the Amsterdam treaty provides for greater access to the documents of EU institutions.

However, these are all superficial changes, and do not address the real issue. The idea that the citizens of the member states also belong to a larger communal entity must take root and grow in their minds if it is to be at all effective. They need to understand the implications of integration, they must see and directly experience the benefits of integration, and they must feel that they can have a real impact on the decisions of the European institutions through meaningful participation before the EU can have real significance in their lives.

Social policy

Effective economic integration demands a reduction in the social differences among Europeans. Without equal pay, equal working conditions, comparable standards on workers' rights and women's rights, a removal of gaps in the quality of working and living conditions, and an expansion of the skilled work force, the foundations of a workable single market will be undermined. Poorer European states will suffer the effects of competition from their wealthier partners in the EU, while those with less progressive employment laws will lose jobs to those that offer better working conditions. These concerns – combined with the long history of welfare promotion in individual western European states – have helped make social policy an important part of the EU agenda.

Social policy deals mainly with questions related to employment, or the rights, opportunities and benefits provided to potential, actual or former workers. One EU scholar argues that the EU has engaged not so much in 'social policy' as in 'social regulation', because it has focused on activities that balance quality of life issues with economic efficiency, and has not tried to replace the welfare programmes of the member states (Majone, 1993, p. 168). These activities have proved controversial, because social policy treads on sensitive ideological and cultural toes. Conservatives and liberals will never agree on the best way of building a level social playing field, and programmes that may be seen as progressive by one member state may be seen as a threat to economic progress or even cultural identity by another. Generally speaking, national labour unions have been in favour of EU social policy, as have the Commission and Parliament (dominated as it was until the 1999 elections by social democratic parties), while business interests and conservative political parties have been opposed, arguing that social policy could make European companies less competitive in the global market (Geyer and Springer, 1998, p. 208).

Relatively little attention was paid to social issues in the early days of the EEC: concern about the competitive implications of different levels of social security payments and labour costs encouraged the EEC Six to avoid addressing social questions head-on during the negotiations leading up to the Treaty of Rome. The treaty ended up being based on the naive assumption that the benefits of the single market would improve life for all European workers. This proved true to the extent that it helped increase wages, but market forces failed to deal with gender and age discrimination, wage disparities, different levels of unemployment, and safety and health needs in the workplace.

The Treaty of Rome made it the Community's business to deal with such matters as the free movement of workers, equal pay for equal work, working conditions, and social security for migrant workers. However, social issues were pushed down the EEC agenda while governments concentrated on completing the single market and resolving battles over agricultural policy, and the movement of workers was heavily restricted. Restrictions began to be eased so that labour shortages in the larger northern economies could be overcome. This led to an influx of immigrants from southern Europe, mostly from non-EC states such as Turkey, Yugoslavia, Greece, Portugal and Spain. By the early 1990s there were an estimated four million foreign workers in the 12 EU member states, about half of whom came from other EU states.

Enlargement in 1973 brought an increase in the disparities in levels of economic wealth within the Community, so social policy was pushed up the political agenda. The European Social Fund was set up in 1974, and the first in a series of four-year Social Action Programmes (SAPs) was launched, aimed at developing a plan of action to achieve full employment, improved living and working conditions, and gender equality. However, a combination of recession and ideological resistance from several European leaders ensured that many of the words failed to be translated into practical change on the ground.

As mentioned above, one of the goals of the Single European Act was to make it possible for Europeans to live and work wherever they liked in the EC, so social policy came to the fore again as questions were raised about the mobility of workers and about 'social dumping', a phenomenon in which money, services and businesses moved to those parts of the Community with the lowest wages and social security costs. The Commission tried to focus the attention of national governments on the 'social dimension' of the single market, but economic recession made sure that the SEA initially lacked such a dimension. This encouraged Commission

Box 6.3   The Social Charter

The core of European social policy is contained in the Social Charter. Adopted in 1989, it brought together all the social policy goals developed at earlier stages in the life of the Community, although it emphasized general goals at the expense of specifics. An action programme lists 47 separate measures that needed to be taken to achieve the goals of the Charter, categorized under the following headings:

1. Improvement of living and working conditions.
2. The right to freedom of movement, including entitlement to equal treatment and the harmonization of conditions of residence.
3. The right to exercise any trade or occupation on the same terms as those applied to nationals of the host state, and to enjoy the same social protection as nationals of the host state in gainful employment.
4. Fair remuneration for all employment.
5. The right to social protection, including a minimum income for those unable to find employment or no longer entitled to employment benefits.
6. The right to freedom of association and collective bargaining.
7. The right to vocational training throughout a worker's working life.
8. The right of men and women to equal treatment.
9. The right to information, consultation and worker participation.
10. The right to health, safety and protection in the workplace.
11. A minimum working age of 16, protection of children and adolescents, and special vocational training for them.
12. A retirement income that is sufficient to allow a reasonable standard of living.
13. The best possible integration of disabled people into working life.

president Jacques Delors – a moderate socialist – to launch an attempt in 1988 to draw more attention to the social consequences of the single market.

The Belgian government had raised the idea of a charter of basic social rights during its presidency of the Council of Ministers in 1987, modelled on its own new national charter. The idea was taken up by Jacques Delors in 1989, and was given a helping hand by the determination of the socialist government of François Mitterrand to promote social policy during the French presidency of the EC. Germany was also in favour (even though it was led by the moderate conservative government of Helmut Kohl), as were states with socialist governments, such as Spain and Greece. However the conservative government in Britain was vehemently opposed: Margaret Thatcher considered it 'quite inappropriate' for laws on working regulations and welfare benefits to be set at the Community level, and dismissed the Social Charter as 'a socialist charter – devised by socialists in the

Commission and favoured predominantly by socialist member states' (Thatcher, 1993, p. 750). When the Charter of Fundamental Social Rights of Workers (or the Social Charter) was adopted at the 1989 Strasbourg summit, Britain refused to go along.

The need for unanimity in the Council of Ministers on social legislation has meant that little progress has so far been made on turning principles into law. Britain under the Major government (1990–97) was usually painted as the leading opponent of the Social Charter, but there have been heated debates involving several member states about issues such as working hours, maternity leave and employment benefits for part-time workers. There were plans to incorporate the Social Charter into Maastricht, but the Major government again refused to go along, so a compromise was reached whereby it was attached to the treaty as a social protocol. Britain was excluded from voting in the Council on social issues while the other 11 member states formed their own ad hoc Social Community. This all changed in 1997 when the newly elected Blair government committed Britain to the goals of the social protocol, and it was incorporated by the Treaty of Amsterdam.

Despite all the rhetoric about social issues, most attention during the 1990s was focused on just one problem: the failure of the EU to ease unemployment, the persistence of which was once described as equivalent to the persistence of poverty in the United States (Dahrendorf, 1988, p. 149). The single market has not been able to generate enough jobs for Europeans, and although unemployment rates in the EU fell during the 1990s, they did not compare well with the US and Japan. By mid-2001, rates in the latter were about 4–5 per cent. In the EU, they ranged from a low of 2–5 per cent in Britain, the Netherlands and Sweden to a high of 9–13 per cent in Belgium, Germany, Italy and Spain (*The Economist*, various issues). The figure for the euro zone was 8.3 per cent, and while this was an improvement on 2000, more than 15 million Europeans were still out of work.

It is unclear why unemployment has remained so high, but at least part of the problem has been the relative weakness of trade unions and the relative ease with which workers can be laid off. Another factor is the size of the informal labour market in Europe, which accounts for as much as one-fifth of GDP in some states and is all but institutionalized in southern Italy, where it overlaps with organized crime. The EU has launched a host of retraining programmes, and is shifting resources to the poorer parts of the EU through various regional and social programmes, but with mixed results. Geyer and Springer (1998, p. 210) argue that EU employment policy has had 'high visibility but little focus', and that the search for solutions is hampered by a lack of support in the member states, which have been responsible for employment policy. They also note that the EU has the problem of trying to create jobs through increased competitiveness while preserving the traditional rights of employees.

One of the changes that came with the Amsterdam treaty was the introduction of a new employment chapter that called on member states to 'work towards developing a coordinated strategy for employment'. However, it only requires the Commission and the member states to report to each other, and most of the responsibility for employment policy still remains with the member states. Unemployment has been high on the agendas of several recent European Council summits, which have agreed common guidelines on employment policy, including a fresh start for the young and the long-term unemployed, and simplified rules for small and medium-sized enterprises. Although millions of new jobs have been created in the EU over the last decade, nearly half are temporary or part-time jobs, many of them are in the service sector, and because most are being filled by men and women new to the job market, they have done little to help ease long-term unemployment.

Another issue on the social agenda has been an improvement in the status of women. The position of women in politics and the workforce in the EU is not that different from their relative position in other liberal democracies, but the situation varies significantly from one member state to another, giving added importance to EU social policy and the goal of building economic and social cohesion. In general, women are in a better position in progressive northern European states such as Denmark, Finland and Sweden, and relatively worse off in poorer southern states such as Portugal, Spain and Greece.

About one in three European workers are women, but career options are still limited, proportionately more women than men are employed in part-time jobs, and women are more likely to work in traditionally feminized jobs – such as nursing and teaching – than in management, and in the less well paid and more labour-intensive sectors of industry (Springer, 1992, p. 66). Unemployment figures are higher for women than for men in most EU states, and women are also paid less than men for comparable work – about 80 per cent of the wages earned by a man. On the other hand, about 75 per cent of working women are employed in the expanding service sector, all EU member states are legally obliged to provide maternity leave, several member states offer parental leave, and the public provision of child care is improving.

Although the rights of working women were mentioned in the Treaty of Rome (which, for example, establishes the principle of equal pay for men and women), it was not until the EEC began to look more actively at social policy in the 1970s that women's issues began to be addressed. The 1974 SAP included the goal of achieving gender equality in access to employment and vocational training, and equal rights at work were promoted by

Box 6.4 Consumer protection policy

The European Community began to dabble in consumer issues in the mid-1970s, but consumer protection was sidelined by the economic goals of the single market programme until it was made a policy objective in its own right by Maastricht. Even then, it was agreed that initiatives by the EU must complement rather than replace national law, and member states are still allowed to implement stronger regulations provided they do not pose a barrier to trade.

The major goals of EU policy are to ensure that consumer interests are taken into account in the development of other policies, to improve the safety of consumer products and services, to improve consumer confidence, and to strengthen the links between the Commission and consumer organizations. The earliest pieces of European law were aimed at the safety of cosmetics, the labeling of foodstuffs, misleading advertising (allowing consumers to complain to courts, which can then make advertisers prove the accuracy of their claims), product liability and the provision of consumer credit. With the single market programme, the generation of new laws increased, focusing on such issues as safety standards for toys and building materials, and new labeling requirements for food and agricultural products.

Notable recent EU initiatives include the following:

- A major 1993 amendment to a 1976 directive banning the marketing of cosmetics that contain ingredients tested on animals; however, because of the slowness of testing methods, it did not come into force until 2000.
- A 1995 directive removing barriers to the free movement of personal data but establishing common standards to protect individual rights and privacy.
- A 1997 directive allowing comparative advertising throughout the EU, thereby expanding a practice already allowed in Britain to member states such as Belgium, France and Germany.
- A 1997 directive requiring retailers clearly to indicate both the absolute price and the unit price of all products, which enables consumers to compare costs more easily. Until then, only France and Sweden had similar legislation.
- A general ban on tobacco advertising, first proposed in 1989, was finally made law in 1998, although Germany challenged the law before the Court of Justice, claiming that it was a health measure rather than a single market measure, and hence did not come under the EU's remit.

new laws such as the 1975 equal pay directive and the 1976 equal treatment directive. Even though direct and indirect gender discrimination are illegal under EU law, however, women still face invisible barriers and glass ceilings.

Elitism and gender bias in the EU are exemplified by imbalances in the staffing of the major EU institutions. There are five women on the 1999–2004 College of Commissioners, but there had been none at all until the appointment of Vasso Papandreou of Greece in 1991. There are many more men than women in the more senior bureaucratic positions in the Commission and Council of Ministers, many more women than men in secretarial and clerical positions, the 1999–2004 European Parliament has about 190 women MEPs (about 30 per cent of the total), there has never been a woman judge on the Court of Justice, and only two women – Margaret Thatcher and former French Prime Minister Edith Cresson – have ever taken part in meetings of the European Council.

Improving accountability

European integration began as an agreement among government leaders to cooperate in selected areas, all the key decisions being taken by those leaders or their representatives. Even as its impact broadened, it remained an elite-driven process, and although citizens now have more influence over the decisions taken by the EU, public opinion is still marginalized. National leaders are held accountable through national elections, party competition, and media comment, but voters have little direct impact on the decisions those leaders take in their name at the European level. EU institutions continue to use a decision making structure that is out of step with new realities, a problem that undermines the credibility and effectiveness of the European Union. As Featherstone (1994, p. 168) puts it, the elitist and technocratic character of institution-building might have served its purpose in the 1950s, but its continuation 'threatens instability and an increasing lack of legitimacy in the system'.

Reformation of the European institutions has been on the agenda of a number of European Council meetings, but progress to date has been limited by the desire of the governments of the member states to keep as much control as possible over the decisions taken in the name of European integration. The discussions leading up to the Amsterdam treaty were an opportunity to address the problem, but they resulted in little substantial change: the equal roles of Parliament and the Council of Ministers in the legislative process were recognized, the legislative process in Parliament was simplified, the powers of the Court of Justice were extended over such issues as asylum, immigration and cooperation in police and judicial matters, and the powers of the Court of Auditors and the Committee of the Regions were increased. The Treaty of Nice was another opportunity to look at how the institutions worked, but produced only changes to the numbers instead of fundamental structural change.

Given that integration is now having so much more impact on the lives of Europeans, it is time for a new effort to be made to improve public understanding of the structure of the EU, and to improve the public accountability of the EU institutions. A good place to start would be with the development of a European constitution. For some, the main barrier to drawing up such a document is that the EU is still evolving – constitutions work best, they argue, when the system of government that is being committed to paper has achieved a high degree of stability and perma-nence, which is not the case in Europe. But the EU could learn much from the model of the United States. Although the US constitution outlined a structure of government that was viewed as permanent, the details of that structure have changed significantly since the constitution was adopted in 1791. For example, Congress was intended to be stronger than the presidency, but the powers of the presidency have grown, particularly since the Second World War, in response to growing needs for national leadership. Similarly, the US Supreme Court was not given the power to interpret the constitution, but won that power through its own decisions.

It could also be argued that the long-term benefits of actively addressing the democratic deficit outweigh short-term concerns about the stage that EU institutions have reached in their evolution. The exercise of developing a European constitution may help focus the minds of leaders and citizens alike, and force them to think more actively about the nature of the entity they are building. Furthermore, democratic constitutions are never the final word, and can be amended and fine-tuned by changes in the law and judgements of a constitutional court.

To date, the powers of EU institutions have been allowed to grow in response to the evolving interests of the EU, but as Europeans better understand the impact that integration is having on their lives, public pressure for institutional reform will inevitably grow. Possible reforms might include the following:

- The European Parliament should become a true legislature. For this to happen the power to initiate the law-making process would have to shift from the Commission to Parliament, the power to take final decisions on the adoption or rejection of new laws would have to shift from the Council of Ministers to Parliament, and Parliament would have to be given greater power over decisions on the EU budget. It should also be sited exclusively and permanently in Brussels, so that it is close to the Commission and the Council of Ministers.

- The Council of Ministers should be replaced by a second, upper chamber of Parliament, providing a different level of representation from that offered by the present chamber. It might be something like the United States Senate, where every state has the same number of representatives, irrespective of size, or the German Bundesrat, where the number of representatives varies according to the population of each state. Alternatively, because it would be difficult to justify giving 420 000 Luxembourgers the same representation as 82 million Germans, the upper chamber might be based instead on providing representation to the more than 200 regions of the member states, or it might be based on sectoral interests, such as industry and the professions. The former have already been given advisory powers through the Committee of the Regions, and the latter through the Economic and Social Committee, so the new chamber might evolve out of one or both of these committees. However the upper chamber is structured, it should have the same powers over legislation as the lower – all proposals would have to go through the same process of introduction, discussion, amendment and adoption before they could become law.
- The president of the European Commission should be directly elected by all eligible voters for a limited number of terms, and should have the right to appoint his or her own Commissioners, either from inside Parliament or – with Parliamentary approval – from outside. The Amsterdam treaty included an agreement that the president be given greater powers over selecting Commissioners and exercising policy leadership, and changes made under Nice will allow the president to reshuffle the membership of the College. Given the growing executive powers of the presidency, however, the time is fast approaching when the decision regarding who becomes president will be taken out of the hands of national governments and given to European voters.
- The power of the European Commission should be restricted to policy implementation. In other words, it would have the same role as a conventional bureaucracy, and be charged with ensuring the execution of laws developed and adopted by Parliament.
- Key appointments – including those to the Court of Justice, the Court of First Instance, the College of Commissioners, the European Central Bank, and other EU institutions – should be made subject to parliamentary approval. Similarly, Commissioners and directors-general should be called more often before Parliamentary committees to answer for their policy decisions and the performance of their departments.

The Amsterdam and Nice treaties fell short of meeting their primary objective of overhauling EU institutions in preparation for an expansion of membership. However Amsterdam includes the agreement that at least one year before the membership of the EU grows to 20 states, an intergovernmental conference will be convened to carry out a 'comprehensive' review of the provisions of the treaties on the composition and powers of the institutions. Negotiations are already under way with six aspirant new members, so that figure will probably be reached – and passed – very soon.

Conclusions

The European Union has helped redefine the relationship among Europeans. Where they have long identified themselves in national terms, and have been tied economically, legally and culturally to one nation-state or another, the reduction of the barriers to trade and to the movement of individuals over the past decade has encouraged Europeans to think of themselves as part of a larger entity with broader interests. Common social policies have resulted in key powers over the lives of individual Europeans shifting to Brussels, so that an increasing number of Europeans feel the effect of decisions made at the EU level. Personal mobility has increased and, cultural barriers aside, Europeans have taken more interest in neighbours who have long been considered as 'foreign' rivals and occasionally a direct threat to their own national interests.

However, while this horizontal integration has been taking place, the ability of Europeans directly to influence the European Union has lagged. Integration has been driven by the priorities and the values of the leaders of the member states, who have made most of their decisions with limited reference to their citizens. The result has been the creation of a European governing structure that is only indirectly accountable to the views of the people who live within it. European law is proposed and implemented by a European Commission whose leadership is not accountable to European voters. Key decisions on the adoption of new laws and policies are taken by national representatives meeting secretly as the Council of Ministers. The only institution that directly represents European citizens – the European Parliament – is denied the power to propose new laws, and must share the power to adopt new laws with the Council of Ministers.

Europeans are divided about the wisdom of integration, with only half of them agreeing that membership has been a 'good thing' for their country. The majority find the EU difficult to understand, admit to being badly informed about critical EU projects such as the adoption of the euro, and are lukewarm to other endeavours, such as expansion of membership into eastern Europe.

As European institutions struggle to sell the concept of integration to the citizens of the member states, they are handicapped by the absence of effective channels of accountability, and by the perpetuation of the democratic deficit. Changes made under the People's Europe programme and as a result of treaty changes have made Europe more real to its citizens, but uniform passports, a European flag and student exchange programmes fall far short of the kinds of changes needed to make Europeans feel as though they are truly connected to the EU. The democratic deficit can only be addressed by a wholesale reform of the EU institutions aimed at making them accountable to the citizens of Europe instead of the leaders of the member states. This, of course, would push the EU further along the road to federalism, something that many Europeans would find hard to accept.

Chapter 7

Economic Integration

The single market
Effects of the single market
The common agricultural policy
Inside the euro zone
Conclusions

> . . . *a profoundly political act.*
>
> Joschka Fischer, German foreign minister,
> describing the creation of the euro, 2001

Economic issues have dominated the life and work of the European Union. Beginning with the experiment in pooling coal and steel production, and moving through the customs union, the common agricultural policy, exchange rate stability, the single market and the single currency, the EU agenda has been driven in large part by matters involving trade, tariffs, markets, currencies, competition and labour mobility. It has only been relatively recently that the agenda of integration has broadened to include a wider variety of policy issues, from social affairs to the environment.

The priority given to economic integration was made clear from the outset in three of the primary goals of the Treaty of Rome:

- The creation of a customs union, by which all tariff barriers and other obstacles to trade among EEC members would be removed, and agreement reached on a common external tariff so that all goods coming into the EEC – no matter where their point of entry – would be subject to the same costs and controls. A related goal was the agreement of a common commercial policy towards third countries (see Chapter 8).
- The creation of a European single (or common) market, meaning agreement on rules that would allow the free movement of people, goods, services and money within the Community. In order to set the groundwork for this, the member states had to develop a common competition policy by minimizing or abolishing state assistance to national industries so as to avoid economic distortions, breaking down monopolies and cartels, and harmonizing national health and safety standards.

- The development of a common agricultural policy by which farmers were paid guaranteed prices for their produce, and agricultural markets were stabilized and food supplies assured.

The customs union was completed without much fanfare in 1968 with the agreement of a common external tariff, but non-tariff barriers to trade among the member states persisted, including variations in technical standards and quality controls, different health and safety standards, and different rates of indirect taxation. Prospects for the single market seemed to move beyond reach in the mid-1970s as recession encouraged member states to protect their national markets. Meanwhile, the common agricultural policy soaked up Community spending, and led to massive overproduction by European farmers.

By the 1980s it had become clear that urgent action was needed to reverse the EC's relative economic decline, and a boost had to be given to the single market programme in order to respond to foreign competition. If duplication of effort could be reduced, joint research encouraged, trans-European corporate mergers promoted, and the final barriers to trans-European business removed, Europe's economies could become more efficient and competitive, and its businesses more profitable. It was this change of thinking that produced the 1985 Schengen Agreement to remove border controls, the 1986 Single European Act aimed at completing the single market, and the ongoing attempts to build exchange rate stability. The latter culminated in 2002 in the most important step towards the final construction of an integrated regional economy: the replacement by 12 member states of their national currencies with a single European currency, the euro.

The single market

At its summit in Brussels in February 1985, the European Council agreed that it was time to refocus on one of the original goals of the European Community: the completion of a single market in which there would be no barriers to trade. Jacques Delors had just taken over as president of the Commission and was keen to proceed, so the trade and industry commissioner, Lord Cockfield, oversaw the drawing up of a white paper outlining the changes that needed to be made (Commission, 1985). This became the basis of the Single European Act, which was discussed at an IGC between September 1985 and January 1986, signed in February 1986, and came into force in July 1987. Its goal was to remove the remaining non-tariff barriers to the free movement of people, goods, services and money by the end of 1992. Those barriers took three main forms: physical, fiscal, and technical.

Physical barriers

The most obvious of the physical barriers to the single market were customs and border checks, which persisted at the EC's internal borders despite the agreement of the customs union in 1968. Member states still controlled the movement of people (they were particularly concerned about illegal immigrants), collected value added tax and excise taxes on alcohol, tobacco and luxury goods, enforced differing health standards, controlled banned products, and sought to prevent the spread of animal and plant diseases. Not only were these checks costly, inconsistent and time-consuming, but they interfered with the free flow of people, goods and services. They were also a psychological barrier to integration, reminding Europeans that they still lived in a region of independent nation-states.

One of the greatest concerns for national governments was international terrorism, which could be checked to some extent with national frontier controls. The problem had been discussed since 1975 by senior officials from justice and home affairs ministries, meeting biannually as the Trevi Group to exchange information. They gradually expanded their interests to take in other security threats, such as those posed by organized crime and football hooligans. A particular concern was the relative ease with which terrorists could enter the Community from third countries through those member states with the weakest controls, such as Greece or Portugal. In order to tighten up the external borders of the EC, the member states began developing common measures on visas, immigration, extradition and political asylum.

In 1984 France and Germany decided to accelerate the reduction of border checks, and in June 1985 joined the Benelux countries in signing the Schengen Agreement. Named for the town in Luxembourg near which it was signed, the agreement set off a series of meetings among the five countries aimed at agreeing and implementing the measures needed to end internal border controls. It was to have come into effect in January 1990, but plans were delayed because of problems setting up the computerized Schengen Information System (SIS), a database of undesirables whose entry to the Schengen area local officials wanted to control. The Agreement remained informal until the Treaty of Amsterdam brought it under the umbrella of the Union. With effect from March 1995 almost all customs and passport controls were finally eliminated by the signatories, which by then included Italy, Greece, Portugal and Spain. Within the Schengen area there is now free circulation of people, common rules on asylum, the right of hot pursuit across frontiers, and a common policy on visas.

Denmark did not sign the agreement until 1996 because of the potential impact of the agreement on the Nordic passport union of Denmark,

Finland, Iceland, Norway, and Sweden. Following negotiations, all five Nordic union members signed on, bringing membership to 15; passport-free travel is now available from the Mediterranean to the Arctic, although all travellers still need to carry some form of identification. Citing concerns about security and its particular needs as an island state, Britain has not signed the agreement, although it has opted into selected elements, including the SIS and police and legal cooperation on criminal matters. Ireland has been unable to join because of its customs arrangements with Britain.

A problem which has worsened in the years since the Schengen Agreement was signed is that of illegal immigration. Just as the United States has long been a magnet for illegal immigrants from Mexico and Latin America, so the EU has begun to feel the same kind of pressures. The smuggling of people into the EU has become a major industry in recent years, with an estimated value running into several billion euros annually. Run mainly by organized crime, the smuggling has grown as a result of a combination of the opening up of eastern Europe and the removal of internal borders among Schengen signatories. There are estimates that as many as half a million people are arriving in the EU each year, entering from North Africa, the Balkans, eastern Europe and Russia via Spain, Italy, Austria, Germany and Finland. Most of the illegal immigrants are Afghans, Albanians, Bangladeshis, Iranians, Iraqis or Kurds. Once inside the EU, many claim to be refugees and apply for asylum (*The Economist*, 20 February 1999).

In order to help deal with concerns arising from the removal of internal border checks, the EU has improved cooperation among national police forces, to which end the European Police Office (Europol) was created in 1995 (although it only formally began operations in 1998). Based in The Hague, Europol was initially defined as an intelligence service, responsible for gathering and analyzing information about drug trafficking in support of the work of national police forces. Its interests have since expanded to include terrorism, illicit trafficking in radioactive and nuclear materials and in people, illegal immigration, money laundering, and organized crime, not only from internal sources, but from Turkey, Poland, Russia, and Colombia. Modelled in part on Interpol, the worldwide police organization, Europol cannot carry out investigations or bring prosecutions. It is building a computer base of information that can be accessed by its liaison offices in the member states, and by national police forces in the interests of building cooperation across borders.

This book went to press shortly after the September 2001 terrorist attacks on the World Trade Center in New York and the Pentagon in Washington DC, and just as the European Council was holding an emergency summit to discuss the implications. What effect the attacks would have on measures taken by the EU to prevent the movement of terrorists was unclear, but they were certain to lead to changes in policy and to greater cooperation among the member states on the movement of undesirables into and around the EU.

Fiscal barriers

The major fiscal barrier to the single market was indirect taxation, which caused distortion of competition and artificial price differences, and as such constituted a handicap to trade. Thanks in part to the influence of the EEC, all member states introduced value added tax (VAT) in the 1970s, but rates in the 1980s varied from as low as 12 per cent in Luxembourg to as high as 22 per cent in Denmark. This was one reason why border controls on the movement of goods persisted; because VAT was paid at the point of purchase, refunds could be claimed for exported goods, and imports possibly subjected to additional charges.

There were also variations in the levels of excise duties among the member states, reflecting different levels of national concern about human health. In the 1980s, for example, smokers in France paid nearly twice as much on cigarettes as those in Spain, smokers in Ireland four times as much, and smokers in Denmark six times as much. The differences were a boon to tourism, because travellers from one country to another could often buy limited quantities of cheaper alcohol, tobacco products, and other consumer items to take home with them. However, they were another barrier to the single market.

In 1991 agreement was reached on a minimum rate of 15 per cent VAT, with lower rates on basic necessities such as food, and in 1992 various minimum rates were also agreed on excise duties. In July 1993 an agreement came into force whereby VAT was collected at the local rate in the country to which the goods and services were going. Agreement was subsequently reached on an EU-wide VAT system in which tax is collected only in the country of origin, the ultimate goal being a single rate of VAT, or at least variations within a very narrow band. Controversially, it was proposed that duty-free sales be abolished for travellers within the EU in 1999; critics charged that the benefits for the single market were marginal, while the costs in terms of lost jobs and reduced sales were substantial.

The idea of minimum rates of VAT has been relatively easy for political and public opinion to accept; much more difficult has been the suggestion that the EU work towards harmonizing tax rates in other areas, notably corporation tax or the setting of minimum withholding tax on savings. Such a suggestion was made by the finance ministers of Germany and France in late 1998, and was immediately opposed by their counterpart in

Britain, Gordon Brown. Talk of tax harmonization, no matter how limited the scope, is seen by many as the first step towards the development of EU authority over the setting of income tax, a notion that is deeply troubling to many Euro-doubters.

Technical barriers

Among the most persistent barriers to the single market was the existence of different technical regulations and standards among the member states. Most were based on different safety, health, environmental, and consumer protection standards, and many seemed petty and inconsequential: different definitions of chocolate that prevented British chocolate being sold in many other member states, for example, or the insistence by Germans that no beer could be sold in Germany that did not meet domestic 'purity laws'. Many of these regulations were in the interests of consumer safety, and were thus welcome, but others amounted to another form of economic protectionism. The Community tried to remove technical barriers by developing EC standards and encouraging member states to conform, but this was a time-consuming and tedious task, and did little to discourage the common image of interfering Eurocrats.

Three breakthroughs helped clear many bureaucratic and political hurdles, and greatly simplified the process of technical standardization. The first came in 1979 with the Cassis de Dijon decision by the Court of Justice, which established the principle of mutual recognition. West Germany had refused to import a French blackcurrant liqueur, Cassis de Dijon, on the grounds that its wine-spirit content was below the minimum set by the West German government for fruit liqueurs. The importer charged that this was a restriction on imports of a kind prohibited under the Treaty of Rome. The Court of Justice agreed, since when member states have had to accept products from other states that meet domestic technical standards. With trade in foodstuffs, for example, the implication was that a member state could not block imports from another member state on the basis of local health regulations. This helped clear the way for free movement in goods and services where there is no specific EU law, greatly easing the workload for the Commission.

The second breakthrough was the 1983 mutual information directive, which required member states to tell the Commission and the other member states if they planned to develop any new domestic technical regulations, and to allow the others three months to respond if they felt these would create new barriers to trade. The third breakthrough was contained in the Cockfield report, which included a 'new approach' to technical regulation: instead of the Commission working out agreements on every rule and regulation, the Council of Ministers would agree laws with general objectives, and detailed specifications could then be drawn up by existing private standards institutes, such as the European Standardization Committee (CEN) or the European Electrotechnical Standardization Committee (CENELEC)

Progress has since been made on removing technical barriers to the single market in a wide variety of areas, from safety and operating standards for road vehicles to the content of processed food. Much work remains to be done in other areas, however, notably the kinds of technical differences that cannot be resolved by the marketplace. For example, television systems are different throughout the EU, obliging manufacturers to make eight different kinds of television set. Similarly, the design of electrical plugs and sockets differs from one member state to another, obliging travellers to take an adapter with them wherever they go. There have been plans afoot since 1992 to develop a common plug, but the cost of rewiring homes and businesses throughout the EU will almost certainly be prohibitive.

An issue of recent interest has been the internet and electronic commerce. An e-commerce directive adopted by the EU in 2001 applied single market principles of free movement of services to e-commerce, allowing operators to provide services throughout the EU. Many of the issues in the directive were technical, including protection of personal data and rules on unsolicited e-mail advertising and the use of online contracts. The EU has also been keen to see reductions in the costs of using the internet, the integration and liberalization of telecommunications markets, and internet access for all schools in the EU. In an effort to improve trans-European links and to pave the way for increased traffic, basic telephone services have been liberalized in most member states, work is underway on an Integrated Service Digital Network which would allow the transmission of voice, data and images through telephone lines, and member states are being encouraged to remove the need for different sets of licences and regulatory approval, and to end monopolies on mobile phone services.

Effects of the single market

The Single European Act was, in its time, the most radical of all the steps taken in the process of European integration since the signing of the treaties of Paris and Rome. It not only accelerated the process of economic integration, but it has also changed the lives of every European, making economic integration more real to millions of people.

Rights of residence

As noted in Chapter 6, the Treaty of Rome allowed Europeans only limited rights to move for any length of time from one member state to another. Migration was seen mainly in economic terms; it was tied to occupation, and anyone who wanted to move to another member state was assessed on the basis of the skills they brought. Since the completion of the single market, the situation has been very different: almost any resident of an EU member state can now live and work in any other EU member state, open a bank account, take out a mortgage, transfer unlimited amounts of capital, and even vote (in some countries) in local and European elections. A few restrictions remain, but they are relatively minor. For example, students are given annual residence permits, must be enrolled on a course of study, and must be able to support themselves. Retirees and people of independent means are given five-year renewable residence permits, and pensions are not yet entirely mobile, although work has been underway to make it possible for workers to move their pensions with them.

Joint ventures and corporate mergers

Transnational corporate mergers have long been a feature of the European business landscape, creating such giants as Unilever and Royal Dutch/Shell (both Anglo–Dutch) or Asea Brown Boveri (Swedish–Swiss). However, despite the existence of many world-leading corporations, western Europe between 1950 and the early 1980s lost markets at home and abroad to competition first from the United States, and then from Japan. Even today, 60 per cent of the companies listed in the *Fortune* magazine list of the world's 100 biggest are American or Japanese, including 15 of the top 20 (*Fortune*, July 2000).

The single market programme helped push competitiveness to the top of the EC agenda, and the Commission in the late 1980s became actively involved in trying to overcome market fragmentation and the emphasis placed by national governments on promoting the interests of often state-owned 'national champions'. The Community also launched new programmes aimed at encouraging research in information technology, advanced communications, industrial technologies, and weapons manufacture (Tsoukalis, 1997, pp. 49–51). The single market has helped take down many of the barriers that national corporations once faced, and increased the number of consumers they can reach. The euro has also made it easier for companies in search of acquisitions to borrow money and buy other companies, which has combined with privatization programmes in many countries and the general trend towards globalization to greatly increase the number of acquisition opportunities, joint ventures and corporate mergers, both within the EU and between European and non-European corporations.

Notable early joint ventures included those between Thompson of France and Philips of the Netherlands on high-definition television, Pirelli of Italy and Dunlop of Britain on tyres, BMW and Rolls-Royce on aeroengines, and among the members of the European Space Agency (ESA). Set up in 1973 in an attempt to promote European cooperation in space research, the ESA now has 14 members: Switzerland, Norway, and all the EU member states except Greece, Luxembourg and Portugal. Twelve European countries have also cooperated in the development of Arianespace, a space-launch consortium owned by governments and state-owned companies (France has a stake of just over 50 per cent). Since the launch of the first in its series of Ariane rockets in 1979 from Kourou in French Guiana, Arianespace has won more than half the global market for launching commercial satellites, eating into a business long dominated by the United States.

The growth of new pan-European businesses seeking to profit from the opportunities offered by the single market, and looking to create 'world-size' companies to compete more effectively with the United States and Japan, has led to a surge in merger and acquisition activities, notably in the chemicals, pharmaceuticals, and telecommunications industries. In 1989/ 90 the number of intra-EC mergers overtook the number of national mergers for the first time (Owen and Dynes, 1992, p. 222), since when the European mergers and acquisitions market has grown to be bigger than that in the United States. Notable recent examples are:

- The 1996 merger between Ciba-Geigy and Sandoz to create Novartis, the world's second largest drug group.
- The merger of British pharmaceuticals companies Glaxo and Wellcome, which in 2000 merged with SmithKline Beecham.
- A string of takeovers by the French insurance company AXA, now ranked among the twenty biggest corporations in the world.
- The mergers and acquisitions which in the space of two years transformed Britain's Vodaphone into one of the world's biggest mobile phone businesses. In 1999 it merged with the US company AirTouch, then with Bell Atlantic in the US to create America's biggest wireless service. In 2000 it took over the much larger German company Mannesmann, which had earlier taken over Orange, Britain's third biggest mobile phone company.

The new opportunities offered at home have been accompanied by remarkable growth in the levels of European foreign direct investment

Box 7.1 Europe and the aerospace industry

Few areas of multinational business have seen quite such dramatic change in recent years as the aerospace industry, where rationalization, competition and other economic pressures have cut the number of large civilian aircraft producers in the world from dozens to just two. Famous names of western European aviation – from Vickers to Hawker Siddeley, Messerschmitt and Dassault – have all gone. In Britain alone, the 19 aircraft producers of the 1940s had been whittled down by 1986 to just one, British Aerospace (Owen and Dynes 1992, pp. 162–3). The same kind of pressures have led to similar changes in the United States, where Lockheed now focuses on military aircraft and McDonnell-Douglas was taken over in 1997 by Boeing, the only remaining American manufacturer of large civilian aircraft.

Much of the responsibility for the changes on both sides of the Atlantic lies with the success of Airbus Industrie, a European consortium founded in 1970, and whose share of the new civil aircraft market had grown from 10 per cent in 1975 to 50 per cent by the late 1990s. The Airbus consortium is 80 per cent owned by the European Aeronautic Defence and Space company (EADS), created in 2000 by a merger between Aérospatiale Matra of France, DaimlerChrysler Aerospace of Germany, and CASA of Spain; the remaining 20 per cent is owned by BAe Systems of Britain, while Finmeccanica of Italy had an option in 2001 on a 5 per cent share. Airbus produces a line of eight different airliners, and has toyed in recent years with the development of the world's largest passenger aircraft, the 555-seat A380.

The creation of EADS was prompted by the argument that economies of scale were giving Boeing an advantage over its European competitors, whose national markets were too small to sustain them. Similar arguments have encouraged transnational cooperation in western Europe on military aircraft and missiles. Individual member states still make competitive products, such as France's Mirage jet fighters, and Britain's Harrier jump jets, but are finding that it makes better commercial sense to pool resources. Successful collaborations include production of the Tornado fighter-bomber and the Eurofighter, both made by a consortium of EADS and Italy's Alenia (which together have 63 per cent interest) and BAe Systems (37 per cent). In April 2001, BAe, EADS and Finmeccanica joined forces to create MBDA, the world's second largest producer of missiles after Raytheon of the United States.

abroad. Between 1997 and 1998 alone, the amount of capital invested more than doubled, from nearly $105 billion to nearly $215 billion. Nearly 60 per cent of those investments were made in the United States, and Britain was both the biggest investor ($63 billion) and the biggest recipient of inward investment (nearly $55 billion) (*Eurecom*, July/August 1999). Among the more notable examples of European companies reaching outside the EU to create large new corporations are:

- The 1998 takeover by British Petroleum of Amoco in the United States, and the subsequent merger between BP Amoco and Atlantic Richfield.
- The 1999 takeover by Germany's Daimler of the US automobile manufacturer Chrysler.
- The 2000 takeover by Germany's Deutsche Telekom of Voicestream in the United States.

Of course, bigger is not necessarily better, because takeovers can reduce competition and consumer choice, and run the danger of creating industries that dominate or monopolize a particular sector. There are also many examples of international mergers failing, sometimes because they have added little value to the participating companies, and sometimes because of language and cultural problems. Out of a concern to make sure that bigger corporations do not become too dominant, the EU has developed a controversial competition policy to avoid abuses such as price-fixing, and to watch out for 'abuses of a dominant position' by bigger companies (Cini and McGowan, 1998). The 1989 merger regulation allows the European Commission to scrutinize all large mergers (even those involving companies based outside the EU that might have an effect on EU business), and the Commission also keeps an eye on the effect of state subsidies on competition in trade (Allen, 1996). Recent targets of Commission investigations have included Microsoft and its Windows 2000 operating system, and planned domestic mergers in the United States between telecom companies MCI/WorldCom and Sprint (which was abandoned), between General Electric and Honeywell (blocked by the Commission), and between computer makers Hewlett-Packard and Compaq.

A European transport system

An important element in the successful operation of markets is integrated infrastructure, such as transport, energy and communications networks. Realizing this, the EU has been actively involved in the development of Trans-European Networks (TENs) aimed at integrating 15 different transport, energy supply, and telecommunications systems. Until 1987, harmonization of the transport sector was one of the great failures of the common market – little of substance had been done to deal with problems such as an airline industry split along national lines (see below), time-consuming cross-border checks on trucks, national systems of motorways that did not connect with each other, air traffic control systems using 20 different operating systems and 70 computer programming languages, and telephone lines incapable of carrying advanced electronic communications. Two phenomena have begun to make a difference.

Firstly, there has been a dramatic increase in tourism. Not only is Europe the biggest tourist destination in the world, capturing nearly 60 per cent of the world tourist trade (World Trade Organization, 1996), but Europeans are now travelling in much greater numbers to each other's countries, which has helped break down prejudices, made Europeans more familiar with each other, and encouraged greater cooperation on transportation by increasing the demand for cheap and easy access. Tourism now employs an estimated 22 million Europeans (about six per cent of the workforce), and generated revenues in 1998 of about €1.04 trillion ($1.15 trillion), or about 14 per cent of the GDP of the EU (World Travel and Tourism Council figures, quoted by Barnard, 1999). The six major tourist destinations are France, Spain, Italy, Britain, Germany, and Austria.

Secondly, rail transport has been revitalized as a cost-efficient and environmentally friendly alternative to road and air transport. The EU has plans to develop a 35 000 km high-speed train (HST) network connecting Europe's major cities, the way being led by France with its high-speed TGV, which needs special new track, and Germany with its ICE network, which can use existing track. With trains travelling at 200–300 kph (some of them with coaches finished to luxurious standards), the HST system has cut travel times considerably. Germany even has hopes over the long term of largely replacing domestic air flights with a system of very high-speed trains (VHSTs) based in part on floating mag-lev technology. Meanwhile, investments have been made in building the tunnels and bridges needed to ensure uninterrupted travel; the completion of the €14 billion Eurotunnel under the channel between Britain and France and of road/rail bridges linking Denmark and Sweden were important pieces in the jigsaw

The development of TENs is now one of the priorities of the EU, and the European Commission has a programme aimed at improving transport links within the EU; it will cost a projected €400 billion by 2010, and will involve the building of 70 000 km of railway track (including 22 000 km of new and upgraded track for HSTs), and 15 000 km of new roads, mainly on the outer edges of the EU. Among the priority projects identified by the European Council: a €20 billion North–South HST link between Berlin and Verona, a €13 billion HST link between Paris, Brussels, Cologne, Amsterdam and London, new motorways for Greece, a motorway link between Portugal and Spain, and a 1400 km Ireland–UK–Benelux road link.

Open skies over Europe

One of the most notable changes brought by the single market programme has been the loosening of regulations on air transport (see Armstrong and Bulmer 1998, Chapter 7). Because most European states are too small to support a significant domestic industry, the majority of air traffic in Europe is international. Until the 1980s, most European countries had state-owned national carriers – such as Air France, Lufthansa, and Alitalia – which played an influential role in making national air transport policy, and had a national monopoly over most of the international routes they flew; the result was that air transport was highly regulated, and expensive for consumers.

Changes began in the mid-1980s when the Thatcher government launched a liberalization programme in Britain that led to the privatization of British Airways in 1987, and negotiated bilateral agreements with several other EU member states. Meanwhile, the European Civil Aviation Conference recommended liberalization, as did a number of national and European interest groups (notably those representing consumers unions), and the idea was taken up in turn by the European Commission and incorporated into the Cockfield report. Britain was most actively in favour, while Germany and France provided limited support, and states with smaller or less efficient national carriers – such as Spain, Italy and Denmark – were opposed. Against this background, three packages of laws and regulations worked their way through the EU institutions in 1987–92, which substantially opened up the market, and led to a restructuring of the air transport market. Big carriers have taken over smaller ones, national carriers have created international alliances, and there has been a growth in the number of cut-price operators such as Virgin Express. More importantly, consumers now have greater choice and can fly more cheaply than before.

Considerable progress has been made since 1987 in moving towards the completion of the single market, but work still remains to be done. In June 1997, the Commission launched a Single Market Action Plan aimed at generating a political commitment for the decisive completion of the single market by January 1999. This divided remaining actions into three groups: those that could be implemented in the short run because they did not need new EU legislation, those that had already been proposed but still needed approval from Parliament and the Council of Ministers, and those that were more complex, such as a reworking of the VAT system. As this book went to press, much progress had been made on implementation of nearly 1340 existing single market-related directives, but the implications of the single market were still not fully understood by Europeans or their leaders, and much still relied not so much on deliberate political decisions as on the pressures of the marketplace to reduce or remove remaining barriers.

The common agricultural policy

Agriculture accounts for only a small fraction of the economic activity of most Western governments, and as a result tends to be fairly low on the policy agenda. Yet it has long been a headline issue in the European Union, because while it employs just five per cent of European workers, and accounts for just three per cent of the combined GDP of the EU, it is the most expensive, most complex, and sometimes most contentious of the policy areas in which the EU has become involved. Compared to other policy areas, the EU has more powers over agriculture, has passed more legislation on agriculture, spends almost as much of its budget on agriculture as on all other policy areas combined, and has seen more political activity on agriculture. Only the foreign ministers meet more often than the agriculture ministers, and the Commission's Agriculture DG is the second biggest of all its directorates-general.

Agricultural policy is also structurally different from other EU policy areas in two important respects. First, while barriers have been removed and markets opened up in almost every area of EU economic activity, agriculture remains heavily interventionist. The EU has taken a hands-on approach to keeping agricultural prices high, drawing criticism not only from within the EU but from the EU's major trading partners. Second, unlike most other EU policy areas, agricultural policy was built in to the Treaty of Rome, where the commitment to a Common Agricultural Policy (CAP) was spelt out more clearly than was the case for any other policy area, although the details were only agreed in the 1960s. Why does agriculture have such a high profile?

First, at the time the Treaties of Rome were being negotiated, agriculture sat high on the agendas of European governments; it was important to their economies, their societies and their cultures. Agriculture accounted for about 12 per cent of the GNP of the Six, and for the employment of about 20 per cent of the workforce. Many farms in the Six were small and therefore vulnerable, and several national governments operated agricultural support and protection programmes that, for political reasons, could not be ended. At the same time, the continued operation of separate national systems might interfere with the common market, so the suggestion was made that there be a Community support system. Furthermore, the Second World War had made Europeans aware of how much they depended on imported food, and of just how prone those imports were to disruption.

The second reason for its prominence is that it was a key element in the trade-off between Germany and France when the launch of the EEC was under negotiation (Grant 1997, pp. 63–8). France was concerned that the common market would benefit German industry while providing the French economy with relatively few benefits. In the mid-1950s France had a large and efficient agricultural sector, which contributed significantly to employment and economic activity. Concerns that the common market would hurt its farmers encouraged the French government to insist on a protectionist system. Even though this was to prove expensive, threats to change the system even today bring protesting French farmers out in their thousands.

Third, agricultural prices are more subject to fluctuation than prices on most other goods, and since Europeans spend about a quarter of their incomes on food, those fluctuations can have knock-on effects throughout the economy. Price increases can contribute to inflation, while price decreases can force farmers to go deeper into debt, perhaps leading to bankruptcies and unemployment. The problem of maintaining minimum incomes has been exacerbated by mechanization, which has led to fewer people working in farming in Europe. European governments felt that subsidies could help prevent or offset some of these problems, encourage people to stay in the rural areas, and discourage them from moving to towns and cities and perhaps adding to unemployment problems.

Finally, farmers in the richer EU states have traditionally had strong unions working for them. As well as national unions, more than 150 EU-wide agricultural organizations have been formed, many of which directly lobby the EU. Among these is the Committee of Professional Agricultural Organizations (COPA), which represents farmers generally on a wide range of issues. Not only are farmers an influential lobby in the EU, but there are many other people who live in rural areas, and many rurally-based services. The residents of small towns and villages add up to a sizable proportion of the population, and of the vote. No political party can afford to ignore that vote, especially as there is little organized resistance to the agricultural or rural lobbies, either at the national or at the EU level.

At the core of agricultural issues in the EU is the Common Agricultural Policy, which has three underlying principles: the promotion of a single market in agricultural produce, a system of protectionism aimed at giving advantages to EU produce over imported produce, and joint financing, meaning that the costs of CAP are to be shared equitably across all the member states. What this has meant in practical policy terms is that EU farmers are guaranteed the same minimum price for their produce, irrespective of how much they produce, of world prices, or of prevailing levels of supply and demand. Meanwhile, the EU's internal market is protected from imports by tariffs, and the member states share the financial burden for making this possible.

CAP is not so much a common agricultural policy as a common agricultural price support system. Annual prices for all agricultural products are fixed by the agriculture ministers meeting in the spring (usually April or May). On the basis of discussions and negotiations that usually have been going on since the previous September and have pulled in the Commission, the Agriculture Council, interest groups, and national governments, the ministers set several kinds of prices:

- *Target prices*, or the prices they hope farmers will receive on the open market in order to receive a fair return on their investments. These are usually set high – above world prices – in order to ensure a minimum standard of living for farmers, and they are supported by levies on imports and subsidies to promote exports.
- *Intervention prices*, or the prices the Commission will pay as a last resort to take produce off the market if it is not meeting the target price.
- *Threshold prices*, or the prices for imports from outside the EU at which levies will be charged in order to make them less competitive.
- *Entry price*, or the minimum price at which a commodity can be imported into the EU.

This price-setting arrangement has become more expensive and more complex as EU farmers have produced more than consumers need. The EU has been obliged to buy up the surplus of commodities such as butter, cereals, beef and sugar. Some of this is stored, while the rest is either sold outside the EU (much to the annoyance of other agricultural countries, such as the United States), given as food aid to poorer countries, or destroyed or converted into another product. For example, excess wine might be turned into spirits, which take up less space, or even into heating fuel. The EU has also tried to discourage production by paying farmers not to produce food.

The costs of CAP come out of the European Agricultural Guidance and Guarantee Fund (EAGGF), which has been the single biggest item on the EU budget since it was launched in 1962 (although agricultural spending has fallen from about 85 per cent of the budget in 1970 to about 45 per cent today). The bulk of funds are spent in the Guarantee Section, which is used to buy and store surplus produce, and to encourage agricultural exports.

Box 7.2 The Common Fisheries Policy

The fishing industry in the EU employs just 0.2 per cent of the workforce, but the state of the industry has implications for coastal communities all around the EU. Disputes over fishing grounds in European waters have also led to sometimes bitter confrontation between EU partners and their neighbours. There were, for example, the infamous cod wars of the 1960s between Britain and Iceland over access to fisheries in the north Atlantic. Similarly, in 1984 French patrol boats fired on Spanish trawlers operating inside the Community's 200-mile limit, and more than two dozen Spanish trawlers were intercepted off the coast of Ireland. Spain's fishing fleet was bigger than that of the entire EC fleet at the time, and fishing rights were a major issue in Spain's negotiations to join the EC. More recently, Spanish fishing boats became an issue in domestic British politics when Eurosceptics in the Major government quoted their presence in traditional British waters as one of their many complaints about the effects of British membership of the EU.

For all these reasons, fishing has been an unusually prominent issue in policy developments in the EU, which since 1983 has pursued a Common Fisheries Policy (CFP). The main goal of this is to resolve conflicts over territorial fishing rights and to prevent overfishing by setting catch quotas. The goals of the policy are pursued in four main ways. First, all the waters within the EU's 200-mile limit have been opened up to all EU fishing boats, although member states have the right to restrict access to fishing grounds within 12 miles of their shores. Second, the CFP prevents overfishing by imposing national quotas (or Total Allowable Catches) on the take of Atlantic and North Sea fish, and by regulating fishing areas and equipment, for example by setting standards on the mesh size of fishing nets. Third, it set up a market organization to oversee prices, quality, marketing, and external trade. Finally, it guides negotiations with other countries on access to waters and the conservation of fisheries.

Most of that money goes to the producers of dairy products, cereals, oils and fats, beef, veal, and sugar. Meanwhile, the Guidance Section is one of the elements that makes up the EU's structural funds (see Chapter 5), and is used to improve agriculture by investing in new equipment and technology and helping those working in agriculture with pensions, illness benefits, and other supports.

In terms of its original goals – increasing productivity, ensuring a fair standard of living for agricultural communities, stabilizing markets, securing supplies, and protecting European farmers from the fluctuations in world market prices – CAP has been an outstanding success. European farmers are wealthier then before, and their livelihoods have become more predictable and stable. The EU is the world's largest exporter of sugar, eggs, poultry, and dairy products, and accounts for nearly 20 per cent of world food exports. Encouraged by guaranteed prices, European farmers have squeezed more and more from their land, so that production has gone up in virtually every area, and the EU is now self-sufficient in almost every product it can grow or produce in its climate (including wheat, barley, wine, meat, vegetables, and dairy products), and produces far more butter, cereals, beef and sugar than it needs. The successes cannot all be ascribed to CAP, however, because farmers have also been helped by intensification, mechanization, and the increased use of agrochemicals.

Unfortunately, CAP has also created many problems:

- EU farmers produce much more than the market can bear. All surplus production is stockpiled throughout the EU, so that there have been – in the past – warehouses full of surplus cereal, powdered milk, beef, olive oil, raisins, figs, and even manure. By the late 1990s, the stockpiles had largely disappeared, but there were warnings that rising world prices could lead to a reappearance of these stockpiles.
- There have been many examples of fraud and the abuse of CAP funds. Differences between EU prices and world prices have meant high refunds that provide an irresistible temptation for less honest farmers and – in Italy – organized crime (Grant, 1997, pp. 99–101).
- CAP has created economic dependency, because many farmers would undoubtedly go out of business if it was abandoned. Furthermore, it has pushed up the price of agricultural land, and has failed to close the income gap between rich and poor farmers. While mechanization and intensification have brought new profits to farmers in states with efficient agricultural sectors, such as Denmark, the Netherlands, and France, those in less efficient states, such as Greece, Italy, and Portugal, remain relatively poor. To make matters worse, spending on productive northern farmers eats in to the support that could be going to less productive southern farmers, undermining attempts to encourage them to stay on the land (Shackleton, 1990, pp. 38–40).
- Environmentalists have criticized the way that CAP has encouraged the increased use of chemical fertilizers and herbicides, and encouraged farmers to cut down hedges and trees and to 'reclaim' wetlands in the interests of making their farms bigger and more efficient.
- CAP has obliged consumers to pay inflated prices for food despite the agricultural surpluses. The contradictions between high prices and warehouses full of stored food has been a major source of public scepticism about the wisdom and benefits of European integration.
- The EU budget is limited to 1.27 per cent of the combined GNP of the member states, so revenues are restricted. Because nearly 45 per cent of

those revenues (nearly €44 billion in 2002) are swallowed up by agriculture, there is much less funding available for other policy areas.
- CAP has distorted world agricultural prices, soured EU relations with its major trading partners, and perpetuated the idea of a protectionist European Union.

With growing political and public pressure for change, a number of attempts have been made to reform EU agricultural policy. The first came at the end of the 1960s when rising concerns about the cost of price supports prompted the suggestion by the Commission that small farmers be encouraged to leave the land, and that farms be amalgamated into bigger and more efficient units. This was vehemently opposed by small farmers in France and Germany.

Following several other failed attempts to reform the system, Agriculture Commissioner Ray MacSharry took up the banner in 1991, warning of the rising volume of stored agricultural produce. He proposed moving away from guaranteed prices, reducing subsidies on grain, beef, and butter, and encouraging farmers to take land out of production. Despite the opposition of many farmers and their unions, the Agriculture Council finally approved the proposals in May 1992 after 18 months of talks. Although they initially made CAP more expensive than before, and led to warnings from the Court of Auditors that they increased the opportunities for fraudulent claims, the changes promised to lead to a medium-term reduction in surpluses, lower food prices for consumers, and – over the longer term – a better use of the money spent on CAP.

In recent years, food surpluses have fallen, farm incomes have risen, and the rise in world cereal prices has helped negate the effects for farmers of CAP price cuts. Proposals were introduced in 1998 by agriculture Commissioner Franz Fischler for price cuts on cereals, beef and milk, for more arable land to be set aside, for more environmental management conditions to be attached to payments to farmers, and for more investment in rural development generally. These would continue to build on EU agricultural reforms as pressures grew on the EU from global trade negotiations under the auspices of the World Trade Organization. Grant argues that agricultural policy might now be considered as a policy of the past rather than of the future of the EU. It was once perhaps the only example of a 'working' Community policy in the sense that it influenced decisions taken by farmers, but its share of the EU budget has fallen as Europe has focused more on other policy areas (Grant 1997, p. 2). However, while it has certainly slipped down the list of media and public concerns in the EU, this does not mean that it has gone away, and it may move back up the agenda as membership of the EU expands eastwards.

Inside the euro zone

In March 2002, after years of controversy and often difficult economic adjustment, 12 of the 15 EU member states took one of the most far-reaching steps so far in the history of integration: they abolished their separate national currencies and replaced them with the new European currency, the euro. It was a move that was a long time coming, which met considerable political resistance and caused economic problems for several member states, yet it was also understood that few barriers to the completion of the single market were so fundamental as the existence of 15 different currencies with fluctuating exchange rates. At the same time, the surrender of national currencies posed many troubling questions about sovereignty and independence, because by giving up their national currencies, the governments of the 12 countries in the euro zone were agreeing to give up control over important domestic economic policy choices, such as the ability to be able to adjust interest rates. Critics also saw the adoption of the euro as another step towards the creation of a unified system of government. Whether or not it will lead to a United States of Europe is a debatable point, but it has certainly changed the way that Europeans do business with each other.

It was understood as early as the 1950s that stable exchange rates would be an important part of the functioning of a single market. Fortunately, that stability was provided by the postwar system of fixed exchange rates. It was only when this system began to crumble in the late 1960s, and finally collapsed with the US decision in 1971 to end the link between gold and the US dollar, that monetary union – the agreement of fixed exchange rates and a single currency – began to move up the agenda of European integration. A committee headed by Luxembourg prime minister Pierre Werner met in 1969–70 to discuss the issue, and concluded that the Community should work towards adopting a single currency in stages by 1980. Community heads of government agreed, and attempts were made using a mechanism called the 'snake in the tunnel' to keep exchange rates steady against each other, and jointly against the US dollar. But international currency turbulence in the wake of the energy crises of the 1970s undermined their efforts, and by 1977 only five of the twelve Community member states were still in the scheme.

A renewed attempt to achieve exchange rate stability and keep inflation under control was made in March 1979 with the launch of the European Monetary System (EMS). An artificial currency called the European Currency Unit (ecu) was created, whose value was based on a basket of European currencies, each weighted roughly according to the size of the economies of the different member states (the deutschemark made up about 30 per cent of the ecu, the British pound about 11–15 per cent, the Italian lira about 9 per cent, and so on). Exchange rates between member states were set in ecus, and countries in the EMS undertook to make sure that those rates fluctuated by no more than 2.25 per cent either way, using a regulatory scheme know as the Exchange Rate Mechanism (ERM). Although several member states again found it difficult to keep their currencies stable relative to the ecu, the EMS contributed to exchange rate stability in the 1980s, and to the longest period of sustained economic expansion since the war. The ecu also helped accustom Europeans to the idea of a single currency.

In 1989 a plan developed under the leadership of Commission president Jacques Delors proposed another staged move towards a single currency: all member states would join the ERM, the band of exchange rate fluctuations would be narrowed and then fixed irrevocably, and the ecu would become the single currency. Despite the near-collapse of the ERM in 1992–93 – when Britain and Italy pulled out, several other countries had to devalue their currencies, and the bands of exchange rate fluctuation had to be widened to 15 per cent – the Maastricht treaty affirmed the basic principles behind the Delors plan. EU member states wanting to adopt the single currency had to meet several 'convergence criteria' that were considered essential prerequisites: a national budget deficit of less than three per cent of GDP, a public debt of less than 60 per cent of GDP, a consumer inflation rate within 1.5 per cent of the average in the three countries with the lowest rates, a long-term interest rate within 2 per cent of the average in the three countries with the lowest rates, and a record of keeping their exchange rates within approved ERM fluctuation margins for two years.

At the Madrid European Council in December 1995, EU leaders decided to call the new currency the euro, and agreed to introduce it in three stages. The first stage came in May 1998 when it was determined which countries were ready: all member states had met the budget deficit goal, but only seven member states had met the debt target, Germany and Ireland had not met the inflation reduction target, and Greece had not been able to reduce its interest rates sufficiently. Maastricht, however, included a clause that allowed countries to qualify if their debt-to-GDP ratio was 'sufficiently diminishing and approaching the reference value at a satisfactory pace'.

In the event, despite the fact that the national debt in Belgium and Italy was nearly twice the target, all but Britain, Denmark (both of which had met all four criteria), Greece and Sweden announced their intention to adopt the euro. Questions were raised in the minds of Eurosceptics about the seriousness with which member states were approaching the convergence criteria, the wisdom of which had already been questioned by many

Box 7.3   The European Central Bank

Although it has – until recently – been one of the least known of the EU institutions, the ECB will play an increasingly important role in the lives of Europeans now that the euro has replaced most national currencies. As it has become increasingly involved in the direction of European monetary policy, however, worrying questions have been raised about its powers, and about the lack of effective checks on those powers.

First proposed in 1988, the framework of the bank was described in the Maastricht treaty. It was founded in 1994 as the European Monetary Institute (EMI), and it was finally established in June 1998 as the European Central Bank. Based in Frankfurt, its main job is to ensure monetary stability by setting interest rates in the euro zone. It has a governing body consisting of the central bank governors from each participating state, and a six-member full-time executive board. Directors serve non-renewable terms of eight years and can only be removed by their peers or by an order from the European Court of Justice. The Bank also has links to non-participating countries through a general council composed of the central bank governors of all EU member states. A new exchange rate mechanism (ERM II) links the euro with the national currencies of non-participating countries, and the ECB is allowed to take action to support non-participating countries so long as this does not conflict with its primary task of maintaining monetary stability among participating countries.

Concerned about the need to convince the sceptical German public that the new European currency would be as strong as the deutschemark (Daltrop 1987, pp. 175–176), Helmut Kohl insisted that the ECB should be an almost direct copy of the famously independent German Bundesbank. In fact, it makes the Bundesbank seem quite restricted by comparison, and was by 1998 already being described as 'the most powerful single monetary authority in the world' (*European Voice*, April 1998). Neither national nor EU leaders are allowed to try to influence the bank, its board, or its constituent national central banks, and the only body that can play any kind of watchdog role over the bank is the monetary subcommittee of the European Parliament, but it so far lacks the resources to be able to hold the Bank or its president – Wim Duisenberg of the Netherlands – particularly accountable. This makes it very different from the United States Federal Reserve, whose chairman is regularly brought to account for its policies before the banking committee of the US Senate.

economists. There were also concerns about the extent to which efforts by governments to meet the criteria had contributed to economic problems in several EU states (notably Germany), and therefore about the strength of the foundations upon which the euro was built.

The second stage came in 1 January 1999 when the euro was officially launched, participating countries fixed their exchange rates, and the new European Central Bank began overseeing the single monetary policy. All its dealings with commercial banks and all its foreign exchange activities were subsequently transacted in euros, which was quoted against the yen and the US dollar. Pause for thought was provided in September 2000 when, in a national referendum, Danes voted against their country adopting the euro. Polls also showed that a majority of Swedes were against adoption, and in Britain found opposition running at three to one. Concerns also arose when the value of the euro against other currencies fell steadily; its value against the US dollar fell from $1.17 to as low as 85 cents. Nonetheless, plans for the transition proceeded, with the printing of 14.5 billion euro banknotes and the minting of 56 billion coins. In January 2001 Greece became the twelfth member state to join the euro zone, having met the targets for reduced inflation and budget deficits.

The final stage began on 1 January 2002, when euro coins and notes became available. The original plan had been for the euro and national currencies to be in concurrent circulation for six months, but it was subsequently decided that Europeans were to be given just two months to make the final transition from national currencies to the euro, and national currencies ceased to be legal tender in the euro zone on 1 March 2002. After centuries of fiscal independence, the 12 members of the euro zone made the final irrevocable step to abolish their national currencies, and deutschmarks, drachmas, escudos, francs, guilders, lire, marks, pesetas, punts and schillings faded into history. The only question that remains now is if and when Britain, Denmark and Sweden will join.

It is still too early to be sure what effect the adoption of the euro will have on European integration. The opinions both of European citizens and of their governments are divided about its implications, and it is probably safe to say that no one chapter in the history of European integration has been approached with so many doubts remaining. It raises questions about the long-term economic effects for Europe, few of which are fully understood, even by economists. The potential benefits include the following:

1. Instead of having to change currencies when they travel from one country to another, and paying for goods and services with unfamiliar banknotes and coins, travellers now use the same currency wherever they go in the euro zone, making them more aware of being part of the common enterprise of integration.

2. There are fewer bureaucratic barriers to the transfer of large sums of money across borders, and businesses no longer have to spend time and money changing currency. This saves everyone transaction costs.
3. Backed by the credibility of the large European market, the euro should be more stable against speculation than the individual currencies of EU member states. Currency instability within the euro zone should decline, as should instability relative to outside currencies. This will help exporters project future markets with greater confidence, promoting economic growth.
4. The stock and bond markets in the euro zone will likely continue their tendency to unify, and investors, instead of focusing on their home markets alone, will become used to the idea of a European stock market.
5. The spread of German-style fiscal responsibility should help lower interest rates across the EU, which should help build the international credibility of the euro. Many European leaders hope and believe that it will become a world class currency in the same league as the US dollar and the Japanese yen. If this happens, the EU will have more power to influence global economic policy, rather than having to react to developments in the US and Japan.
6. Greater price transparency is now available, because instead of costs being expressed in different currencies from one country to another, they are all expressed in euros, and consumers can make easy comparisons. This should promote competition as businesses try to make their goods and services available at similar prices throughout the single market.

At the same time, the adoption of the euro is a gamble. Never before has a group of sovereign states with a long history of independence tried combining their currencies into one on a similar scale, and the risks are significantly greater than those involved in completing the single market. Furthermore, all the key preparatory decisions about the euro were taken by European national leaders with little or no regard to public opinion, which was often hostile to the idea, and uncertain about the implications. The potential costs of the euro include the following:

1. Different countries have different economic cycles, and separate currencies allow them to devalue, borrow, adjust interest rates, and take other measures in response to changed economic circumstances. Such flexibility is no longer available in the euro zone, because the European Central Bank cannot follow different fiscal policies for different parts of the EU. The members of the euro zone will have to sink or swim together.

2. Some economists were concerned about the underlying weaknesses in EU economies in 1997–98, and raised questions about the extent to which figures relating to the convergence criteria were being fudged to allow countries that had not met those criteria to take part. Some feared that these weaknesses could result in a high-credibility deutsche-mark being replaced with a low-credibility euro, undermining economic health throughout the EU. The most sceptical doubted that all the countries that adopted the euro would be able to keep within the ERM, and that some might find their domestic economic problems forcing them to fall by the wayside before 2002. This did not happen, but at what costs was it avoided, and just how strong are the foundations of the euro?

3. Unless Europeans learn each other's languages and are able to move freely in search of jobs, the euro could perpetuate the pockets of poverty and wealth that already exist across the EU, thereby interfering with the development of the single market. Having a common currency in a country as big as the United States works mainly because people can move freely; this is not true of the EU, where there are still physical, fiscal, technical and social barriers to movement.

One of the principal motives behind European integration has been the argument that Europe must create the conditions in which it can meet external economic threats without being undermined by internal divisions. For many, the adoption of the euro represents the crowning achievement of exactly fifty year's-worth of effort (1952–2002) aimed at removing the barriers to trade among Europeans and the construction of a single market that will allow Europe to compete on the global stage from a position of strength. It has been argued that European monetary integration has been driven in large part by external forces and the pressures of an international monetary system dominated by the US dollar (Loedel, 1998). While its effects on the domestic economies of Europe are debatable, there is little question that the adoption of the euro has made the EU a substantial new actor in that international system.

Conclusions

Although the work of the European Union has been driven most obviously by economic factors – and particularly by the goal of free trade in a single market – European leaders have found, through neofunctionalist logic, that economic integration has had a spillover effect on many other policy areas. Most notably, they have found that completion of the single market was a much more complex notion than originally expected. The primary objective of the single market was the removal of tariffs and non-tariff barriers to trade, but behind that seemingly harmless term – non-tariff barriers – lay a multitude of problems, handicaps, and obstacles.

Among other things, economic integration has meant removing cross-border checks on people and goods, controlling the movement of drugs and terrorists, agreeing standard levels of indirect taxation, harmonizing technical standards on thousands of goods and services, agreeing regulations in the interests of consumer safety, reaching agreement on professional qualifications, allowing Europeans to take capital and pensions with them when they move to another country, opening up the European market for joint ventures and corporate mergers, developing trans-European transport and energy supply networks, providing the means by which Europeans can communicate with each other electronically, developing common approaches to working conditions, establishing common European environmental standards, promoting the development of poorer rural and urban areas in order to avoid trade distortions, and creating an equitable and efficient agricultural sector.

In a sense, however, everything that was agreed during the 1960s, the 1970s, and the 1980s – the thousands of decisions taken by prime ministers, chancellors, presidents, ministers, and European bureaucrats, and the thousands of directives, regulations, and decisions developed and agreed by the different EU institutions – was simply a prelude to the biggest project of all, the conversion to a single currency. In March 2002, 12 of the 15 member states abolished their national currencies and adopted the euro, while 3 – Britain, Denmark, and Sweden – opted to remain out, at least temporarily. Many questions remained about the wisdom of the positions taken both by the champions and the opponents. Have the former been too hasty in their decision to press on, regardless of their domestic economic problems? Are Britain and Denmark being wisely cautious or typically Eurosceptic in their decisions to wait and see? Will the adoption of the euro prove to be a disruptive step too far, or one of the most far-sighted and creative decisions ever taken by Europe's leaders?

Whatever happens over the next few years, the single market has had widespread and irreversible implications for everyone living in the European Union, and for all the EU's trading partners. It has helped create new wealth and opportunity, has brought down many of the economic barriers that have for decades divided Europeans, and has paved the way for the creation of trans-European economic ties that have reduced national differences and promoted the idea of Europe as a powerful new actor on the world stage.

Chapter 8

The EU and the World

Building a European foreign policy
Towards a European defence policy
Europe as an economic superpower
Relations with the United States
Relations with eastern Europe
Development cooperation
Conclusions

> *[Western Europe is] largely an American protectorate, with its allied*
> *states reminiscent of ancient vassals and tributaries.*
>   Zbigniew Brzezinski, former US national security adviser, 1997

The world does not know what to make of the European Union, mainly
because the European Union does not know what to make of itself. The
key actors in international relations are states and international
organizations, but the EU is neither one nor the other – and yet it has
elements of both. Under the circumstances, how are non-member
governments to think of the EU? Should they relate to the 15 member
states separately, or should they work with the European Union as a
whole?

The answer depends on the issue at stake, because the EU presents
multiple personalities to the rest of the world. When trade negotiations are
on the agenda, outside parties must deal with the EU as a whole, because
the member states usually allow the Commission to represent their
collective interests. But on defence and security issues, the member states
often go their own ways. The lack of focus, the long-time absence of
leadership on foreign policy, and the frustration felt by other countries was
neatly summed up in a question once posed by former US Secretary of
State Henry Kissinger: 'When I want to speak to Europe, whom do I call?'
The problem was resolved to some extent in 1999, when a single external
relations portfolio was created in the Commission, and a High Representative was appointed who would be the first point of contact on issues of
common foreign and security policy.

If the EU were a military union, its combined armed forces would make
it one of the two biggest powers on earth. But it does not yet have a

common defence policy, and its armed forces are divided among countries with often different priorities and capabilities. This became particularly obvious during the 1991 Gulf War and the crises in Iraq in 1998, when member states adopted different policy positions. It has also been obvious in the varied responses to problems in the Balkans, from Bosnia in the early 1990s to Kosovo in 1998 and Macedonia in 2001. The seeds of a common defence force have been planted in the Eurocorps, founded by France and Germany in 1992, but much remains to be done before the EU can present a common face to the world on security matters.

In contrast, few doubts remain about the status of the European Union as an economic superpower, or about its dominant role in global trade negotiations. It is home to a growing number of world-leading corporations, and is the world's biggest and richest marketplace, with 375 million consumers, more than 28 per cent of global GDP, 36 per cent of imports, and 38 per cent of exports. Its influence over the global economy will presumably grow even further as the euro takes root, because the US dollar and the Japanese yen will face some formidable competition, and there will be greater coordination within the euro zone on economic policy.

Europe may have been unprepared for the crises in the Gulf and the Balkans, lacking both political unanimity and military preparedness, but there has been progress on the development of common foreign policies. As Christopher Hill put it in 1992 (pp. 135–6), setbacks have produced renewed efforts at policy cooperation, which has followed a path of 'peaks and troughs along a gradual upward gradient . . . (and) consensus has become more habit-forming'. This chapter looks at the reasons for those peaks and troughs, and at how the role of the EU as an actor on the global stage has changed. It shows how European integration has moved beyond economic issues, and how western Europe – once a bystander in the Cold War – now exerts a new and potent influence over world affairs.

Building a European foreign policy

The development of a common European foreign policy has always been one of those issues – like the single currency – that Eurosceptics believe will lead inexorably to the surrender of national sovereignty and the creation of a European federation. In their attempts to work together, EU leaders have thus found themselves being pulled in two directions. On the one hand it is clear that the member states will have more power and influence in the world if they act as a group rather than independently. On the other hand there is the fear that coordination will interfere with the freedom of member states to address matters of national rather than of European interest. The tension between these two views has interfered from the beginning with attempts to build common policy positions, let alone a common foreign policy.

The Treaties of Rome make no mention of foreign policy, and the EEC long focused on domestic economic policy, although the logic of spillover implied that the development of the single market would make it increasingly difficult to avoid developing common external policies. There were several abortive moves in that direction in the early years of integration, including the European Defence Community (EDC) and the European Political Community, and Charles de Gaulle's plans for regular meetings among the leaders of the Six to coordinate foreign policy. The EDC was proposed in 1950, was pursued most actively by the French, and was to have been built on the foundations of a common European army and a European 'minister of defence'. However Britain was opposed to the idea, preferring to pursue the goals of the Treaty of Brussels (see below) and to bring Italy and West Germany into the fold. All prospects of an EDC finally died in 1954 when the French National Assembly turned it down (Urwin, 1995, pp. 60–8).

European integration subsequently focused on building the single market, and it was only at the 1969 Hague summit that Community leaders decided to look again at foreign policy. They agreed in 1970 to promote European Political Cooperation (EPC), a process in which the six foreign ministers would meet to discuss and coordinate foreign policy positions. However, EPC was not incorporated into the founding treaties. It remained a loose and voluntary arrangement outside the Community, no laws were adopted on foreign policy, each of the member states could still act independently, most of the key decisions on foreign policy had to be unanimous, and no new institutions were to be created, although the European Council was launched in 1974 in part to bring leaders of the member states together to coordinate policies.

The need to develop common positions was helped by the creation in 1975 of the Conference on Security and Cooperation in Europe (CSCE), a trans-European security body with members from western and eastern Europe. Although Community member states acted as a group in the CSCE, and subsequently consulted with each other on virtually every aspect of foreign policy, they were reluctant to give up too many of their independent powers. Nevertheless, EPC was given formal recognition with the Single European Act, which confirmed that the member states would 'endeavour jointly to formulate and implement a European foreign policy'. (In 1994, the CSCE became the Organization for Security and Cooperation in Europe.)

The EPC process was strictly intergovernmental, and was overseen by the foreign ministers meeting as the Council of Ministers, with overall leadership coming from the European Council. Regular meetings of senior

Box 8.1 The EU on the world stage

How does the EU fit in to the global system? It can adopt laws that are binding on its member states, but can it also negotiate with third parties on behalf of the member states, and enter into binding agreements with those parties? The answer depends on where one looks.

The Treaty of Rome included a Common Commercial Policy for the Community, which gave the Commission the authority to negotiate with third parties, and the power to make recommendations to the Council of Ministers on agreements with third parties generally. It also allowed the Council to authorize the Commission to open and conduct the necessary negotiations. But there were questions about the policy areas to which this applied, and it took a 1971 case before the Court of Justice (*Commission* v. *Council (AETR)*) to clarify matters.

The immediate issue was a dispute between the Commission and the Council over an international agreement on road transport. The Commission claimed that it had competence, because the power to develop a common transport policy included the right to reach agreements with third parties. The Council disagreed, arguing that the Treaty of Rome only allowed the Commission to reach such agreements in areas specifically listed in the treaty. The Court sided with the Commission, arguing that there were implied powers for the Commission to conclude treaties with third parties in areas which may flow from 'other provisions of the Treaty and from measures adopted . . . by the Community institutions'. In other words, the Court concluded that whenever the Community adopted common rules in a particular area, the member states no longer had the right – individually or collectively – to enter into agreements with third parties that affected those rules: 'as and when those rules come into being, the Community alone is in a position to assume and carry out contractual obligations with third countries affecting the whole sphere of application of the Community legal system'.

The result was that in policy areas within which the EU has sole authority, or a large measure of authority, the Commission can sign an international agreement without the member states also signing. These areas include the Common Agricultural Policy, the Common Commercial Policy, competition, and common policies on fisheries and air transport. In such cases, the EU has only one vote. Conversely, in policy areas where the EU has little or no competence – including criminal justice, education, and taxation – the member states alone have the power to sign, in which case they have 15 independent votes. However, because there are political and practical difficulties in defining the boundaries between domestic and external policy, and between economic and non-economic policy, authority is sometimes shared, and the result is what are called 'mixed agreements': they are signed both by the EU and the member states (Smith, 1997).

officials from all the foreign ministries provided continuity, and a small secretariat was set up in Brussels to help the country holding the presidency of the Council of Ministers, which provided most of the momentum. Larger or more active states such as Britain and France had few problems providing leadership, but policy coordination put a strain on smaller and/or neutral countries such as Luxembourg and Ireland. The shifting of responsibilities every six months gave each member state its turn at the helm, but complicated life for non-Community states, which had to switch their attention from one member state to another, and to establish contacts with ministers and bureaucrats in six, then nine, then 12 capital cities.

The Gulf War of 1990–91 proved to be a turning point. Following the August 1990 Iraqi invasion of Kuwait, the United States orchestrated a multinational campaign involving 13 countries in the defence of Saudi Arabia, a six-week air war against Iraq, and a four-day ground war in February 1991. In contrast to the relatively decisive stance of the Americans, Community states responded very differently to the crisis (van Eekelen, 1990; Anderson, 1992):

- Britain was strongly in favour of using force, and placed a substantial military contingent under US operational command. France also made a large military commitment, but put more emphasis on diplomatic resolution in order to maintain good relations with Arab oil producers and protect its weapons markets.
- Germany was constrained by a strong postwar tradition of pacifism and constitutional limits on the deployment of the German troops.
- Out of fear of retribution, Belgium refused to sell ammunition to Britain and, along with Spain and Portugal, refused to allow its naval vessels to be involved in anything other than minesweeping or enforcing the blockade of Iraq. Ireland, meanwhile, maintained its neutrality.

For the Luxembourg foreign minister the Community's response underlined 'the political insignificance of Europe'. For the Belgian foreign minister, it showed that the EC was 'an economic giant, a political dwarf, and a military worm' (*New York Times*, 25 January 1991). More significantly, the divisions over the Gulf War – coupled with the dramatic changes then taking place in eastern Europe and the former USSR – underlined the need for Europe to address its foreign policy more forcefully, and political pressure began to grow for a review of EPC. Commission President Jacques Delors noted that while the member states had taken a firm line against Iraq on sanctions, once it became obvious that the situation would have to be resolved by force, the EC realized that it had neither the institutional machinery nor the military force to allow it to act as one (Delors, 1991).

Integrationist states now began to press for the use of qualified majority voting on foreign policy issues, and for new emphasis to be placed on the development of a common defence policy. The result was the decision under Maastricht to replace the EPC with a Common Foreign and Security Policy (CFSP), which became one of the three pillars that now make up the European Union. Despite the new label, the goals of the CFSP are only very loosely defined, with vague talk about the need to safeguard 'common values' and 'fundamental interests', 'to preserve peace and strengthen international security', and to 'promote international cooperation', and there has been little real change in the practice of European foreign policy. Smith (1998) identifies just four differences between EPC and the CFSP: the CFSP represents a stronger commitment to common policies, joint action can be initiated and/or implemented by qualified majority voting in the Council (although unanimity is the norm), security issues are fully included in the CFSP, and the CFSP is part of the institutional structure of the EU.

The record since Maastricht has been mixed. On the one hand there has been a steady convergence of positions among the member states on key international issues, helped by the fact that their ambassadors to the United Nations meet every week to coordinate policy, and the EU states mainly vote together on resolutions in the Security Council, where the EU – through Britain and France – holds two of the five permanent seats. Among the results have been a number of 'joint actions', such as transporting humanitarian aid to Bosnia and sending observers to elections in Russia and South Africa, 'common positions' on EU relations with other countries, and the rapid expression of support for the United States and for anti-terrorist operations following the attacks in New York City and Washington DC in September 2001. The EU has also flexed its economic muscle to political ends, for example becoming embroiled in several trade disputes with the United States in the late 1990s (see below).

The EU also coordinates Western aid to eastern Europe, Russia and the former Soviet republics, has become a major supplier of aid to developing countries, and has been a magnet for foreign investment from the United States and Japan. The president of the European Commission attends meetings of the G8 alongside the leaders of Russia and the seven most industrialized countries, four of which are EU member states. The significance of the EU as an actor on the global stage is also reflected in the fact that almost every country in the world now has diplomatic representation in Brussels (both for Belgium and for the EU), and that the Commission has opened more than 130 overseas delegations.

On the other hand there are many examples of weakness and division, including the failure of the EU to broker peace in Bosnia (a job subsequently completed under US leadership), and its failure to act on a 1996 dispute between Greece and Turkey over an uninhabited Aegean island, which prompted Richard Holbrooke, the US assistant secretary of state for European affairs, to accuse the EU of 'literally sleeping through the night'. Perhaps the most serious recent example of EU hesitancy was its feeble response in 1998–99 to the crisis in the Yugoslav province of Kosovo. When ethnic Albanians in Kosovo began agitating in mid-1998 for independence from Serb-dominated Yugoslavia, the government of Slobodan Milosevic responded with force, and by August 1998 there was a massive refugee problem, and growing reports of massacres of both Kosovars and Muslims. The West's initial position on the conflict seemed to be aimed at discouraging separatism rather than stopping the violence, and the Milosevic government took this as a signal to continue its offensive. When the military response eventually came, in March 1999, it was led not by the EU, but by the United States under the auspices of NATO.

The problems have in part been a consequence of weaknesses in the institutional machinery of the EU. For example, while the Commission carries out trade negotiations on behalf of the EU as a whole, discussions on the CFSP rest more firmly with the Council of Ministers, and are thus more intergovernmental. Changes made to the CFSP by the Treaty of Amsterdam were designed to respond to such problems. As well as opening the possibility of limited majority voting on foreign policy issues, the rotation of countries holding the presidency of the EU was changed; this was previously arranged in alphabetical order by the name of each member state in its national language, but it is now arranged so that large member states alternate with small ones, thereby more effectively balancing the leadership of large and small states.

Amsterdam also brought institutional changes. First, a Policy Planning and Early Warning Unit (PPEWU) was set up in Brussels to help the EU anticipate foreign crises. It consists of 20 members: one each from the member states, the Western European Union and the European Commission, and three from the Council of Ministers. Second, the old habit of having four different regional external affairs portfolios in the European Commission was replaced with the creation of a single foreign policy post and the appointment of a High Representative on foreign policy; the first office-holder was Javier Solana, former secretary-general of NATO.

Ironically, while the leaders of the member states have had difficulty reaching common positions, and are divided on the idea of relinquishing more powers over foreign policy to the EU institutions, there is widespread public support for the idea of common European foreign and defence policies. Eurobarometer polls have found that about 68–75 per cent of Europeans favour a common defence policy, and 63–69 per cent favour a common foreign policy. Italians generally show the most enthusiasm (as high as 74 per cent in favour and only 11 per cent against), about two-thirds of Germans, French, Dutch and Belgians are in favour, and there is even strong support in neutral Ireland (more than half in favour and only about one-fifth against). Among the British, about half are in favour and about one-third are against.

Towards a European defence policy

The credibility of the EU on the world stage will continue to be handicapped until it has the ability to back up its words with military action. Together the 15 member states constitute a formidable military power: they have more than two million troops, 22 000 tanks, 21 000 artillery pieces and 6300 combat aircraft, and between them account for 85–95 per cent of the military capacity of western Europe. Britain and France are both nuclear powers, and the European corporate world includes some of the biggest arms manufacturers in the world, such as British Aerospace, Matra-Défense of France, and Finmeccanica of Italy. However, European governments tend to have independent opinions and priorities when it comes to committing their forces, there is still only limited coordination on policy, and progress on setting up a European defence force has been slow.

The fundamental problem lies in a philosophical division between Atlanticists such as Britain, the Netherlands and Portugal, which emphasize the importance of continuing the security relationship with the United States, and Europeanists such as France, Italy, Spain and sometimes Germany, which look more towards European independence. During the Cold War (1945–91), Atlanticists had the upper hand as defence was pushed down the agenda of European integration by the emphasis on economic policies, the failure of the European Defence Community, and the fact that the main defence issue was security against a Soviet attack, something that fell squarely under the remit of the US-dominated North Atlantic Treaty Organization (NATO). Furthermore, member states had different policy positions and different defence capacities: the British and the French had special interests in their colonies and former colonies, the Germans and the Dutch saw their armed forces as part of the broader NATO system, and several countries – notably Ireland – were neutral. Nevertheless the Europeans became used to coordinating their defence policies within the NATO framework, guided by US leadership.

Europeanists appeared to gain ground in the late 1990s in the wake of changes in US policy. President Kennedy had spoken during his inauguration of the willingness of the United States to 'bear any burden' and 'meet any hardship . . . to assure the survival and success of liberty', but post-Cold War American public opinion turned against such an idea, and the term 'burden sharing' became more common in transatlantic discussions, with demands for the EU to take on greater responsibility for addressing its own security threats. There were also signs that the US, particularly under the administration of George W. Bush, was more inclined to take positions at odds with its European allies. Meanwhile, the ability of the EU to respond to security threats was clearly inadequate, a problem that has become more critical over the last ten years as US defence expenditure has fallen (Barber, 1998).

The terrorist attacks on the World Trade Center in New York and on the Pentagon in Washington DC in September 2001 brought new issues into the equation. The meaning of 'war' and 'defence' had already been changing, but the attacks, and the response to the attacks, brought new elements into the consideration of defence policy on both sides of the Atlantic: terrorism (especially when it involved suicide attacks) could not be met with conventional military responses, it transcended national borders and was not a problem that could be resolved by interstate conflict, and it showed that the United States still needed the help of the Europeans for intelligence-gathering, diplomatic ventures, and bases from which to launch military responses. While the EU does not have the capacity to launch conventional military operations, the nature of terrorism suggests that it will need to look in new directions to define the future of its defence and security policies. It is difficult to see how this will be done without working in close cooperation with the United States.

Maastricht stated that one of the goals of the EU should be 'to assert its identity on the international scene, in particular through the implementation of a common foreign and security policy including the eventual framing of a common defence policy'. But while the CFSP moved defence more squarely onto the EU agenda, Maastricht provided a loophole that could be used to slow down the development of common defence policy: it committed member states to defining and implementing a common policy that 'shall include all questions related to the security of the Union, including the *eventual* framing of a common defence policy, *which might in time* lead to a common defence' (emphasis added).

There are two critical elements missing from the development of a European defence capability. First, there is no common defence policy. Nothing illustrates this quite so clearly as the independent stance taken by France over the years. Since withdrawing its forces from the integrated NATO military command in 1966, France has more often preferred to go its own way than cooperate with either NATO or its European partners. Driven by a combination of its concern about US influence in Europe through NATO, and its own political marginalization, it has adopted policy positions that have often run counter to those of its neighbours, and of the EU as a whole. For example, it tried to prevent the creation of a new consultative council bringing together NATO countries and former Warsaw Pact members, it refused to place its warships under NATO command during the UN blockade of Serbia and Montenegro in 1993–96, it has pursued its own independent interests in its former African colonies, and it unilaterally resumed nuclear testing in the Pacific in 1995.

Second, Europe lacks the necessary institutional machinery to manage a defence capability. The growing sense that the Europeans should be taking care of their own security, independently of NATO, led to the revival in the 1990s of the Western European Union (WEU). The WEU traced its roots back to the Brussels Treaty for collective self-defence, signed in 1948 by Britain, France and the Benelux countries, which created the Western Union. It was quickly sidetracked by the 1949 treaty creating NATO, and the Western Union's defence functions were shifted to NATO so as to avoid duplication of effort. The Brussels Treaty remained in force, however, and the Western Union became the WEU in 1954 when Germany and Italy joined. Its political objective was to help Germany contribute to the defence of western Europe without taking part in the kind of European army envisioned by the European Defence Community. NATO was clearly the major actor in European defence, however, and it was only in 1984, following the failure of a plan to give EPC a security dimension (van Eekelen, 1990), that the WEU was reactivated.

The WEU passed its first modest test in 1987–90 when it coordinated minesweeping by its members in the Persian Gulf during the Iran–Iraq War, but the 1990–91 Gulf War stretched it beyond its limits. Coincidentally, the end of the Cold War brought a redefinition of NATO's role and of the US attitude towards the defence of western Europe. In 1991, NATO ministers welcomed the development of the CFSP and the reinforced role of the WEU as 'the defence component of the process of European unification and as a means of strengthening the European pillar of [NATO]'.

In June 1992, the WEU foreign and defence ministers – meeting at Petersberg, near Bonn – issued a declaration outlining the responsibilities of the WEU. Under the 'Petersberg tasks', military units from member states, acting under the authority of the WEU, could be used for humanitarian, rescue, peacekeeping and other crisis management jobs, including peacemaking, in cooperation with the OSCE and the UN Security Council. Thus the WEU worked with NATO in monitoring the UN embargo on Serbia and Montenegro, helped set up a unified Croat–Muslim police force to support the administration of the city of Mostar in Bosnia in 1994–96, and helped restructure and train the Albanian police force in 1997.

With its membership expanding and the acknowledgement under the terms of Maastricht that it was 'an integral part of the development of the [EU]', the WEU underwent a substantial overhaul. In order to improve liaison with NATO, the WEU secretariat was moved from London to Brussels in January 1993. In 1997, the Amsterdam treaty resulted in closer association between the WEU and the EU, and the Petersberg tasks were incorporated into the EU treaties. That same year, Tony Blair became prime minister of Britain and signalled his willingness to see Britain play a more central role in EU defence matters. In December 1998, Britain and France issued a joint statement after a meeting in St. Malo declaring that the EU needed to be in a position to play a full role in international affairs, to which end the EU 'must have the capacity for autonomous action,

Box 8.2 Prospects for a European army

Although there was talk of the construction of a European army as long ago as the late 1940s and early 1950s, when the idea was mooted in Germany and France, it is only over the last decade that practical steps have been taken to set up experimental European military units. Known collectively as the Forces Answerable to WEU (FAWEU), they include a British–Dutch amphibious force and two bodies consisting of personnel from France, Italy, Spain and Portugal: a 20 000-strong Rapid Deployment Force (EUROFOR) head-quartered in Florence and designed for humanitarian or peacekeeping operations in the Mediterranean area, and a non-permanent European Maritime Force (EUROMARFOR).

The most likely foundation for a European army, though, may be Eurocorps, created in May 1992 by Germany and France to replace an experimental Franco–German brigade set up in 1990. Headquartered in Strasbourg, the 60 000-member Eurocorps has been operational since November 1995 and has been joined by contingents from Belgium, Luxembourg and Spain. It was conceived as a step towards the development of a European army that would give substance to the Common Foreign and Security Policy, give the EU an independent defence capability, and provide insurance should the United States decide to withdraw its forces from Europe.

Germany insists that the Eurocorps would complement NATO, and that it would be placed under NATO 'operational command' in the event of a threat to western European security, but Britain, the Netherlands and the United States suspect that France's objective – as it has been since the time of de Gaulle – is to displace the US dominance of NATO. Britain preferred that the Eurocorps operate under the auspices of the WEU, while France preferred to see the WEU and Eurocorps as the basis of an EU defence wing, and for the WEU eventually to merge with the EU. The latter view eventually won the day.

backed up by credible military forces, the means to decide to use them and a readiness to do so'.

WEU resources were steadily merged into the EU, and the European Council in December 1999 agreed that by the year 2003, the EU should be able – at 60 days notice – to deploy and sustain forces capable of carrying out the Petersberg tasks. It also agreed to establish the political and military committees needed to make this possible. The WEU was seen as a staging post in the process of the EU taking greater responsibility for its own security; by 2002 virtually all its responsibilities had been merged into the EU. However, while an embryonic EU defence force exists in the form of the Eurocorps and the various other specialist units that answer to the WEU (Box 8.2), and while the quote by Zbigniew Brzezinski at the beginning of this chapter may be an overstatement, much work remains to be done before the EU has a meaningful and effective security capability.

Europe as an economic superpower

While the prospects of the EU becoming a major military power are uncertain, there are no doubts at all about its new status as an economic superpower. The common external tariff is in place, the single market is complete, most of the member states have adopted a single currency, the Commission has powers to represent the governments of all the member states in negotiations on global trade, and it is now well understood by everyone that the EU is the most powerful actor in those negotiations. There has also been rapid economic growth in most parts of the EU over the last twenty years, with even some of the poorer parts catching up as a result of the opportunities opened up by the single market and investments made under the structural funds.

The figures paint a very clear picture of the EU's economic power:

- It is the world's largest economic bloc. With just 6.3 per cent of the world's population, it accounts for 28.3 per cent of global GDP (Table 8.1).
- It is the world's biggest trader, accounting for more than 38 per cent of world exports by value, twice as much as NAFTA and five times as much as Japan (Figure 8.1). Six of the EU member states rank among the world's dozen largest importers and exporters.
- With a population of more than 375 million, the EU is the biggest market in the industrialized world, and one of the most open. Just as multinational corporations have found it essential since the Second World War to sell to the US market in order to maximize their profits, so the European market is becoming increasingly important, and more

Table 8.1   *The EU in the global economy*

	Population (million)	% share of world population	GDP ($US billion)	% share of world GDP
Germany	82.1	1.4	2112	7.0
UK	59.5	1.0	1441	4.8
France	58.6	1.0	1432	4.8
Italy	57.6	1.0	1171	3.9
Spain	39.4	0.7	596	2.0
Netherlands	15.8	0.3	394	1.3
Belgium	10.2	0.2	248	0.8
Sweden	8.9	0.1	239	0.8
Austria	8.1	0.1	208	0.7
Denmark	5.3	0.09	174	0.6
Finland	5.2	0.09	130	0.4
Greece	10.5	0.2	125	0.4
Portugal	10.0	0.2	114	0.4
Ireland	3.7	0.06	93	0.3
Luxembourg	0.4	0.006	20	0.07
EU total	*375.3*	*6.27*	*8497*	*28.3*
United States	278.2	4.7	9152	30.5
Canada	30.5	0.5	635	2.1
Mexico	97.0	1.6	429	1.4
NAFTA total	*405.7*	*6.8*	*10216*	*34.0*
Japan	126.6	2.2	4347	14.5
China	1253.6	20.1	989	3.3
Russia	146.2	2.4	401	1.3
WORLD total	*5978.0*	*100.00*	*29995*	*100.00*

Source: Population and GDP figures from World Development Indicators Database, World Bank Web site 2001, http://www.worldbank.com. All figures are for 1999.

accessible thanks to the completion of the single market and adoption of the euro.

- One-third of the corporations in the Fortune 100 list of the world's largest industrial corporations in 2000 were European – mainly German, French, British, Italian and Dutch. They included DaimlerChrysler, Royal Dutch/Shell, BP Amoco, Volkswagen, Siemens, Fiat and TotalFinaElf.

Figure 8.1   *The EU share of world trade*

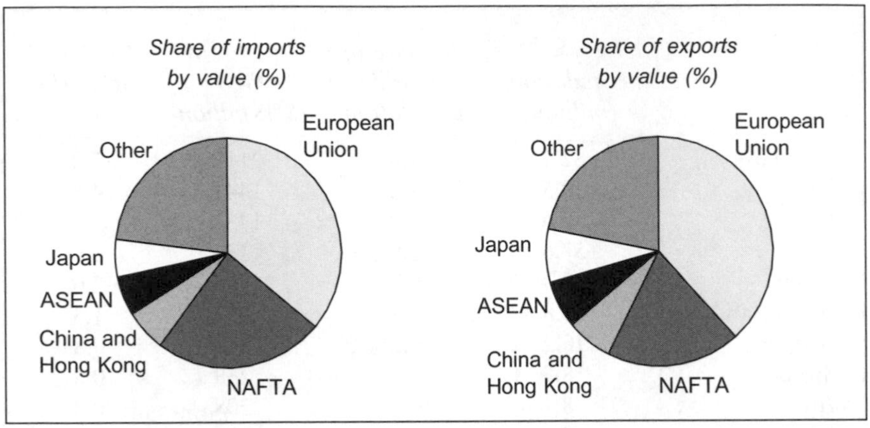

Source: World Trade Organization Web site, 2001, http://www.wto.org. All figures are for 1999.

The removal of trade restrictions and the lowering of customs barriers has been a goal of the EU since the Treaty of Rome. This treaty outlined a Common Commercial Policy (CCP), stating that the Community would contribute 'to the harmonious development of world trade, the progressive abolition of restrictions on international trade, and the lowering of customs barriers'. To this end the EU has built a complex network of multilateral and bilateral trading networks and agreements, some based on proximity (agreements with eastern Europe and Mediterranean states), some on former colonial ties (see the section on development cooperation below) and some on expediency (agreements with the United States and Japan).

The economic power of the EU has been helped by an institutional structure that promotes common positions among the member states. The Council of Ministers is responsible for making the final decisions, but it uses qualified majority voting, and the Commission plays an active role at every level. The latter generates policy initiatives, is responsible for investigating and taking action against unfair trading practices, and makes suggestions to the Council of Ministers when it thinks that agreements need to be negotiated with other countries or international organizations. Most importantly, once the member states have agreed a position among themselves, they leave it up to the Commission to negotiate almost all external trade agreements on behalf of the EU as a whole. So if anyone were to ask to whom they should speak in Europe regarding trade matters, the answer would be clear.

The central issue in international trade is the extent to which states take action to protect their domestic industries. In good times the pressures diminish because there are fewer threats to those industries from abroad. In bad times, however, governments may be more inclined to protect their industries from cheap imports, and may either impose tariffs on imports (taxes that make imports more expensive and provide a source of government revenue) or impose non-tariff barriers such as quotas and higher technical standards. Since the Second World War there has been an ongoing programme of international negotiations aimed at removing trade restrictions and liberalizing trade. These took place under the auspices of the General Agreement on Tariffs and Trade (GATT) until 1995, when it was replaced by the World Trade Organization (WTO). The principle underlying GATT/WTO is that economic welfare is best promoted by exploiting comparative advantage – that is, countries should specialize in what they produce best. Meanwhile, the United States argues that trade liberalization helps consumers by opening markets to cheaper goods, taxpayers by cutting subsidies to inefficient industry, producers by giving them access to bigger markets, and workers by creating new jobs.

Negotiations under the auspices of GATT/WTO have been carried out in successive rounds lasting several years, the lengthiest and most contentious of which was the Uruguay round, launched in 1986 by 105 countries (there were 117 by the time it concluded in 1993). The EC had been involved in several earlier rounds of negotiations, but the Uruguay round promised to be particularly controversial because its scope was broadened to include trade, thereby posing a direct challenge to the most protectionist of all Community policy areas.

The United States and the Community's other major trading partners called for cuts of 90 per cent in EC export subsidies and 75 per cent in other farm support over a period of ten years, arguing that they gave European farmers an unfair advantage. The EC countered with the offer of a 30 per cent cut in farming subsidies and refused to reform the Common Agricultural Policy. A breakthrough was finally achieved in 1992 thanks in part to CAP reforms agreed by the EC, including production and price reductions and a switch away from subsidies to farmers based on production. Although the Europeans eventually made concessions on production and export subsidies, and the Uruguay round was finally concluded in December 1993, the attitude of the Community towards the negotiations underlined some of its protectionist tendencies, and some of the problems that had emerged from its focus on completing the single market without paying due attention to its global implications. At the same time, the European experience during the Uruguay round clearly showed the benefits of policy collaboration and speaking with a single voice (Woolcock and Hodges, 1996).

Despite its support for free trade, the EU's external economic policies have caused concern among some of its major trading partners. Most fundamentally, the Community was not founded until ten years after GATT came into force, and it was never formally recognized under GATT rules. A combination of the EC's position on global trade negotiations, its focus on internal economic issues and its promotion of special arrangements with ACP states (see below) subsequently led to talk about 'Fortress Europe', particularly from political and corporate leaders in the United States worried about the implications of the single market and about the EC's unwillingness to cut agricultural subsidies as part of global trade negotiations. The charges of protectionism have proved unfounded, however; not only has the creation of the single market led to the reduction of internal and external barriers to trade, but the EU has become the primary champion of global trade liberalization under the auspices of the WTO.

The EU today faces some challenging realignments in world trade:

- The United States remains the EU's largest trading partner, accounting for about one-fifth of imports and exports, but these figures may fall as the United States builds closer economic ties with the Pacific rim.
- The United States is keen to see agriculture at the top of the agenda in future trade negotiations, presenting another challenge to the EU to reform the Common Agricultural Policy. At the same time though, the role of the Commission as a negotiator will give the EU more influence than it had during the Uruguay round.
- India, China, Japan and Australasia are more likely to strengthen the trading links among themselves than to build their trade with the EU. The EU's relationship with Japan has been dominated for many years

Figure 8.2 *EU trade with the world*

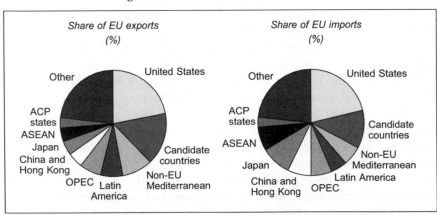

Source: European Commission, Trade DG, 2001. All figures are for 1998.

by a substantial trade deficit, with Japan currently exporting about 40 per cent more to the EU than it imports from the EU. The presidents of the Commission and the Council meet annually with the Japanese prime minister, and a variety of cooperative links have been established, including an executive training programme that takes European business executives to Japan for a year of in-house training. The relationship will remain unbalanced, however, as long as Japan continues to protect its domestic market.

While the EU faces challenges abroad, there are also substantial new opportunities closer to home, most notably on the Mediterranean rim, in central and eastern Europe – with nearly 122 million consumers and enormous productive potential – and in Russia and the former Soviet republics of eastern Europe – with about 218 million consumers and a wealth of largely untapped natural resources. The challenge for the EU is to help them continue to make the transition to free market economics, and to help Russia, Romania, Bulgaria and other troubled states in the region achieve stability.

Relations with the United States

The transatlantic relationship has blown hot and cold, which is only to be expected given that the EU and the United States are both major allies and major competitors. Relations were strong after the Second World War, the United States playing a critical role in European integration with the investments it made under the Marshall Fund and the security blanket it provided for western Europe during the Cold War. US administrations saw integration as a way of helping western Europe recover from the ravages of war and of improving European (and American) security in the face of the Soviet threat. Relations cooled in the early 1960s with Charles de Gaulle's concerns about American influence in Europe, and they continued to cool as the Europeans fell out with the United States over Vietnam, and over German diplomatic overtures to eastern Europe.

The 1971 collapse of the Bretton Woods system precipitated by the decision of the Nixon administration to abandon the gold standard not only marked the beginning of a steady withdrawal of the US responsibility for global leadership, but also emphasized to many Europeans the unwillingness of the United States always to take heed of European opinion. The Community was by then rapidly catching up with the United States in economic wealth, it traded less with the United States and more with eastern Europe, and the revival of the western European antinuclear movement in the early 1980s placed a further strain on transatlantic relations.

Trade was the focus of early EC–US relations, the United States preferring to deal with security matters either through NATO or bilaterally with allies such as Britain and West Germany. The end of the Soviet hegemony in eastern Europe in the late 1980s led to a new volatility in Europe that encouraged the Bush administration to call for stronger transatlantic ties on political matters. The result was the signature in November 1990 of a Transatlantic Declaration committing the US and the Community to regular high-level meetings. Contacts were taken a step further in 1995 with the adoption of a New Transatlantic Agenda and a Joint EU–US Action Plan under which both sides agreed to move from consultation to joint action aimed at promoting peace and democracy around the world, expanding world trade, and improving transatlantic ties. Biannual meetings have since taken place between the presidents of the United States, the Commission and the European Council, between the US secretary of state and EU foreign ministers, and between the Commission and members of the US cabinet.

The EU is the largest market for US exports, the largest destination of US foreign investment and tourism, and the largest source of foreign direct investment in the United States. Despite their cooperation, and despite the fact that the EU and the US continue to hold many common views on foreign policy, divisions of opinion have become more common and more substantial with time. This is hardly surprising, because there has been a reassertion of European economic power, a relative decline of US influence, a revision of US economic and security priorities, and a recalculation of international relations in the vacuum left by the collapse of the USSR. Early examples of disagreements included the slowness of the Community to criticize the 1979 Soviet invasion of Afghanistan, and the unwillingness of any EC member state except West Germany to support the resulting US-led boycott of the 1980 Moscow Olympics. Since then, the two sides have disagreed over Israeli policy on the West Bank, over how to deal with Iraq after the 1990 invasion of Kuwait and since, and over the issue of farm subsidies during the Uruguay round of GATT negotiations.

Particular controversy broke in March 1996, when President Clinton signed into law the Cuban Liberty and Democratic Solidarity Act (the Helms–Burton Act). Ostensibly a response to the shooting down by the Cuban government of two civilian aircraft associated with the anti-Castro movement, its objective was to increase economic pressure on Cuba by discouraging foreign investment in land and property expropriated by the Castro regime. Had it applied only to US companies the matter might have ended there, but it made provision for foreign companies investing in Cuba to be sued in US courts, and for executives from those companies to be refused entry into the United States.

The Act was strongly criticized by the major trading partners of the United States, notably Canada and Japan, and was met with outrage by the EU, which threatened sanctions against US firms and citizens. It also added fuel to the flames of a transatlantic dispute over another US law, which required that sanctions be imposed on foreign firms investing in the oil industries of Iran and Libya. A disputes panel was set up within the World Trade Organization to investigate the matter, and regular meetings took place between US trade representatives and the European Commission. The problem was finally resolved in May 1998 when the United States agreed to a progressive lifting of the sanctions imposed on European companies, and to waive the ban on European executives entering the United States. Eleven months later another simmering economic dispute ended when the EU conceded to US demands that it open its markets to bananas from Latin America, instead of favouring bananas from former European colonies in the Caribbean.

Another fallout occurred in 2001 when, within weeks of taking office, President George W. Bush signalled his intention to withdraw the United States from its commitments under an international agreement to reduce the emissions of carbon dioxide (CO_2) implicated in the problem of global warming. An international treaty had been agreed in 1992, and a protocol to the treaty was agreed in Kyoto, Japan, in 1997, committing signatories to specific percentage reductions in CO_2 emissions. The Bush administration argued that the Kyoto protocol was unrealistic, and objected to the fact that India and China were not obliged to make reductions (although they contribute only a small percentage of global emissions, whereas the US is the source of about one quarter of those emissions). EU member states were strongly critical of the Bush position, and even more critical of the manner in which he announced his intention of unilaterally withdrawing the US from the protocol.

Transatlantic trade disputes were forgotten in late 2001 following the terrorist attacks on New York City and Washington DC. The EU was quick to come to the support of the United States, although the level and the nature of that support varied by member state. There was agreement on the need to fight international terrorism, and police and intelligence-gathering cooperation in the search for members of the al-Qaeda terrorist network, but only Britain was involved in the US-led attacks on the Taliban regime in Afghanistan. Following the defeat of the Taliban, military personnel were sent or offered by several EU member states, including Britain, France, Germany and Italy. Unfortunately, the active role played by British prime minister Tony Blair in providing moral, political and military support to the United States once again emphasized the difficulties of developing a common EU foreign and security policy.

Relations with eastern Europe

The dominant presence of the United States in the external relations of the EU has been supplanted to some extent in recent years by the growing importance of central and eastern European countries (CEECs). Not only has the EU become the major source of foreign aid for the eastern bloc, but several CEECs are expected soon to join the EU, with important political and economic implications for both sides.

A common EU response to changes in eastern Europe was agreed at the December 1988 Rhodes European Council. With the encouragement of the United States, the EU took responsibility for coordinating Western economic aid to the east, a role that was formalized at the July 1989 meeting of the Group of Seven industrialized countries (G7), and strengthened in December 1989 with the launch of a programme to help with economic restructuring in Poland and Hungary. Known as PHARE, the programme has since been extended to other eastern European states and the Baltic states, and €1.6 billion was budgeted under the programme in 2001.

Trade and cooperation agreements have been signed by the EU with almost all eastern European states, several billion euros in loans have been made available by the European Investment Bank, the EU has sent food aid to the east, and several programmes have been launched to help eastern European social reform, including help to upgrade university departments in the east under the Tempus programme. The Commission now coordinates the aid efforts of the G24 countries: the EU, what remains of EFTA, and the United States, Canada, Japan, Australia, New Zealand and Turkey. The EU's leading role in this programme has not only helped define EU foreign policy, but has also made the EU a major independent actor in the economic and political future of eastern Europe.

The EU's influence was also boosted by the creation in 1990 of the European Bank for Reconstruction and Development (EBRD), which has channelled public money from the EU, the United States and Japan into development of the private sector in the east. Based in London, the EBRD is not actually part of the EU, but its foundation was an EU initiative, it derives 51 per cent of its capital from the EU, deals in euros, and has had a growing influence on EU decisions. Much like the International Bank for Reconstruction and Development (the World Bank), the EBRD was founded to provide loans, encourage capital investment and promote trade, but its specific focus is on helping eastern European countries make the transition to free-market economics. Both eastern and western European states are members, as are the United States and Russia.

The end of the Cold War produced a growing number of eastern European requests for associate or full membership of the EU. Germany

Box 8.3 The implications of eastward expansion

Ten central and eastern European countries are on the shortlist for the next round of EU expansion: the Czech Republic, Estonia, Hungary, Poland and Slovenia (with which negotiations began in 1998), and Bulgaria, Latvia, Lithuania, Romania and Slovakia. They all applied for membership in 1994–96, negotiations opened with the first group in 1998, and the general assumption is that the first wave of new members may join by 2004–5, and will most likely include the Czech Republic, Hungary, and Poland, and perhaps Estonia and Slovenia.

In order to prepare them for membership the EU agreed 'pre-accession strategies' with all ten, and began publishing reports every year on the progress each country was making towards aligning their national laws and standards with those of the EU. The Copenhagen summit of the European Council in 1993 set down three conditions they had to meet before being allowed to join:

- proof of respect for democratic principles, the rule of law, human rights and the protection of minorities.
- functioning market economies that are able to cope with the competitive pressures and market forces of the EU.
- the ability to take on all the obligations of membership, including incorporating into their national legal system all the laws agreed by the EU.

Several applicant countries complained in the late 1990s that much more was being expected of them prior to accession than had been the case with earlier entrants. Furthermore, they were being expected to wait longer; while Greece, Spain and Portugal joined the EU 7, 11 and 12 years respectively after freeing themselves from dictatorship, the first eastern European entrants (the former East Germany excepted) will have had to wait perhaps as long as 14 years from the end of the Cold War.

There are strong political and economic arguments in favour of eastern expansion: EU membership is likely to underpin the democratic transition for these states in the same way as it did for Greece, Portugal and Spain, it will open up new investment opportunities, and it will pull them into a strategic relationship with the west that could be useful if relations with Russia deteriorate. The promise of eastward expansion has also forced a reappraisal of the EU decision-making process, which has been adjusted regularly since 1958 but is still founded on a club of six countries. Under the Treaty of Nice, arrangements were agreed for a redistribution of seats in the European Parliament, a revised weighting of votes in the Council of Ministers, and a rethinking of the balance of national representation in the Commission.

(and Chancellor Helmut Kohl) was particularly active in promoting the idea, in part because of its historic links with the east, while the Major government in Britain also supported eastward expansion, but mainly to slow down the process of integration. Europe Agreements came into force in 1994 with Hungary and Poland, in 1995 with Bulgaria, the Czech Republic, Romania and Slovakia, and in 1998 with the three Baltic states. The agreements were seen as a step beyond associate membership, and were designed to integrate eastern European economies with those of the EU as quickly as possible through the staged removal of barriers to trade in industrial and agricultural goods, and of barriers to the movement of workers. The Treaty of Amsterdam paved the way for eastward expansion, which was confirmed in 1998 when membership negotiations began with the Czech Republic, Estonia, Hungary, Poland, and Slovenia (Box 8.3).

Enlargement to poorer states such as Greece, Portugal and Spain created problems enough in the 1980s – which have been partly overcome by huge EU investments in infrastructure in the three countries – but the challenge promises to be much greater with eastern Europe. Its governments and citizens are still struggling with the job of transforming their economies from central planning to the free market, and their political systems from one-party authoritarianism to multiparty democracy. Eastern Europe is also poor. While per capita GNP is in the range of $20–32 000 in most EU states, it is in the $1000–5000 range for most eastern European states. If all ten CEECs were to join, they would increase the EU population by 28 per cent but its GDP by just 4 per cent.

In order to help these countries make the transition and prepare them for EU membership, the EU launched the Agenda 2000 programme in 1997. Essentially a working programme for the EU until 2006, it includes a list of all the measures that the Commission believes are needed to bring the CEECs into the EU without risking institutional paralysis and substantially increased costs for the existing members. The measures include reform of the structural funds to ensure that they are spent in the regions of greatest need, the reduction of subsidies under CAP and a new focus under PHARE on training local specialists in fields such as law and administration. The Commission also used Agenda 2000 to make a new appeal for institutional reform. Following the disappointment of Nice, another IGC is in the pipeline, aimed at overhauling the EU decision making process in preparation for enlargement.

Development cooperation

The long history of European colonialism has left the European Union with a heritage of close economic and political ties to the South: Latin

America, south Asia and Africa. Several of the founding members of the Community – notably France and Belgium – still had large colonies when the Treaty of Rome was signed, and from the time of the first unsuccessful French attempts to have its overseas territories accorded associate status of the EC, the South has been a significant factor in the external relations of the EU. At the heart of that relationship has been a programme of aid and trade promotion involving several dozen former European colonies in sub-Saharan Africa, the Caribbean and the Pacific – the so-called ACP states (Table 8.2).

Table 8.2   *The ACP states*

Africa (48)	Mali	Cuba
Angola	Mauritania	Dominica
Benin	Mauritius	Dominican Republic
Botswana	Mozambique	Grenada
Burkina Faso	Namibia	Guyana
Burundi	Niger	Haiti
Cameroon	Nigeria	Jamaica
Cape Verde	Rwanda	St Kitts and Nevis
Central African	Sao Tome and	St Lucia
Republic	Principe	St Vincent and
Chad	Senegal	Grenadines
Comoros	Seychelles	Suriname
Congo (Brazzaville)	Sierra Leone	Trinidad and Tobago
Congo (Kinshasa)	Somalia	
Djibouti	South Africa	*Pacific (14)*
Equatorial Guinea	Sudan	Cook Islands
Eritrea	Swaziland	Fiji
Ethiopia	Tanzania	Kiribati
Gabon	Togo	Marshall Islands
Gambia	Uganda	Micronesia
Ghana	Zambia	Nauru
Guinea	Zimbabwe	Niue
Guinea Bissau		Palau
Ivory Coast		Papua New Guinea
Kenya	*Caribbean (16)*	Samoa
Lesotho	Antigua and Barbuda	Solomon Islands
Liberia	Bahamas	Tonga
Madagascar	Barbados	Tuvalu
Malawi	Belize	Vanuatu

EU development aid policies are based partly on remedying quality of life issues such as poverty and hunger, but there are also less altruistic motives: the South accounts for more than one third of EU exports (more than the United States and Japan combined), and the EU continues to rely on the South as a source of oil and of key raw materials such as rubber, copper and uranium. Food aid, humanitarian aid and cooperation with developing countries accounted in 2002 for 2.8 per cent of the EU budget (about €2.7 billion), adding to the more than $25 billion in bilateral aid flows from the member states individually.

The EU aid programme has several different aspects. As well as allowing all Southern states to export industrial products to the EU tariff- and duty-free (subject to some limitations on volume), the EU provides food and emergency aid, and sponsors development projects undertaken by non-governmental organizations. The EU has also negotiated a series of cooperative agreements with the ACP countries. These began with the 1963 and 1969 Yaoundé Conventions (named after the capital of Cameroon, where they were signed), which gave 18 former colonies preferential access to Community markets. The 18 in turn allowed limited duty-free or quota-free access by the EC to their markets. The provision of trade concessions was expanded by the four Lomé Conventions (named after the capital of Togo), which were signed in 1975, 1979, 1984 and 1989.

Lomé IV, which covered the period 1990–2000 and was revised in 1995, had three main elements. First, it provided financial aid to 71 ACP states under the European Development Fund, in the form mainly of grants for development projects and low-interest loans. Second, it provided free access to the EU for products originating in ACP countries, with the exception of agricultural products covered by CAP. About 95 per cent of ACP exports entered the EU duty free, compared to just 10 per cent of agricultural goods from other countries, and other goods were subject to tariffs in the range of 17–23 per cent. Finally, it offered an insurance fund for ACP exports called Stabex, designed to offset falls in the value of 50 specified ACP agricultural exports. If prices fell below a certain level, Stabex made up the deficit. If they went above that level, ACP countries invested the profits in the fund for future use.

Opinions were mixed about the effects of the Yaoundé and Lomé conventions. On the one hand, they helped build closer commercial ties between the EU and the ACP states, and there was an overall increase in the volume of ACP exports to Europe from the 1960s to the 1990s. On the other hand, the conventions were widely criticized for promoting economic dependence, and for perpetuating the flow of low-profit raw materials from the ACP to the EU, and the flow of high-profit manufactured goods from the EU to the ACP. Questions were also raised about the extent to which they helped the ACP states invest in their human capital, and helped them develop greater economic independence.

Other problems were structural. Stabex did not help countries that did not produce the specified commodities, payments from the European Development Fund were small by the time the fund had been divided among 71 countries, the ACP programme excluded the larger Southern states that had negotiated separate agreements with the EU (for example India and China), too little attention was paid to the environmental implications of the focus on cash crops for export, and the programme neither helped deal with the ACP debt crisis nor really changed the relationship between the EU and the ACP states.

The biggest problem was internal to the ACP countries themselves. They mostly failed to diversify their exports, to invest in infrastructure, to build up a more skilled labour force and to become more competitive in the world market. The EU provided them with a generous set of trade preferences, and yet imports from the ACP as a share of the EU total fell from 6.7 per cent in 1976 to just 3 per cent in 1998. Oil, diamonds, gold and other industrially related products accounted for about two-thirds of ACP exports to the EU, the balance being made up by agricultural products (30 per cent) and fish (5 per cent). Four countries – Nigeria, Ivory Coast, Cameroon and Mauritius – between them accounted for more than 40 per cent of EU imports from the ACP countries. At the same time, economic growth in many sub-Saharan African states was sluggish, and there was very little trade taking place among African ACP states.

Negotiations began in 1998 on a new EU–ACP agreement, which was signed in Contonou, Benin, in 2000. Designed to run for twenty years, with revisions every five years, the Contonou agreement added seven more countries to the ACP group, including Cuba. It places a stronger require-ment on ACP states to improve domestic political, economic and social conditions, and it emphasizes the importance of human rights and democracy, its objectives including the promotion of the interests of the private sector, gender equality, sustainable environmental management, and the replacement of trade preferences with a progressive and reciprocal removal of trade barriers. Whether this will be enough to address the structural problems of the ACP programme remains to be seen.

Meanwhile, the EU has become the single biggest source of official development assistance in the world. Its member states collectively accounted for 48 per cent of the total in 2000 (OECD Homepage, 2001), which was much more than the 25 per cent provided by Japan or the 18 per cent by the United States. Most EU aid (15 per cent of which is channelled through the EU) goes to sub-Saharan Africa, but an increasing proportion is going to Latin America. The EU also provides emergency humanitarian aid (nearly €500 million in 2001), much of which has gone in recent years to the victims of conflicts in Afghanistan, Armenia, Azerbaijan and Tadjikistan. It has also become the second largest provider of food aid in the world after the United States, supplying food worth about €500 million per year.

Conclusions

The process of European integration was born as a way to help western Europe rebuild itself after the Second World War, and to remove the historical causes of conflict in the region. Over time the EC/EU has become increasingly extroverted, and integration now has implications not just for internal European relations, but for Europe's relations with the rest of the world. While the EEC initially focused on bringing down the barriers to internal trade, it very quickly became involved in external trade matters, and the EU over the past decade has turned its attention to common foreign and security policies. The process has steadily acquired consistency and regularity, and the CFSP now makes up one of the three pillars that constitute the European Union. Unfortunately the EU is trying to develop its common foreign policy at a time of great change in the world.

One of the sparks that led to the creation of the EU was the obvious security threat posed by the Soviet Union, but that threat has since been replaced by less easily definable economic concerns, by more specific regional security problems such as those in the Balkans and the Middle East, and by less easily defined potential threats such as international terrorism, nationalist pressures in Russia, the movement of political refugees, the spread of nuclear weapons, the implications of new technology, and environmental problems. Meanwhile globalization is proceeding under the auspices of the World Trade Organization, and the United States is shifting its economic interests more towards the Pacific rim. Finally, the wealth and competitiveness of China, India and other newly industrializing countries continue to grow, altering the balance of global economic power.

The most important medium-term issue in EU external relations is the expansion of membership into eastern Europe. There is no question that this will happen, it is simply a matter of determining which countries will join and when. Enlargement promises not only significant economic and social change in eastern Europe, but a substantial reordering of the balance of power within the EU. It was once an exclusive club of half a dozen members, dominated by the relationship between France and Germany. It now has 15 members, and could soon have at least 20, and eventually 25 or more, many of them quite poor.

All these changes make it essential for the EU to give its own identity clearer definition, and to build the kind of defensive capability and credibility that it needs as a new economic superpower.] While most of the questions about the economic weight of the EU have been answered, it is likely to be some time before the world wakes up to the sight of multilingual soldiers, sailors and pilots going to war under the colours of the European flag, following an agreement reached by Europe's political leaders. [However, while the EU may still present a rather confused and confusing image to the outside world, the outline of that image is slowly becoming sharper.]

Appendix: A Chronology of European integration, 1944–2002

1944	July	Bretton Woods conference
1945	May	Germany surrenders; European war ends
	June	Creation of United Nations
1947	September	Launch of Marshall Plan
1948	January	Creation of Benelux customs union
	April	Organization for European Economic Cooperation founded
1949	April	North Atlantic Treaty signed
	May	Council of Europe founded
1950	May	Publication of Schuman Declaration
1951	April	Treaty of Paris signed, creating the European Coal and Steel Community
1952	March	Nordic Council founded
	May	Signature of draft treaty creating the European Defence Community
	August	ECSC comes into operation
1953	November	Plans announced for a European Political Community
1954	August	Plans for EDC and EPC collapse
	October	Creation of Western European Union
1956	October	Suez crisis
1957	March	Treaties of Rome signed, creating Euratom and the European Economic Community
1958	January	Euratom and EEC begin to operate
	February	Benelux Economic Union founded
1960	May	Creation of European Free Trade Association
1961	February	First summit of EEC heads of government
	August	Britain, Ireland and Denmark apply for EEC membership
1962	April	Norway applies for EEC membership
1963	January	De Gaulle vetoes British membership of the EEC; France and Germany sign Treaty of Friendship and Cooperation
1965	April	Merger treaty signed

1966	May	Britain, Ireland and Denmark apply for the second time for EEC membership (Norway follows in July)
1967	December	De Gaulle vetoes British membership of the Community
1968	July	Agreement of a common external tariff completes the creation of an EEC customs union; Common Agricultural Policy agreed
1970	June	Membership negotiations open with Britain, Denmark, Ireland and Norway; concluded in January 1972
1971	August	US leaves gold standard; end of the Bretton Woods system of fixed exchange rates
1972	September	Referendum in Norway turns down EEC membership
1973	January	Britain, Denmark and Ireland join the Community, bringing membership to nine
1974	January	Creation of the European Social Fund
1975	January	Creation of the European Regional Development Fund
	March	First meeting of the European Council in Dublin
	June	Greece applies for Community membership; negotiations begin in July 1976
1977	March	Portugal applies for Community membership; negotiations begin in October 1978
	July	Spain applies for Community membership; negotiations begin in February 1979
1979	March	European Monetary System comes into operation
	June	First direct elections to the European Parliament
1981	January	Greece joins the Community, bringing membership to ten
1984	January	Free trade area established between EFTA and the EC
1985	June	Schengen Agreement signed by France, Germany and the Benelux states
1986	January	Spain and Portugal join the Community, bringing membership to twelve
	February	Single European Act signed in Luxembourg
1987	June	Turkey applies for Community membership
	July	Single European Act comes into force
1989	April	Delors report on economic and monetary union
	July	Austria applies for Community membership
	December	Adoption of the Social Charter by eleven EC member states; rejection of Turkish membership application

1990	July	Cyprus and Malta apply for Community membership
	October	German reunification brings former East Germany into the Community
1992	February	Treaty on European Union (Maastricht Treaty) signed
	June	Following a popular referendum, Denmark rejects the terms of Maastricht
1993	May	Referendum in Denmark leads to acceptance of terms of Maastricht
	November	Treaty on European Union comes into force
		European Community becomes a pillar of the new European Union
1994	January	Creation of the European Economic Area
	March	Poland and Hungary become associate members of the EU
	May	Opening of the Channel Tunnel, linking Britain and France
	June–Nov	Referendums in Austria, Finland and Sweden go in favour of EU membership, but Norwegians say no
1995	January	Austria, Sweden and Finland join the European Union, bringing membership to fifteen
	March	Schengen Agreement comes into force
	July	Europol Convention signed
1997	October	Treaty of Amsterdam signed
1998	March	EU membership negotiations open with the Czech Republic, Cyprus, Estonia, Hungary, Poland and Slovenia
	June	Establishment of the European Central Bank
		Treaty of Amsterdam comes into force
1999	January	Eleven member states announce they will adopt the euro
2000	December	Treaty of Nice signed
2001	March	Switzerland votes against membership of the EU
	June	Following a popular referendum, Ireland rejects the terms of Nice
2002	March	Twelve EU member states make the final switch to the euro

Sources of Further Information

The literature on the European Union has grown dramatically in the last few years, the number of new books, journal articles and Web sites increasing to match the pace of change in the EU itself, and of expanding interest in EU affairs. The sources listed here are not designed to be comprehensive, but to give a taste of what was available as this book went to press. To keep up with developments, you might want to monitor new acquisitions at your nearest library, keep an eye out for new books from the publishers with the best lists on the European Union (including Lynne Rienner, Oxford University Press, Palgrave, Routledge, and Rowman & Littlefield), and search online book dealers such as Amazon.com.

Books

Among the growing number of general introductions to the European Union are Dinan (1999), Nugent (2002), Archer (2000), Van Oudenaren (2000), George and Bache (2001), and Wood and Yesilada (2002). Edited collections on recent developments in the EU include Laurent and Maresceau (1998), Cram *et al.* (1999), and Cowles and Smith (2001). For general surveys of the history of the EU, see Black *et al.* (1992), Pinder (1995), and Urwin (1995).

After a long dry spell, the number of books on EU institutions has grown rapidly in the last few years. The Commission in particular has been the subject of a rash of new studies, notable among which are Cini (1996), Edwards and Spence (1997), and Nugent (1997, 2001). Surveys of Parliament are offered by Westlake (1994), Corbett (1998), and Lodge (2001), and political parties are the focus of a book by Hix and Lord (1997). Most studies of the Court of Justice are written in legal jargon, and there are few general introductions beyond Lasok (1998), Dehousse (1998), and Brown and Kennedy (2000). For an explanation of the EU legal system, see Shaw (2000).

Despite its critical role in the EU, the Council of Ministers has been the subject of surprisingly little scholarly literature so far, the only recent full-length studies being Hayes-Renshaw and Wallace (1997), and Sherrington (2000). For an assessment of the role of the presidency of the Council of Ministers, see Kirchner (1992), and for the European Council, see Johnston (1994) and Bulmer and Wessels (forthcoming). For surveys of EU institutions and decision making, see Peterson and Bomberg (1999), Hix (1999), and Warleigh (2002).

For edited collections dealing with a variety of EU policy areas, see Wallace and Wallace (2000), and Richardson (2001). Tsoukalis (1997) has a general survey of economic policy, while there are now an increasing number of studies of EU activities in many specific policy areas, including agriculture (Grant, 1997), competition (Cini and McGowan, 1998), energy (Matláry, 1997), the environment (McCormick, 2001), foreign policy (Rhodes, 1998; Whitman, 1998; White, 2000), social policy (Hantrais, 2000; Roberts and Springer, 2001), and technology (Peterson and Sharp, 1998).

Periodicals and EU publications

The Economist. A weekly news magazine that has stories and statistics on world politics, including a section on Europe (and occasional special supplements on the EU). Selected headline stories can be found on the *Economist* Web site:

http://www.economist.com

The Economist also publishes two series of quarterly reports that are treasure-houses of information, but they are expensive, and not every library carries them: *Economist Intelligence Unit Country Reports* (these cover almost every country in the world, and include a series on the European Union), and *European Policy Analyst*. Both provide detailed political and economic news and information.

The Economist also publishes *European Voice*, a weekly newspaper published in Brussels that is packed with all the latest news and information on the EU. Selected headline stories can be found on its Web site:

http://www.european-voice.com/

Journal of Common Market Studies. This quarterly academic journal is devoted to the EU and contains scholarly articles and book reviews. Many other academic journals include articles on the EU, but the most consistently useful are *West European Politics*, *International Organization* and *Parliamentary Affairs*.

There are several official sources of EU information, all of which are available on the Web through the Europa Web site:

http://europa.eu.int

Official Journal of the European Communities. Published daily, this is the authoritative source on all EU legislation, proposals by the Commission for new legislation, decisions and resolutions by the Council of Ministers, debates in the European Parliament, new actions brought before the Court of Justice, opinions of the Economic and Social Committee, the annual report of the Court of Auditors, and the EU budget.

General Report on the Activities of the European Union. This is the major annual report of the EU, with a record of developments in all EU policy areas, and key statistical information.

Bulletin of the European Union. Published ten times per year, this is the official record of events in (and policies of) all the EU institutions. It contains reports on the activities of the Commission and other EU institutions, along with special feature articles. Supplements contain copies of key Commission documents, including proposed legislation.

Directorate-General Documentation. Every DG in the Commission publishes its own periodicals, reports and surveys dealing with its specific areas of interest. One of the most useful of the regular publications is the series of biannual Euro-barometer opinion polls. These have been carried out in the EU since 1973, mainly to provide EU institutions and the media with statistics on public attitudes towards European integration.

Eurostat. An acronym for the Statistical Office of the European Communities, Eurostat collects and collates statistical information of many different kinds from the EU member states. Much of this is available on the Web; all of it is published in the form of yearbooks, surveys, studies and reports.

EUR-Lex. This is the definitive source on EU legislation, containing all the directives, regulations and other legal instruments adopted by the EU, as well as internal and external agreements.

Web sites

The variety of useful Web sites changes often, as do their URLs, so instead of listing useful sites here, I have set up a short series of links on my home page. The URL is:

http://php.iupui.edu/~jmccormi/

Palgrave also has a Web page for books in the European Union series which provides information on key developments and links to other internet sources. The URL is:

http://www.palgrave.com/politics/eu/

Bibliography

Allen, David (1996) 'Competition Policy: Policing the Single Market', in Helen Wallace and William Wallace (eds), *Policy-Making in the European Union*, 3rd edn (Oxford: Oxford University Press).

Anderson, Scott (1992) 'Western Europe and the Gulf War', in Reinhardt Rummel, *Toward Political Union: Planning a Common Foreign and Security Policy in the European Community* (Boulder, CO: Westview).

Archer, Clive (2000) *The European Union: Structure and Process*, 3rd edn (New York: Continuum).

Armstrong, Harvey (1993) 'Community Regional Policy'', in Juliet Lodge (ed.) *The European Community and the Challenge of the Future* (New York, NY: St Martin's Press).

Armstrong, Kenneth and Simon Bulmer (1998) *The Governance of the Single European Market* (Manchester: Manchester University Press).

ASEAN Homepage (2001) World Wide Web < http://www.asean.or.id/ >.

Aspinwall, Mark and Justin Greenwood (1998) 'Conceptualising Collective Action in the European Union: An Introduction', in Mark Aspinwall and Justin Greenwood (eds), *Collective Action in the European Union: Interests and the New Politics of Associability* (London: Routledge).

Bainbridge, Timothy and Anthony Teasdale (1995) *The Penguin Companion to European Union* (London: Penguin).

Barber, Lionel (1998) 'Sharing Common Risks: The EU View', *Europe*, no. 374, pp. 8–9

Barnard, Bruce (1999) 'Business is Booming in the World's Biggest Tourist Market', in *Europe*, no. 384, pp. 22–4.

Barnes, Ian and Pamela M. Barnes (1995) *The Enlarged European Union* (London: Longman).

Black, Cyril E. *et al.* (1992) *Rebirth: A History of Europe Since World War II* (Boulder, CO: Westview).

Bradford, Michael (1998) 'Education and Welfare', in Tim Unwin (ed.), *A European Geography* (Harlow: Longman).

Brewin, Christopher and Richard McAllister (1991) 'Annual Review of the Activities of the European Community in 1990', in *Journal of Common Market Studies*, vol. 29, no. 4 (June), pp. 385–430.

Brown, L. Neville and Tom Kennedy (2000) *The Court of Justice of the European Communities*, 5th edn (London: Sweet & Maxwell).

Bugge, Peter (1995) 'The Nation Supreme: The Idea of Europe 1914–1945', in Kevin Wilson and Jan van der Dussen (eds), *The History of the Idea of Europe* (London: Routledge).

Bulmer, Simon and Wolfgang Wessels (forthcoming) *The European Council: Decisionmaking in European Politics*, 2nd edn (Basingstoke: Palgrave).

Carr, William (1987) *A History of Germany, 1815–1985*, 3rd edn (London: Edward Arnold).

Cini, Michelle (1996) *The European Commission: Leadership, Organization and Culture in the EU Administration* (Manchester: Manchester University Press).

Cini, Michelle and Lee McGowan (1998) *Competition Policy in the European Union* (Basingstoke: Palgrave).

Collins, Ken and David Earnshaw (1993) 'The Implementation and Enforcement of European Community Environment Legislation', in David Judge (ed.), *A Green Dimension for the European Community: Political Issues and Processes* (London: Frank Cass).

Commission of the European Communities (1973) *Report on the Regional Problems of the Enlarged Community* (The Thomson Report), COM(73)550 (Brussels: Commission of the European Communities).

Commission of the European Communities (1985) *Completing the Internal Market* (The Cockfield Report), COM(85)310 (Brussels: Commission of the European Communities).

Commission of the European Communities (2001) *European Governance: A White Paper*, COM(2001)428 (Brussels: Commission of the European Communities).

Coombes, David and Nicholas Rees (1991) 'Regional and Social Policy', in Leon Hurwitz and Christian Lequesne (eds), *The State of the European Community* (Boulder, CO: Lynne Rienner).

Corbett, Richard (1998) *The European Parliament's Role in Closer EU Integration* (New York: St Martin's Press).

Cowles, Maria Green and Michael Smith (eds) (2001) *The State of the European Union: Risks, Reform, Resistance, and Revival* (Oxford: Oxford University Press).

Cram, Laura, Desmond Dinan and Neill Nugent (eds) (1999) *Developments in the European Union* (Basingstoke: Palgrave).

Dahrendorf, Ralf (1988) *The Modern Social Conflict* (London: Weidenfeld & Nicolson).

Daltrop, Anne (1987) *Politics and the European Community* (London: Longman).

Dehousse, Renaud (1998) *The European Court of Justice* (Basingstoke: Palgrave).

Delanty, Gerard (1995) *Inventing Europe: Idea, Identity, Reality* (New York: St Martin's Press).

Delors, Jacques (1991) 'European Integration and Security', in *Survival*, vol. 33, no. 2 (Spring), pp. 99–109.

den Boer, Pim (1995) 'Europe to 1914: The making of an idea', in Kevin Wilson and Jan van der Dussen (eds), *The History of the Idea of Europe* (London: Routledge).

de Rougemont, Denis (1966) *The Idea of Europe* (London: Macmillan).

Dinan, Desmond (1999) *Ever Closer Union? An Introduction to European Integration*, 2nd edn (Boulder, CO: Lynne Rienner/Basingstoke: Palgrave).

Edwards, Geoffrey and David Spence (eds) (1997) *The European Commission*, 2nd edn (London: Cartermill).

Europa Homepage (2001) World Wide Web < http://europa.eu.int > .

Featherstone, K. (1994) 'Jean Monnet and the "democratic deficit" in the EU', in *Journal of Common Market Studies*, vol. 32, no. 20, pp. 149–70.

Fernández-Armesto, Felipe (ed.) (1997) *The Times Guide to the Peoples of Europe* (London: Times Books).

Franklin, Mark (1996) 'European Elections and the European Voter', in Jeremy Richardson (ed.) *European Union: Power and Policy-Making* (London: Routledge).

Gallagher, Michael, Michael Laver and Peter Mair (1992) *Representative Government in Modern Europe*, 2nd edn (New York: McGraw-Hill).

George, Stephen (1996) *Politics and Policy in the European Community*, 3rd edn (Oxford: Oxford University Press).

George, Stephen and Ian Bache (2001) *Politics in the European Union* (Oxford: Oxford University Press).

Geyer, Robert and Beverly Springer (1998) 'EU Social Policy After Maastricht: The Works Council Directive and the British Opt-Out', in Pierre-Henri Laurent and Marc Maresceau (eds), *The State of the European Union, Vol. 4* (Boulder, CO: Lynne Rienner).

Gillingham, John (1991) *Coal, Steel, and the Rebirth of Europe, 1945–1955* (Cambridge: Cambridge University Press).

Grant, Wyn (1997) *The Common Agricultural Policy* (Basingstoke: Palgrave).

Greenwood, Justin (1997) *Representing Interests in the European Union* (Basingstoke: Palgrave).

Haas, Ernst B. (1964) 'Technocracy, Pluralism and the New Europe', in Stephen R. Graubard (ed.), *A New Europe?* (Boston, MA: Houghton Mifflin).

Haas, Ernst B. (1968) *The Uniting of Europe: Political, Social, and Economic Forces, 1950–57* (Stanford, CA: Stanford University Press).

Hantrais, Linda (2000) *Social Policy in the European Union* (Basingstoke: Palgrave).

Hardgrave, Robert L. and Stanley A. Kochanek (2000) *India: Government and Politics in a Developing Nation* (Fort Worth, TX: Harcourt College Publishers).

Hay, David (1957) *Europe: The Emergence of an Idea* (Edinburgh: Edinburgh University Press).

Hayes-Renshaw, Fiona and Helen Wallace (1997) *The Council of Ministers* (Basingstoke: Palgrave).

Heater, Derek (1992) *The Idea of European Unity* (New York: St Martin's Press).

Heisler, Martin O. with Robert B. Kvavik (1973) 'Patterns of European Politics: The "European Polity" Model', in Martin O. Heisler (ed.), *Politics in Europe: Structures and Processes in Some Postindustrial Democracies* (New York: David McKay).

Hill, Christopher (1992) 'EPC's Performance in Crises', in Reinhardt Rummel (ed.), *Toward Political Union: Planning a Common Foreign and Security Policy in the European Community* (Boulder, CO: Westview Press).

Hix, Simon (1999) *The Political System of the European Union* (Basingstoke: Palgrave).

Hix, Simon and Christopher Lord (1997) *Political Parties in the European Union* (Basingstoke: Palgrave).

Hobsbawm, Eric (1991) *The Age of Empire 1848–1875* (London: Cardinal).

Hogan, Michael J. (1987) *The Marshall Plan: America, Britain, and the Reconstruction of Western Europe, 1947–52* (New York: Cambridge University Press).

Ionescu, Ghita (1975) *Centripetal Politics: Government and the New Centres of Power* (London: Hart-Davis McGibbon).

Johnston, Mary Troy (1994) *The European Council: Gatekeeper of the European Community* (Boulder, CO: Westview Press).

Keating, Michael and Liesbet Hooghe (1996) 'By-passing the Nation State? Regions and the EU Policy Process', in Jeremy Richardson (ed.), *European Union: Power and Policy-Making* (London: Routledge).

Keegan, Victor and Martin Kettle (1993) *The New Europe* (London: Fourth Estate).

Keohane, Robert O. and Stanley Hoffmann (1990) 'Conclusions: Community Politics and Institutional Change', in William Wallace (ed.), *The Dynamics of European Integration* (London: Royal Institute of International Affairs).

Keohane, Robert O. and Stanley Hoffmann (eds) (1991) *The New European Community: Decisionmaking and Institutional Change* (Boulder, CO: Westview Press).

Kirchner, Emil Joseph (1992) *Decision-Making in the European Community: The Council Presidency and European Integration* (Manchester: Manchester University Press).

Lasok, Dominik (1998) *Law and Institutions of the European Communities*, 7th edn (London: Lexis Law Publishing).

Laurent, Pierre-Henri and Marc Maresceau (eds) (1998) *The State of the European Union, Vol. 4: Deepening and Widening* (Boulder, CO: Lynne Rienner).

Lindberg, Leon N. (1963) *The Political Dynamics of European Economic Integration* (Stanford, CA: Stanford University Press).

Lindberg, Leon N. and Stuart A. Scheingold (1970) *Europe's Would-Be Polity: Patterns of Change in the European Community* (Englewood Cliffs, NJ: Prentice-Hall).

Lindberg, Leon N. and Stuart A. Scheingold (1971) *Regional Integration: Theory and Research* (Cambridge, MA: Harvard University Press).

Lodge, Juliet (2001) *The 1999 Elections in the European Parliament* (Basingstoke: Palgrave).

Loedel, Peter H. (1998) 'Enhancing Europe's International Monetary Power: The Drive Toward a Single Currency', in Pierre-Henri Laurent and Marc Maresceau (eds), *The State of the European Union, Vol. 4: Deepening and Widening* (Boulder, CO: Lynne Rienner).

Majone, Giandomenico (1993) 'The European Community Between Social Policy and Social Regulation', in *Journal of Common Market Studies*, vol. 3, no. 2, pp. 42–58.

Mancini, G. Federico (1991) 'The Making of a Constitution for Europe', in Robert O. Keohane and Stanley Hoffmann (eds), *The New European Community: Decisionmaking and Institutional Change* (Boulder, CO: Westview Press).

Matláry, Janne Haaland (1997) *Energy Policy in the European Union* (Basingstoke: Palgrave).

Mazey, Sonia and Jeremy Richardson (1996) 'The Logic of Organisation: Interest Groups', in Jeremy Richardson (ed.), *European Union: Power and Policy-Making* (London: Routledge).

McCormick, John (1995) *The Global Environmental Movement*, 2nd edn (London: John Wiley).

McCormick, John (2001) *Environmental Policy in the European Union* (Basingstoke: Palgrave).

Menon, Anand, Anthony Forster and William Wallace (1992) 'A Common European Defense?', in *Survival*, vol. 34, no. 3, pp. 98–118.

Milward, Alan S. (1984) *The Reconstruction of Western Europe, 1945–51* (Berkeley, CA: University of California Press).

Minshull, G. N. and M. J. Dawson (1996) *The New Europe Into the 21st Century*, 5th edn (London: Hodder and Stoughton).

Mitrany, David (1966) *A Working Peace System* (Chicago, IL: Quadrangle).

Mitrany, David (1970) 'The Functional Approach to World Organisation', in Carol A. Cosgrove and Kenneth J. Twitchett (eds), *The New International Actors: The UN and the EEC* (London: Macmillan).

Monnet, Jean (1978) *Memoirs* (Garden City, NY: Doubleday).

Nugent, Neill (ed.) (2000) *At the Heart of the Union: Studies of the European Commission*, 4th edn (Basingstoke: Palgrave).

Nugent, Neill (2001) *The European Commission* (Basingstoke: Palgrave).

Nugent, Neill (2002) *The Government and Politics of the European Union*, 5th edn (Basingstoke: Palgrave).

Nye, Joseph S. (1971) 'Comparing Common Markets: A Revised Neofunctionalist Model', in Leon N. Lindberg and Stuart A. Scheingold (eds), *Regional Integration: Theory and Research* (Cambridge, MA: Harvard University Press).

OECD Homepage (2001) World Wide Web, < http://www.oecd.org >.

Owen, Richard and Michael Dynes (1992) *The Times Guide to the Single European Market* (London: Times Books).

Palmer, Michael (1968) *European Unity: A Survey of European Organizations* (London: George Allen & Unwin).

Peterson, John and Elizabeth Bomberg (1999) *Decision-Making in the European Union* (Basingstoke: Palgrave).

Peterson, John and Margaret Sharp (1998) *Technology Policy in the European Union* (Basingstoke: Palgrave).

Pinder, John (1995) *European Community: The Building of a Union*, 2nd edn (Oxford: Oxford University Press).

Pye, Lucien (1966) *Aspects of Political Development* (Boston, MA: Little, Brown).

Rhodes, Carolyn (ed.) (1998) *The European Union in the World Community* (Boulder, CO: Lynne Rienner).

Richardson, Jeremy (ed.) (2001) *European Union: Power and Policy-Making*, 2nd edn (London and New York: Routledge).

Roberts, Ivor and Beverley Springer (2001) *Social Policy in the European Union: Between Harmonization and National Autonomy* (Boulder, CO: Lynne Rienner).

Rosamond, Ben (2000) *Theories of European Integration* (Basingstoke: Palgrave).

Salmon, Trevor and Sir William Nicol (eds) (1997) *Building European Union: A Documentary History and Analysis* (Manchester: Manchester University Press).

Schultz, D. Mark (1992) 'Austria in the International Arena: Neutrality, European Integration and Consociationalism', in Kurt Richard Luther and Wolfgang C.

Muller (eds), *Politics in Austria: Still a Case of Consociationalism?* (London: Frank Cass).

Shackleton, Michael (1990) *Financing the European Community* (New York: Council on Foreign Relations Press).

Shaw, Josephine (2000) *Law of the European Union*, 3rd edn (Basingstoke: Palgrave).

Sherrington, Philippa (2000) *The Council of Ministers: Political Authority in the European Union* (London: Pinter).

Smith, Michael (1997) 'The Commission and External Relations', in Geoffrey Edwards and David Spence (eds), *The European Commission*, 2nd edn (London: Cartermill).

Smith, Michael (1998) 'What's Wrong with the CFSP? The Politics of Institutional Reform', in Pierre-Henri Laurent and Marc Maresceau (eds), *The State of the European Union, Vol. 4* (Boulder, CO: Lynne Rienner).

Springer, Beverly (1992) *The Social Dimension of 1992: Europe Faces a New EC* (Westport, CT: Praeger).

Taylor, Paul and A. J. R. Groom (1975) 'Functionalism and International Relations', in A. J. R. Groom and Paul Taylor (eds), *Functionalism: Theory and Practice in International Relations* (London: University of London Press).

Thatcher, Margaret (1993) *The Downing Street Years* (New York: HarperCollins).

Tsoukalis, Loukas (1997) *The New European Economy Revisited: The Politics and Economics of Integration*, 3rd edn (Oxford: Oxford University Press).

Union of International Associations Homepage (2001) World Wide Web < http://www.uia.org/welcome.htm > .

Urwin, Derek (1995) *The Community of Europe*, 2nd edn (London: Longman).

van Eekelen, Willem (1990) 'WEU and the Gulf Crisis', in *Survival*, 32:6, pp. 519–32.

Van Oudenaren, John (2000) *Uniting Europe: European Integration and the Post Cold-War World* (Lanham, MD: Rowman & Littlefield).

Wallace, Helen (1992) 'What Europe for Which Europeans?', in Gregory F. Treverton (ed.), *The Shape of the New Europe* (New York: Council on Foreign Relations Press).

Wallace, Helen and William Wallace (2000) *Policy-Making in the European Union*, 2nd edn (Oxford: Oxford University Press).

Wallace, William (1990) *The Transformation of Western Europe* (London: Royal Institute of International Affairs).

Wallace, William (1996) 'Government Without Statehood: The Unstable Equilibrium', in Helen Wallace and William Wallace (eds), *Policy-Making in the European Union*, 3rd edn (Oxford: Oxford University Press).

Warleigh, Alex (2002) *Understanding European Union Institutions* (London: Routledge).

Weigall, David and Peter Stirk (eds) (1992) *The Origins and Development of the European Community* (London: Pinter).

Westlake, Martin (1994) *A Modern Guide to the European Parliament* (London: Pinter).

Wexler, Immanual (1983) *The Marshall Plan Revisited: The European Recovery Program in Economic Perspective* (Westport, CT: Greenwood).

White, Brian (2000) *Understanding European Foreign Policy* (Basingstoke: Palgrave).

Whitman, Richard G. (1998) *From Civilian Power to Superpower? The International Identity of the European Union* (New York: St Martin's Press).

Williams, Shirley (1991) 'Sovereignty and Accountability in the European Community', in Robert O. Keohane and Stanley Hoffmann (eds), *The New European Community: Decisionmaking and Institutional Change* (Boulder, CO: Westview Press).

Wood, David and Birol Yesilada (2002) *The Emerging European Union*, 2nd edn (London: Longman).

Woolcock, Stephen and Michael Hodges (1996) 'EU Policy in the Uruguay Round', in Helen and William Wallace (eds), *Policy-Making in the European Union* (Oxford: Oxford University Press).

World Trade Organization (1996) *Compendium of Tourist Statistics 1989–94* (Madrid: World Trade Organization).

Zurcher, Arnold J. (1958) *The Struggle to Unite Europe, 1940–58* (New York: New York University Press).

Index

acquis communitaire 77
Adonnino committee 149–51, 155
Adenauer, Konrad 56, 58, 65
Africa Caribbean Pacific (ACP)
    programme 81, 215–17
African Union 27
Agenda 2000 214
airline deregulation 179
Airbus Industrie 176
Amsterdam, Treaty of (1997) 76, 148,
    162
  content/effects of 79–81, 109, 119,
      160, 164–5, 169, 203, 214
  signature 79
Andean Group 21
Arab Common Market 25
Arab League 25
Arab Monetary Fund 25
Arianespace 175
Asia Pacific Economic Cooperation
    (APEC) 22–3
assent procedure 108
Association of Southeast Asian Nations
    (ASEAN) 23–4
Atlanticists vs. Europeanists 200–1
Austria 58, 72, 77–9

Balkans 40
Belgium 59, 197
Benelux Economic Union 59, 66
Blair, Tony 203
Bretton Woods conference/system 60,
    73, 209
Briand, Aristide 36
Britain
  and European integration 66, 69
  and Gulf War 197
  joins EEC 69–70
  postwar 59, 63
Brussels, Treaty of (1948) 202

Charlemagne 32, 34
Chirac, Jacques 46
Christian democracy 47
Churchill, Winston 63
citizenship *see* European Union
civil society 132–5
codecision procedure 78, 108
cohesion 74–6, 124, 125
Cohesion Fund 125, 127
Cold War 1, 36–8, 40, 41, 56, 63
Committee of Permanent
    Representatives *see* COREPER
Committee of the Regions 97, 127,
    164
Common Agricultural Policy
    (CAP) 68–9, 125, 168, 180–6,
    196, 207
  principles of 181–2
  problems with 184–5
  reform of 185
Common Commercial Policy 196, 206
Common Fisheries Policy 183
Common Foreign and Security Policy
    (CFSP) 78, 198, 199, 201
  failures 198–9
  successes 198
common market *see* single market
competition policy 167, 177
confederalism 6–9
Conference on Security and
    Cooperation in Europe
    (CSCE) 195
consultation procedure 108
consumer protection policy 161
Contonou Convention (2000) 217
cooperation procedure 108
COREPER 96, 98
corporate mergers 174, 175–7
Coudenhove-Kalergi, Count
    Richard 36, 37

Council of Arab Economic Unity   25
Council of Europe   63–4
Council of Ministers   95–9, 147, 196,
      206
   presidency   96–8
   reform of   164
Court of Auditors   97
Court of First Instance   111, 112
cultural policy   153
customs union   68, 167, 168

defence policy   *see* security policy
Delors, Jacques   73, 91–2, 158, 197
democratic deficit   141–2, 146–9,
      165
   closing   162–5
Denmark
   and EC application   69–70
   and EU law   131
   and Maastricht treaty   77, 144
   postwar   59
development cooperation   214–18
direct actions   112
dual executive   45, 46

East African Community   25–6
eastern Europe   *see* European Union,
      enlargement
economic and monetary union
      (EMU)   73
Economic and Social Committee   97,
      164
Economic and Community of West
      African States (ECOWAS)   26–7
electoral systems   47–8, 106
electronic commerce   173
employment policy   76, 159–60
enlargement   *see* European Union,
      enlargement
environmental policy   128–32,
      139–40
euro   57, 72–3, 78, 81, 144, 174,
      186–91, 192
   development   186–9
   pros and cons   189–91
Eurocommunism   47
Eurocorps   203

Europe
   administrative structure   49–50
   boundaries   31, 38–41
   economic structure   50–4, 122–3,
      128
   nature   30–8
   languages in   38–9, 151–2
   modern features   41
   political structure   45–9
   population density   53–4
   quality of life   52
   unity   30–1, 33–8
European Aeronautic Defence and
      Space company (EADS)   176
European Agency for the Evaluation of
      Medicinal Products (EMEA)   97
European Atomic Energy Community
      (Euratom)   67
European Bank for Reconstruction and
      Development (EBRD)   212
European Central Bank   97, 188, 189,
      190
European Coal and Steel Community
      (ECSC)   16–17, 56, 64–6, 67
European Commission   68, 88–95,
      131–2, 146–7, 147–8, 164, 196, 199,
      206, 208
European Council   99–103, 146
European Court of Justice   109–13,
      147, 172
European currency unit (ECU)   73,
      186–7
European Defence Community   66–7,
      195
European Economic Area (EEA)   77–9
European Economic Community
      (EEC)   56–7
   creation   67
   development   68–9
European elections   106–8, 155
European Environment Agency
      (EEA)   97, 131
European Environmental Bureau
      (EEB)   134
European Free Trade Association
      (EFTA)   69, 77–9
European Investment Bank   97, 212

European Monetary System
(EMS) 73, 186
European Parliament 103–9, 147, 163, 164
elections 106–8, 155
European Political Community 67, 76
European Political Cooperation 75, 76–7, 195–7
European Regional Development Fund
(ERDF) 75, 125, 126, 127
European Social Fund 75, 125, 157
European Space Agency 175
European Union
character and nature 4–6, 135–9, 193–4, 196
citizenship 78, 154
civil society in 132–5
confederal features 8–9, 113
'constitution' 85–8, 163
as economic superpower 194, 204–9
enlargement 69–72, 77–9, 83, 144, 212–14, 218
external relations 94
federal features 11–12, 50, 140
flag 149–50, 156
and Gulf War 197
integrative pressures 13–18, 115–16
interest groups in 132–5
legal system 89, 109–10, 130
motives behind creation of 57–60, 63–4
passport 149
policies of *see* public policies of the
EU *or under subject headings*
public opinion about 142–4, 189, 199–200
public understanding of 145
relations with eastern
Europe 212–14
relations with South 214–18
relations with United States 209–11
and terrorist attacks in 2001 211
treaties 89
Europol 78, 97, 170
Exchange Rate Mechanism
(ERM) 73, 187, 191
executives 46

federalism 9–12, 49–50
Finland 59, 77–9
foreign policy 76, 78, 80, 81, 194–200
France
and the Common Agricultural
Policy 181
and Germany 70
postwar 58, 64–5
Free Trade Area of the Americas 22
functionalism 14–15

Gasperi, Alcide de 59
Gaulle, Charles de 70, 195, 209
General Agreeement on Tariffs
and Trade (GATT) 69, 207, 208, 210
see also World Trade Organization
Germany
beer purity laws 172
and the Common Agricultural
Policy 181
confederalism in 8
and EU law 131
federalism in 49–50
and France 70
and Gulf War 197
postwar 58, 60–2, 63, 64–5
Greece 60, 70, 131

heads of state 45–6
Hitler, Adolf 36

Iceland 59, 79
immigration 150–1, 157, 174
illegal 170
integrative potential 17–18
interest groups 133–5
intergovernmental conferences
(IGCs) 67, 77, 82, 137
intergovernmental organizations 5, 65
intergovernmentalism 4, 6, 136
internal market *see* single market
international organizations 4–5
Ireland 59, 69–70, 128, 144
Italy 58–9

Japan 208–9
joint ventures 174–5

Keynes, John Maynard 60
knowledge deficit 145

language issue 38–9, 151–2
Latin American Free Trade Association
　(LAFTA) 21–2
legislatures 46–7
Liechtenstein 79
Lomé conventions (1975–89) 216–17
Luxembourg 59

Maastricht treaty (1992) 146
　content/effects of 78, 94, 127
　signature 77
Major, John 50, 159
Malta 72
Marshall Plan 61
Members of the European
　Parliament 105
Mercosur 22
Merger Treaty (1965) 68
Mitrany, David 14–15
monetary union *see* euro
Monnet, Jean 15, 16, 56, 64–5, 66, 67,
　135, 137
mutual recognition principle 172

Napoleon 35
nations 3
neofunctionalism 15–18, 72
Netherlands 59, 131
Nice, Treaty of (2000) 82, 103, 163
　content/effects of 99, 111, 119, 164
Nordic Council 59
North American Free Trade Agreement
　(NAFTA) 18–21
North Atlantic Treaty (1949) 62
North Atlantic Treaty Organization
　(NATO) 62, 200, 201–3
Norway 59, 70, 77

ombudsman 154–5
Organization for European Economic
　Cooperation (OEEC) 61, 64

Paneuropa 37
Paris, Treaty of (1951) 66
people, movement of 150–2, 152–4,
　174
People's Europe 149–56
Petersburg tasks 202, 203, 204
pillars of the EU 78, 198
political integration 13
political parties 47, 107
　in European Parliament 107
　green parties 129–30
Portugal 59–60, 72, 197
preliminary rulings 112
Prodi, Romano 92
proportional representation 47–8,
　106
public policies of the EU
　agriculture 68–9, 125, 168, 180–6,
　　207
　commercial 196, 206
　competition 167, 177
　consumer protection 161
　culture 153
　development cooperation 214–18
　employment 76, 159–60
　environment 128–32, 139–40
　fisheries 183
　foreign 76, 80, 81, 194–200
　People's Europe 149–56
　regional 74–5, 121–8, 139
　security 76–7, 193–4, 200–4, 218
　social 74–5, 156–62
　trade 207–9
　transport 177–9

qualified majority voting 99, 100,
　198

realism 13–14
regional integration
　in Africa 25–7
　in Asia 23–4
　in Latin America 21–3
　in Middle East 24–5
　motives behind 12–18
　in North America 18–21
regional policy 74–5, 121–8, 139

regionalism in Europe   123, 125–6
Rome, Treaty of (1957)   67, 69, 72,
     167–8, 180, 196

Santer, Jacques   92
Schengen Agreement (1985)   81, 119,
     168, 169–70
Schuman, Robert   15, 16, 56, 64, 65
Schuman Declaration   56, 65
security policy   193–4, 200–4, 218
single currency   *see* euro
Single European Act (1986)   56, 68,
     73, 150, 168
   content/effects of   75, 126, 151,
        173–80, 192
   signature   74, 168
single market   68, 72, 74, 81, 167,
     168–80
Social Charter   75–6, 119, 158
social democracy   47
social policy   74–5, 156–62
South Asian Association for Regional
     Cooperation (SAARC)   24
sovereignty   ‑10
Spaak, Paul-Henri   67
Spain   3, 59–60, 183, 197
spillover   15, 17
states   2–4
structural funds   75, 123, 125, 183
subsidiarity   118
Suez crisis   62–3
supranationalism   5–6, 136
Sweden   59, 77–9, 131
Switzerland   8, 49, 79

terrorism   169, 170–1, 198, 201, 211
Thatcher, Margaret   50, 158–9, 162

tourism   151, 178
trade policy   207–9
Trans-European Networks   177–9
transport policy   177–9
Treaty on European Union   *see*
     Maastricht treaty
Turkey   40–1, 72, 79

unemployment   76, 159–60
unitary administration   49
United Kingdom   *see* Britain
United States of America
   and Bretton Woods   73
   confederalism   7–8
   constitution   87, 163
   federalism in   9–11, 12
   and Gulf War   197
   and postwar Europe   60–3
   relations with EU   209–11
   and trade with EU   207, 208, 210–11
   see also North American Free Trade
        Agreement

value added tax   171, 180

Western European Union (WEU)   62,
     199, 202–4
women in the EU   160–2
worker mobility   *see* people,
     movement of
World Trade Organization
     (WTO)   185, 207, 208, 211, 218
   see also General Agreement on
        Tariffs and Trade

Yaoundé conventions (1963/69)   69,
     216